STORY
AND
CONTEXT

STORY
AND
CONTEXT

An Introduction to Christian Education

DONALD E. MILLER

90
ABINGDON PRESS
Nashville

Story and Context: An Introduction to Christian Education

Copyright © 1987 by Abingdon Press

This book is printed on acid-free paper.

Library of Congress Cataloging-in-Publication Data

Miller, Donald Eugene.
  Story and context.

  Bibliography: p.
  Includes index.
  1. Christian education. I. Title.
BV1471.2.M465   1987   207   86-14111
ISBN 0-687-39644-1 (soft: alk. paper)

ISBN 0-687-39644-1

Scripture quotations in this publication are from the Revised Standard Version of the Bible, copyrighted 1946, 1952, © 1971, 1973 by the Division of Christian Education of the National Council of the Churches of Christ in the U.S.A., and are used by permission.

MANUFACTURED BY THE PARTHENON PRESS AT
NASHVILLE, TENNESSEE, UNITED STATES OF AMERICA

CONTENTS

PART TWO: STORY

PART THREE: FAITH

PART FOUR: TEACHING

STORY
AND
CONTEXT

INTRODUCTION

The purpose of this book is to provide an introduction to the field of Christian education. The 1970s and 1980s have seen a revival of interest in Christian education as well as in other ministries of the church. With the revival of interest have come a number of new approaches to education and nurture, which have varied from focusing on worship and reconceptualizing faith development to exploring the educative functions of church life. The richness of writing on Christian education increases the need for basic surveys of the field.

An introductory summary of a field assists readers to gain an overview in a relatively short time. At the same time, introductions have the inherent weakness of overly schematizing subject matter that is richer and more varied than presented. Such is the case here. Christian education, like all fields, needs introductory discussions, but an introduction is only a map of terrain that requires further investigation. Chapters in this book on theology, ethics, and biblical study raise questions that can't be answered in a few pages. However, this book will serve its purpose if it indicates something of the structure of Christian education and something of the way that its issues are being discussed.

This book should be of special use to college and seminary students. Professional educators will likely be familiar with most of the materials, but they may find it helpful as an overview of the field. Pastors should find the book useful as a guide to how they may relate to the educative and nurturing functions of the church. Lay teachers may also find the book of interest. Anyone who wants to know the relationship of education to other Christian ministries should discover useful material here.

The model of Christian education explored is that of the faith community as teacher. But a survey of the field must attempt to account for all the trends in religious educational practice, giving some balance to them. Some educators have stressed revelation and instructional content, while others have featured growth, maturation, and conversion. Some have aimed primarily at promoting common faith and public responsibility, while others are concerned about the support and renewal of the religious community. My intention is to discuss all these issues from the vantage point of the community of faith as the context of teaching and learning.

The discussion that follows conceives of Christian education as taking place within four intersecting dimensions: community, story, faith, and teaching. Three chapters are given to discussion of each dimension. Part 1 focuses on the faith community as the context for teaching and learning. Chapter 1 considers the structure and process of community life, as well as the interplay of religious and secular communities. Chapter 2 briefly surveys the teaching strategy of the faith community from the time of the Hebrew Bible to the present. Chapter 3 looks at the purpose of Christian education.

Part 2 treats the relation of the Christian story to the faith community as teacher. Teaching the Bible is the subject of chapter 4. The relation of theology and education is discussed in chapter 5. Education as practical theology and ethics is set forth in chapter 6.

Part 3 is entitled "Faith" and focuses on personal transformation and worship. Chapter 7 reviews the various theories of faith and moral development. Chapter 8 sets forth a view of the faith journey featuring one's way of life in its community context. The relation of education and worship is considered in chapter 9.

Part 4 turns to matters of teaching and administration. Theories of learning and instruction are described in chapter 10. Curriculum is the subject of chapter 11. Finally, chapter 12 deals with questions of administration and leadership of Christian education.

Two particular emphases stand out: the use of story and the community context. Both concepts have their limits. Story refers to stories told in church school, personal life stories, congregational histories, and the Christian story. I believe the current discussion of narrative will allow such multiple useof the term "story." Nevertheless, this book experiments with the concept of narrative to discover how well it can hold together the dimensions of Christian education. The concept of community refers to small groups, congregations, local areas, regional areas, denominational groups, ecumenical groups, and the kingdom of God. Though the primary referent is to the congregation, the term "community" must not be identified only with the congregation or with the denomination. I believe that sociological and theological considerations allow for such a broad use of the term and that furthermore it provides a frame for coherent discussion of the field of Christian education. The reader should keep the multiple uses of both story and community in mind.

My hope is that this book can be a special study resource not only in the academic classroom, but also for congregations and perhaps also for teacher training. There are various study aids, including exercises to be carried out, discussion questions, and recommendations for further reading.

A work of this kind requires the assistance of many people. I am especially indebted to Allen and Mary Elizabeth Moore, both of whom teach at the School of Theology at Claremont. The book was first conceived and planned in discussion with them, although I am wholly responsible for what is written here. Pierce Ellis, former editor at Abingdon Press, encouraged me to proceed when otherwise I likely would not have done so. Discussion with faculty colleagues and classes at Bethany Theological Seminary have been more significant than I can tell in shaping my ideas. A very special word of appreciation goes to Barbara Stewart, who spent many hours, often in the evening and on weekends, typing and correcting the imperfect copy I gave to her. Finally, I want also to mention Tom France, my teaching assistant, who was willing to work at some of the more tedious tasks of completing a manuscript. Their help and encouragement made this work possible.

I
CONTEXT

Chapter One:

THE FAITH COMMUNITY AS TEACHER

A COMMUNITY PERSPECTIVE

The model of Christian education explored in this book is that of the faith community as teacher. Though a faith community model has been implicit in discussions of religious education at least since Horace Bushnell,[1] recently the idea has gained renewed interest. Indications of declining vitality, or at least change, in the Sunday school movement have prompted a search for alternative models of religious education. In the past several decades a number of serious studies of the community model have become available.[2] At the same time, theological and biblical studies have been more and more influenced by the methods of sociology.

The aim of this book is to bring the community models of education, theology, and biblical studies together. A community model is certainly not the only way to coordinate the concepts, materials, and activities of religious education.[3] Perhaps it is not the most adequate way. However, to make such a judgment requires a careful and full description of the community model. I shall attempt to portray a community model of education that gives careful attention to theological understanding, biblical awareness, responsibility, and justice, as well as to learning theory and teaching methods. Throughout, the perspective remains that of the faith community as teacher.

The community model developed here consists of a dynamic relationship between a living story, shared practices, and individual persons. Questions about personal commitment and change are relevant to a community model, which always relates personal experience to interactions between persons. We shall therefore be very concerned about the living story, the community context, and the life journey of individuals. The processes of education and nurture occur in the interaction between these three realms.

THE DYNAMICS OF COMMUNITY LIFE

All communities have a number of dynamic elements in common: interacting individuals, normative practices, symbolized meanings, and a shared environment.[4] We may therefore define a community as a group of persons sharing common commitments, norms of behavior, symbolic culture, and living within a shared environment. Shared commitments refers to individual loyalty to the community; shared norms, both to formal institutions and to customary practices; and shared symbols, to language, thought, and the whole range of cultural expression. The shared environment is the place of residence and activity, the nexus of causes that condition the common life, and the various conditions that shape patterns of interaction. All of the elements are present when a group is a community in the fullest sense.

Persons interacting in the same place normally develop rules, roles, customs, institutions, traditions, and sym-

bolic culture. Individuals within a community are shaped
by community patterns and at the same time give shape to
those patterns. For example, the free use of first names is
usually received as an act of warmth, openness, and
friendliness in the United States. In many places outside
the United States, quickness to use first names connotes
disrespect, thoughtlessness, and lack of consideration.
Such practices and symbols grow within a community as
interaction becomes patterned and takes on common
significance for those who so interact. Individuals may
give different interpretations to an accepted practice, but
its very existence implies some shared meaning.[5]

Symbols and practices that have become customary for a
group have the capacity to shape and direct the persons
who gave rise to them. Newcomers, whether visitors,
immigrants, or children, enter into communities with
certain practices, customs, and meanings already given.
Children are born into families in which an established
language is already being spoken. Any one person or family
will rarely change the language pattern to any great extent.
Nevertheless, language does change across the years, as is
evident from considering that the English of the King
James Bible is often difficult for contemporary readers to
understand. Patterns of behavior adopted and practiced by
a community have a profound effect upon anyone who
enters that community.

Community patterns transcend any one person, but not
completely. The behavioral patterns of a community have
a life of their own, and that life can be studied and
described independently of individuals. Yet such patterns
exist only as they are practiced by individuals. The
particular manner in which a pattern is practiced by one
individual will begin to reshape the community when
others adopt that practice. The capacity of every individual to accept or reject, continue or alter, interpret or

criticize any given community practice means that every individual transcends the community patterns, but not completely. To some extent community patterns of behavior transcend every individual within the community, but in another sense every individual transcends the community patterns. Such double transcendence constitutes the living, dynamic process of community life.

Individuals and groups within a community are sometimes able to make significant changes in the environment, in local practices, or even in the self-understanding of a community. Conversely, shared practices and meanings are able to change individuals and groups. A change in the environment may affect persons, group practices, and meanings. Education has always emphasized the importance of understanding and meaning, but education should also be seen within the context of values, practices, social interests, commitments, and environmental influences.

THE COMMUNITY OF FAITH

Like every community, a community of faith is a group of interacting persons sharing a commitment to norms and symbols within a shared place. What distinguishes a community of faith is that its commitments, norms, and symbols are related to and affected by the widest horizon of meaning, the final center of value, its ultimate concern, and the sense of absolute dependence—by faith in God.[6] A faith community is one in which the widest horizon of meaning is symbolized (no matter how ambiguously), the final center of value is acknowledged (even if only partially), and the story of God's will and providence is the subject of the community's symbolic culture. To some extent every community has a common story, a common ethos, and a common loyalty. In a faith community, the sense of the ultimate is at the center of these three.

In a limited sense, every community is a community of faith. The common stories, ethos, and loyalties intimate what it views as finally ultimate and absolute. However, when the stories do not represent the absolute, when the ethos does not represent the final center of value, and when the loyalties do not represent an unconditional commitment, but are nevertheless treated as though they do, then the community has become idolatrous.[7] Secular communities create their own stories, values, and commitments without great regard to faith in the wider horizon and the rich immediacy of what is ultimately being given to them.

The faith of the Christian community is unique; everything centers in the saving power of God in Jesus Christ. The common story is of God who created the world and who, when humanity became alienated from God, entered into the world in the person of Jesus Christ to suffer the power of alienation, and to enable humanity to be renewed in the love of God and of one another. The common ethos is centered in the community's active love of God and of one another. The common commitment is centered in the community's loyalty to and experience of God's forgiving and directing providence in Jesus Christ. The common environment is whatever location within the world they find themselves as the particular locus of God's forgiveness and love.

The process of committed individuals interacting within a community of faith inevitably leads to norms and meanings. Equally characteristic is the influence of norms and symbolic culture upon interacting individuals within the community setting. To interact within any community is to be shaped by it to some extent. To be engaged with a community over a longer period of time is to be even more deeply shaped by it. But time alone is not the most important criterion of engagement with a community. The quality of the participation is of greater importance. Every person within a community is learning simply by being in the community. To interact is to be already participating in the loyalty, ethos, and symbolic culture of the community. The learning may be customary and habitual rather than conscious and intentional, or it may be quite intentional and conscious. Common stories may be confused, loyalties may be mixed, and individuals may disagree about which norms have priority. In fact, all these tendencies are present in every faith community. Nevertheless, to be engaged at all is to be learning in relation to the community process, consciously or unconsciously, intentionally or unintentionally.

The relationship between learning and the interior life of the faith community is picked up in the biblical concept of "Torah," which can mean either covenant or instruction. The Torah was the fundamental reality of the Hebrew community, and was at the same time the learning, the instruction. In the same way, faith in Jesus Christ, based upon the living covenant with him, is the central reality of the Christian community of faith. Faith in Christ cannot be separated from hearing, learning, deciding, and believing, any more than faith in God can be separated from Torah in the Hebrew community.

EDUCATION AND UNDERSTANDING

Participation in a community of faith may be a learning process, but not all learning is education. To see the place of education within the faith community we must examine the meaning of education.[8] A moment's consideration should convince the reader that education is to be distinguished from any form of indoctrination, habituation, forced response, or mind control. The process by which prisoners of war are starved until they give verbal consent to certain propaganda can hardly be called education. Nor can education conceivably include terror-ism that brutalizes persons until they agree to a point of view. A captive may be starved, beaten, threatened, and otherwise terrorized until he or she agrees to accept the captor's point of view, but surely such forced mind control cannot in any sense be called education.

The question of habit formation is more ambiguous. At one level habits can be formed without any voluntary control. For example, Pavlov's experiments which condi-tioned a dog to salivate at the ring of a bell did not require the voluntary cooperation of the dog. Persons can be conditioned to behaviors that avoid pain and seek pleasure in the same way as Pavlov's dog. One thinks of the projection of subliminal cues on television, cues of which the viewer is not consciously aware, but which clearly influence the viewer's behavior. Such advertising has been outlawed because it violates the viewer's freedom to decide. Involuntary influence can certainly be eliminated from what it means to be educated.

Persons sometimes intentionally set up a conditioning program for themselves. Students often are quite willing for a teacher to mete out rewards and punishments toward the establishment of desirable habits. Such habit forma-tion we call training. Is training identical with education? One might be well trained in playing the piano, and yet know very little about music. One might also be quite well trained in the technique of writing without being knowledgeable about writing. In every field one can be well trained without being well educated.

We conclude that education must include a fuller understanding of what is being studied. When voluntary, training is not alien to education. Indeed, since the process of understanding always includes some habit formation, if none other than the habit of inquiry, education will always include some element of training. However, education must include a fuller understanding that is not necessary to training. To consider a person well educated in any subject without their having gained a wider perspective, a fund of information, a variety of basic metaphors, and a way of deciding is a contradiction in terms. The "self-educated" person has gained such fuller understanding in his or her own way.

We arrive, then, to this point: education includes the voluntary participation of the learner. If the voluntary element is limited or eliminated, the process takes on the characteristics of indoctrination or thought control. Education is a process of engaging the interest of the learner. We commonly speak about compulsory public education. Such education is compulsory in the sense that parents are required by the state to send their children to school. Children can be compelled to attend school, but they cannot be compelled to learn. Indeed, some public schools resemble a prison where students are forced to submit to certain assignments. However unless the students become interested and voluntarily engaged, there can be no education—only indoctrination or thought control. Similarly, in the faith community the learning process must engage the voluntary cooperation and interest of participants before it can properly be called education.

EDUCATION AS PROCESS

Education has still another characteristic: it is a long process that cannot be reduced to a momentary change. If a momentary radical change were the sum and substance of education, then the process that led up to the change and that following it would be irrelevant to education. Education would become identical with "snapping"—a reorientation that occurs in an instant. Momentary changes may occur and there may be sudden turns along the way, but the education cannot be reduced to those changes and turns.

Very likely, a learner cannot come to a fuller understanding unless there are transforming moments.[9] Almost all learning theories suggest that there are moments of insight when learning comes in a flash, newly conceiving what was heretofore not so understood. To exclude the transforming moment from education would eliminate the possibility of understanding. So education must include the possibility and anticipation of the transforming moment, but, still, it cannot be reduced to such "flashes." It is a longer and deeper process of coming to a fuller understanding, that cannot be completed in an hour or a day. One may very well be informed in a brief period, but one can hardly be educated in such brief encounters.

Furthermore, education requires a guide. Guides may employ a variety of different methods. There may also be more than one teacher, and where there is a common discipline, there may be a whole community of teachers. In a very important sense the entire community may serve as teacher. The collective experience and understanding of the whole is immensely richer than that of any one individual. Traditionally a school is made up of a community of scholars known as faculty, which is the major teaching resource. In the faith community, the entire community is the basic teaching resource, and whatever formal teaching is done is representative of the whole.

There is a more profound sense in which the spirit of truth, the Holy Spirit, is the teacher. This might also be stated as the Spirit of God or the Mind of Christ. The prayer of the faith community is to be led by the Spirit of God. When a Christian community is led by the spirit of alienation or by a local, divisive spirit, it can offer only an impoverished Christian education. Therefore the community is constantly tested by the Scriptures; by the perceptions, convictions, and admonitions of the various members of the community; and by sensitive appeal to the Holy Spirit for guidance. Each faith community will also have its authorities and polity, which also test the spirit. Yet nothing should be allowed to replace the Spirit of God in a community seeking to come to a fuller understanding of its faith. The Holy Spirit comes in the interrelationship between individuals, the community, and the story. Spiritual leading comes as persons together search the Scriptures, encourage one another to find a common vision, work together to carry it out, and hope always to be open to the Holy Spirit.

Education is a self-motivated, self-interested process of being helped to discover a fuller awareness of what is true by experienced guides or by the whole community. This concept of education does not suggest how the process should take place, other than that it be voluntary, continuous, purposeful, and mutual. Nor does this concept suggest the character of the object of knowledge other than that it be true.

EDUCATION AND CHRISTIAN FAITH

If we accept this description of education, we may ask whether education can be Christian. This may seem a strange question, since the church has been interested in education for the two thousand years of its existence. However, the question deserves a thoughtful answer. The relationship between faith and education is complicated, and we can do no more here than to suggest an answer. Suffice it to say that Christians may at least engage in education if it does not contradict the character of their faith. The Christian faith presumes a voluntary response, as does education. Christianity is not only or merely a momentary transformation, but also a "way," a longer process. Christian faith does not preclude a fuller understanding. Both Hebrew and Christian believers have taught that understanding leads to faith, or at least that faith can be enriched by understanding. Even if faith is considered qualitatively different from understanding, faith nevertheless is thought to be deepened by it. Faith does not preclude a human teacher or a community of teachers.

There are two ways in which education can be Christian. First, the object of study may be the Christian faith. The subject matter is then Christian, although perhaps only in a very objective sense. Buddhists and Moslems can make the Christian faith an object of their study. Second, the teacher can teach out of a deep belief in the Christian faith. Put otherwise, when teaching and learning take place in a community of those for whom the Christian faith is a matter of deep loyalty and ultimate concern, then teaching and learning will be shaped by the Christian understanding of truth. Education becomes Christian in the fullest sense when both criteria are followed: the teaching occurs within a community deeply committed to the Christian faith and the subject matter is the Christian faith.

Education may enhance our understanding of faith, it may serve to express that faith, and it may lead others to an acceptance of that faith. The emphasis in this book is on not only the Scripture and the history of the Christian faith, but also on the faith community as the context for teaching. The lived relationships within the community become the primary context for understanding the meaning of faith. The diversity of experience and understanding within the community goes beyond what any one teacher is capable of giving. While the idea of faith does not entail the idea of understanding, faith has an affinity for understanding. The community of faith always teaches its ethos and symbolic culture. Therefore, we are not surprised to find that Christian communities have always been accompanied by schooling and education from elementary to university levels.

EDUCATION AS NURTURE

We have just described education as the process of being led into a fuller understanding. Another approach to Christian teaching was classically described by Horace Bushnell in the middle of the nineteenth century.[10] Bushnell's thesis was that "the child is to grow up a Christian, and never know himself as being otherwise."[11] He felt there is an organic connection between parents and children such that the character, practice, and beliefs of the parents are naturally taken in by the children.

Bushnell called for parents to surround children with Christian faith, piety, and discipline so that they are naturally formed in the Christian life. They become Christian in habit and belief by being a part of a family and a Christian community that shapes their personalities and character. Since the "organic laws" of the family shape the values of children, the child should be surrounded by good manners, good grooming, rules that reflect spiritual concern, wholesome play, celebration, and prayer. Children should be taught, but only as they ask, and they ought to be taught what they are ready to hear and not forced to learn what they do not understand. Bushnell is particularly critical of teaching children that they are sinners and that they must begin living a life of good works. He does not aim primarily for fuller understanding, but rather for character, mood, belief, habit, and awareness. He calls for a molding of personality and piety by the natural relation-

28

ships to parents and by the patterns of life in the community of those who care.

Bushnell's approach gives priority to nurture rather than education. Religious education in the twentieth century is carried on between the poles of nurture and education. Nurture focuses upon relationships and common practices, while education focuses upon a fuller understanding. The two are not contradictory, but in a given setting one must have priority over the other. The discussion in this volume of the faith community as teacher attempts to keep a balance between questions of nurture and of education. Story and community process are very close to Bushnell's concept of nurture, but they do not exclude formal teaching.

THE PLURALISM OF COMMUNITIES

Communities are organized around certain predominant interests.[12] Marriage is organized around sexual and intimacy needs. Families are organized around the need to bear and socialize children. Businesses are organized around the need to exchange goods and services. Schools are organized around educational needs. Voluntary groups are organized around special interests. Police are organized around the needs of people for protection. The list can go on and on. We have already suggested that faith communities are organized around commitment to ultimate value and meaning, that is, to faith in God. Religious education takes place within the competition of various interests for allegiance. Churches cannot avoid being influenced by the interests of groups around them. For instance, churches tend to take on the characteristics of one or another social class.[13] Some denominations tend to be upper class; others tend to be middle or lower class. Similarly, churches reflect regional differences. There are northern and southern, eastern and western differences in most denominations. Different denominations also predominate in both northern and southern Nigeria, each tending to represent a particular tribal background. One can see sharp national differences as well. The Orthodox are predominantly Eastern European. There are Swedish Lutherans, Norwegian Lutherans, Danish Lutherans, and German Lutherans, all of which are different denominations outside those countries.

Competing groups also dramatically influence the education that takes place in a given faith community. Much of the teaching of a community of faith has to do with confrontation and interaction with competing communities at the level of symbolic meaning, normative ethos, personal commitment, and creative context. Sometimes the influence of the teaching in the faith community is decisive, and sometimes the influence of the competing community is decisive.[14]

THE ECOLOGY OF EDUCATION

In their study of the Sunday school, Robert Lynn and Elliott Wright spoke of the ecology of education present at the beginning of the twentieth century. By this they meant the interrelationship between institutions in its effect upon religious education. Lynn and Wright saw the development of the Religious Education Association in relation to the missionary enterprise, the new industrialism, advances in public school education, and a new vision of internationalism.

A more recent study argues convincingly that the ecology of education at the turn of the century was not radically different from that of the mid-nineteenth century.[15] By that time Horace Mann had persuaded public opinion to accept public schooling, complemented by religious education in churches. Public schools adopted an organizational model of graded classrooms, specific objectives, and a controlled curriculum. The new industrialism, the move to consolidate schools, and a centralized organizational model were all in place. The turn of the century simply saw a working out of principles that had already been established.

The two studies just mentioned discuss the institutional ecology influencing the churches' teaching. Gabriel Moran has written forcefully about the contemporary ecology of education. He finds that work, leisure, mass communication, and family patterns have radically shifted. The radical pluralism of late-twentieth-century America is quite different from the social ethos of a previous century. The majority of people no longer live in agricultural settings. Many make their living in service and professional occupations as well as in factories. Many women are now in the work force. People have more free time, and a whole new leisure industry has arisen. Television has transformed people's awareness of the world. Family patterns have changed radically. Nearly half of all families now have one parent rather than two. Many persons are divorced, unmarried, widowed, or otherwise single. The level of education has risen dramatically in the past century. In sum, the whole ecology of education is quite different than it was a half century or century ago.

In previous generations the church could depend on the continuity of family traditions. Most persons were in touch with extended families, and the stability of the family was an assumption of Bushnell's suggestions about Christian nurture. But the church can no longer assume such stability. In fact, the church would do well to become more aware of family and life-journey stress. The church is now in a position of nurturing family life, including that of single parent families and many single persons. The congregation has become the stabilizing force for the family, not the other way around.[16]

Religious teaching often has a dramatic effect upon public issues. Without doubt, the teaching of churches affected people's attitudes about slavery in the nineteenth century. Often churches upheld slavery, but some also initiated the call to free the slaves. In the same way, black churches were a center of the civil rights movement in the 1960s. Critics have said that the church, particularly the church school, is the basic source for the legitimation of racism, narrow nationalism, militarism, and other strongly self-centered views. However, churches have also been centers of criticism of such views. The attitude toward the public is formed and influenced in the preaching and teaching of congregations and denominations.

Communities of faith can also contribute to what has been called the "civil religion."[17] Like all communities, the wider public searches for images to interpret its ongoing story. Frequently, these images have originated in communities of faith. Images of faith gave Abraham Lincoln words to plumb the tragedy of the Civil War. Bonhoeffer, Barth, and Niebuhr have given images to interpret mid-twentieth-century life. Congregations are capable of giving images that shape the civil religion. Whether the teaching be for God's justice or self-serving provincialism is a primary concern in the chapters that follow.

CHURCHES, DENOMINATIONS, AND SECTS

Faith communities tend to relate to competing values and institutions in several characteristic ways.[18] One way is that of the sect group. By definition, a sect group in one or several practices stands in sharp contrast to predominant social norms and values. The ethos of the sect group contrasts decisively with the wider public ethos. Christianity was a Jewish sect in its origin and a Roman sect as it grew. When Christianity became predominant, it lost its sectarian character. However the monastic movement continued the sectarian dimension of Christianity. The various sect movements of the fifteenth century anticipated the Reformation. The early sixteenth-century reformers took a sectarian stance, in the sense just given, but they repudiated that position as the Reformation grew. This left the Anabaptist groups as the predominant sects of the time. The Levelers were a significant sect during the English revolution of the seventeenth century.[19]

In contrast to the sect, churches give symbolic and normative support to the public ethos. The church may raise questions of justice, but always in the name of total community commitments. The classic example of the church is the medieval Roman Catholic Church. Most of the Reformation religious bodies aspired to be churches, e.g., the Lutheran, Reformed, and Anglican churches. The various Orthodox churches also meet these criteria.[20]

Besides sects and churches there are denominations. The denomination accepts the wider community ethos, but interprets it in contrasting ways. Denominations differ from the larger culture primarily at the symbolic level, while sect groups differ primarily at the normative level. Church groups do not intend to differ sharply from the wider culture either symbolically or normatively. They do have a vision of a transformed society, but they are willing to compromise with the cultural ethos and symbol system. While denominations may and often do take a prophetic stance in relation to questions of justice, they do not intend to break with the wider culture. The Church of the Brethren intends to be prophetic about peace in the United States but wants to do so within a stance of political responsibility. The Old Order Brethren refuse to be drafted, which they see as obeying God rather than man. They refuse to vote or to otherwise accept responsibility for political process.

Such a typology clearly has its limitation. One can see all three tendencies in almost any religious group. Nevertheless the classification does allow us to see the range of responses of faith communities to competing groups.

RELIGIOUS EDUCATIONAL STRATEGIES

Churches, denominations, and sects tend to educate in different ways. Churches normally expect governments to sponsor and finance religious education, the content of which is directed by the church. The church, then, in liturgy, sacrament, and custom gives spiritual expression to wider cultural values. The denomination sets up supplementary religious instruction beside public education, since an imperative of the denomination's mission is the continuation of its interpretation of the common ethos. The sect group fights against public education either by asserting its own ethos to counteract the common ethos in the public school, or by setting up private schools to transmit its own ethos.[21]

Any one of these groups may have continuity within itself from one country to another and nevertheless relate differently to the wider culture in disparate countries. Jews who function like a denomination in America can at the same time function like a church in Israel. Catholicism can be a denomination in America and a church in Italy. The importance of making the distinction is that churches, denominations, and sects educate in different ways. The educational strategy of a faith community is conditioned by the character of its relationship to the wider culture. A church, denomination, or sect may adopt other educational strategies than those discussed here, but the influence of other institutions must still be taken into account.

METHOD AND TERMINOLOGY

Our approach to the faith community moves dialectically on two levels. On the one side we describe the processes of every community of faith. To that extent we may speak of education as religious education. On the other hand we stand within a confessing community; clearly, our loyalties have influenced our selection and organization of materials. From a confessional perspective one may speak of Christian education or Jewish education. Our aim has constantly been to allow the faith community perspective and the confessing community perspective to inform one another.

Perhaps a further word about method should be added. All persons and communities inevitably speak from the point of view of their own commitments and confessions. Yet it is very important that we develop ways to understand one another beyond our own confessional loyalty. Our conviction is that this is best done by constantly attempting to acknowledge the principles of selectivity within one's own perspective and by constantly describing life from a religious perspective transcending confessional limitations. A wider perspective allows for public discourse and for dialog with scientific disciplines. Yet every such attempt at a larger perspective is a limited perspective with its own principles of selectivity. No perspective, no matter how universal, can escape its own confessional limitations. This leads to the method of describing the faith community in publicly immediate and inclusive ways, but expressing those assertions within the perspective of one's own particular faith and commitment to Jesus Christ as the center of all faith communities. We presume that others will want to state these assertions from their own perspectives: Jewish, Orthodox, or other. We intend that statements about the faith community be the subject of the widest public debate and that the confessing statements encourage and enrich faith.

A particular problem for religious education in the twentieth century has been whether the field should be designated religious education or Christian education. In view of the preceding, we are willing to follow the suggestion of Thomas Groome[22] to speak of "Christian religious education." Sometimes we speak of "religious" education, especially when our perspective is the public perspective on faith communities. At other times we speak of "Christian" education, when our perspective is the confessing Christian community. The use of both terms does not indicate contradiction or inconsistency. Rather, they hold together two sides of a dialectic, both of which must be included if both clarity and commitment are to be represented. We prefer the phrase "education in the Christian community."

STUDY SUGGESTIONS

Exercises

1. Choose several groups with which you are familiar, perhaps your family, youth group, or your class. In the above section, "The Dynamics of Community Life," the following elements were mentioned: interacting persons, widely accepted practices, symbolized meanings, and

shared environment. Give examples of each of these elements for the groups you have selected.

2. The section entitled "The Community of Faith" suggests that to interact in a group is already to participate in habitual and customary behavior. For a group with which you are familiar, perhaps in a group discussion, list ways by which the group shapes persons who participate in it.

3. Consider whether Christian teaching is more on the side of developing fuller understanding or nurturing faithful character. Ask a panel of persons to make a case for either side. Perhaps give four persons two minutes to speak for one view and four persons for the other view. Alternate speakers. Then continue the discussion with everyone present.

4. Trace the national and ethnic background of the religious group to which you belong. Present your findings to others in your religious group and then discuss the extent to which ethnic and national traditions still prevail among you.

5. Ask a number of persons in your congregation, men and women, younger and older, to tell others about how the church's teaching affects them where they work. This might be a panel presentation. After those on the panel have spoken, ask others to share similar stories from their own lives. What are your observations about the interaction of the church's teaching and the demands of the work world?

6. Obtain a curriculum for television awareness from your denominational headquarters. Let a group of you pledge to watch certain programs and then discuss the question, How does the

Christian faith address the topic of this TV program? Become acquainted with the problem of violence on TV. Let your group write a letter to a TV network about the presence or absence of violence in that network's shows.

7. Survey the number of single persons, single-parent families, and other non-traditional family patterns in your congregation. Discuss with some of these persons what the church contributes to their way of life. What is your conclusion about your church's ministry to non-traditional families? How do these family patterns affect the educational program of the church?

8. Visit a religious community that has its own elementary or high school. Observe some of the teaching in both formal and informal settings. Talk to teachers and students to discover the aims of the school and the methods used. How does the teaching of an intentional community differ from that of another congregation with which you are familiar?

Questions for Discussion

1. What are the elements of a community model of Christian education? What are its strengths and limitations?

2. What changes in common practice have occurred in your church during your lifetime?

3. What doctrine of the church is assumed in the present chapter?

4. To what extent does education require a more experienced teacher as guide? Can a community carry this function?

5. What is the relationship between conversion and Christian education?

6. To what extent does the Christian faith require right teaching?
7. What is the relationship between Christian nurture and Christian education?
8. Describe the present "ecology of education," as that term is used in this chapter.
9. To what extent can or should Christian education contribute to the wider public faith?
10. Is it important to develop ways of understanding beyond one's own confessional limitations? How can this be done?

Suggestions for Further Reading

Peter L. Berger and Thomas Luckmann, *The Social Construction of Reality.*
A scholarly account of the relationship of symbol, social practice, individual, and community.
Charles R. Foster, *Teaching in the Community of Faith.*
A brief account of a faith community model of Christian education.
C. Ellis Nelson, *Where Faith Begins.*
A readable book that turned the attention of religious educators to cultural and social considerations.
Larry O. Richards, *A Theology of Christian Education.*
Focuses on the nurturing community from a conservative point of view.

Chapter Two:

THE FAITH COMMUNITY IN HISTORY

STORY AND CHANGE

Beliefs, customs, loyalties, and circumstances are constantly changing, and the community's story is the narrative of those changes. Teaching and learning are therefore related to the institutional patterns of an era. One may not simply pick up the educational methods of a previous generation and apply them. They belong to their time just as other methods belong to this time. The ongoing story brings out the relationship between teaching and its institutional setting.

Radical changes in shared norms and customs are evident in the twentieth century. For example, at the turn of the century the church was often the social center of a community. Nowadays few churches, other than strongly intentional congregations like the Sojourners Community in Washington, D.C., can make this claim. Customs about modesty, sexual propriety, and courtesy have shifted as well.

Shared commitments and experiences have also changed. Families become strongly committed in one year, and then lose interest the next. The shift may be due in part to the changing ages of children or to a change of jobs. The many women who are working lessen the number who are willing to give long hours of volunteer service to the church. Both men and women are simply not willing to give long time commitments to church school teaching as was true in earlier generations.

Finally, the environment of the church has changed. Modern transportation makes people much more mobile. Modern communications make people much more knowledgeable about the world. The increasing level of education makes people less dependent upon an educated minister for a learned opinion. Leisure time activities and mass media give people many interesting activities.

The sum of these changes is a constant movement in the story of the faith community. The previous story takes on different significance in new situations. In addition to the change of significance is the fact that the shift in customs, commitment, and environment is itself part of the ongoing story. The story must take these trends into account. Every community is therefore narrating its own story.

In addition to the changes first mentioned, certain conflicting elements are always present. The struggle between the local interpretation of events and interpretation by the larger community is to be found everywhere. Local interpretations conflict with regional meanings, and they in turn with national meanings. National meanings contradict the global. The observation about local and translocal conflict is also true with regard to customs and commitments.

Always, a struggle between evolutionary and revolutionary change is present. An evolutionary change is one in which continuity with the past is strong; a revolutionary change, one making a radical break. Some periods in history evolve slowly, and other periods explode with change.

There is also a dialectic between the various individual and social factors on the one hand and the ongoing story on the other. Very often interaction gives rise to the story, but sometimes the story changes the interaction. Christian education takes place between the local and the global, the evolutionary and the revolutionary, the social practices and the story. Therefore, the faith community always lives in history, and living in history is part of its story. When we look to different historical examples, we see that they evidence these elements of interaction and change.

ISRAEL AND THE TORAH

Consideration of religious education in ancient Israel should not begin with methods of teaching, but with the meaning of Torah within the social setting of the time.[1] Torah was the heart of the community. The word has the double meaning of both covenant and instruction. As a covenant, Torah was the promise, loyalty, and commitment to God that was understood to hold the people together. If the people forget the covenant, then God will forget the people and they will be forsaken.

Keeping the covenant was based upon remembering. The whole people were to remember the covenant, including young children, adults, and the elderly. This was accomplished in various ways. Observation of the laws contained in the covenant, the liturgical celebration of the historic events surrounding the covenant's disclosure, and public reading of the Scriptures were three prime methods. There was continual, daily discussion of how the requirements of the covenant could be carried out in various circumstances. Family ceremonies and discus-

43

sions were also reminders, and retelling the story within the family was encouraged to stimulate the questions of children. Another covenantal reminder was private devotion and prayer. When the nation lost its political independence, schools were set up to train children and youth in the Scriptures. Special leaders, teachers, and prophets developed schools, such as those who followed Isaiah or those in the Qumran community. The community also sought to collect and preserve a body of literature in which the covenant was most vividly portrayed. In all these ways the covenant was preserved in the people's memory.

The Torah was collected in the midst of the political struggles of Israel. The struggle between the northern and southern kingdoms can be seen in the strands of the tradition. Yahweh may perhaps represent the voice of democratic rural people against the walled cities of Israel.[2] In the face of the fall of the northern kingdom, the reform of Josiah called for greater unity of worship and greater depth of devotion, emphases evident in the book of Deuteronomy. The fall of the southern kingdom led to the writing of the tradition, to schools, and to development of liturgy. The final form of the canon (Jamnia A.D. 90) came after the fall of Jerusalem in A.D. 70 . The rise of liturgy, schools, canon, and special communities of disciples coincided with the threat of loss of the tradition. The canon itself reflects political struggles, differences of interpretation, and a drive to preserve the covenant.

Not all of what we have just described can be called education, at least in the formal sense. However, it is a process of being guided toward a fuller understanding of the truth, and it occurred at all levels of the community. The stories of the Hebrew faith's formative events were recounted and dramatized both publicly and in the family.

Patterns of behavior were connected to stories in the family, the celebrative community, special schools (prophets, synagogue, Qumran) and the two nations. Questions of justice and the meaning of being a holy people were constantly before the people. The Pharisaic movement attempted to extend both normative justice and ceremonial practices. Christianity as proclaimed by the apostle Paul transformed normative ceremonial practices and located justice in God's grace and the committed response of believers. In his interpretation of the gospel Paul saw himself to be carrying out the intent of the tradition.

THE EARLY CHURCH AND THE GOSPEL

Discussion of religious education in the New Testament does not begin with a consideration of Jesus' methods of teaching. It begins, rather, with the meaning of the gospel as a community-forming event. For the Pauline tradition, gospel is the heart of the new community. In Jesus of Nazareth, God has established a new covenant, a covenant of grace rather than of law. The character of that covenant of grace is its basis in the transforming deed of God in Christ, extending forgiveness to everyone who will receive it. God's grace is a resurrecting event, lifting us individually and communally out of our bondage to death. The newness of life in Christ is at the same time a personal renewal and a reconciliation with others.

The new covenant has the character of Torah. This character is most evident in the Gospel of Matthew, where the new covenant is set beside the old. The new is seen to be a fulfillment of the old, moving from external ritual to the depths of the heart, which was actually the intent of the old covenant. The covenant involves both a doing and a teaching. "Whoever then relaxes one of the least of these

45

commandments and teaches men so, shall be called least in the kingdom of Heaven" (Matthew 5:19*a* RSV). Each individual's deepest commitment is at the same time a community commitment. The new teaching that has come in Christ is actually a genuine renewal of the old. The community is drawn into a new enterprise of interpretation and of acting faithfully in constantly changing circumstances.

The social setting for Matthew seems to be a community in the Pharisaical tradition like the one at Jamnia. They seem to have been studying how the tradition is most intensively expressed in the life, death, resurrection, and teaching of Jesus. It is presumed that God's saving power comes to humanity as a covenant, that the bearer of that new covenant is Jesus of Nazareth, that covenant is community-forming, and that a community of interpretation is an inevitable expression of covenant.

The context for the Pauline letters seems to be that of wandering prophets moving among settled communities. Paul moves from those who know the word of God to those who do not, from Jews to Gentiles. The gospel breaks the wall of separation between the two (Ephesians). The social setting of moral and religious commitment is presumed as part of God's ongoing work. Paul is a minor artisan who supports himself, but who defends the claim of those who minister to be cared for. Yet he establishes communities where sexual differences (male and female), economic differences (rich and poor), caste differences (slave and free), and religious differences (Jew and Gentile) are overcome. Ritual, preaching, singing, discussion of Scriptures, letter writing, and organization of communities seem to be the ways that Paul spreads the gospel, and such processes are his primary modes of teaching.

We may also speak of the Lukan tradition. The setting seems to be that of defending the gospel to a well-placed

Roman citizen. Luke argues that the gospel has power to bring about justice that is not found in Roman law. The gospel brings into being the ideals of Roman justice. The teaching of God's Word forms a group where social justice is actually being practiced in spite of ongoing injustice. The incredible power of the Spirit moves and convinces people of God's righteousness (Luke 4:18).

We could also speak of John where, again, a community of the faithful is presumed. In this case, the community seems to be persecuted by others, but they are not to be surprised at hatred and persecution. Christ comes as light and power, and to be near him is to find the way. To know him is to love one another. To participate in a community where the presence of Christ informs all that is said and done is to know God. People will reject such a community, because the false always reject the true. Still, constant and extended dialog occurs between the true and the false. Some are able to see and some are not, yet the dialog continues. So the community carries out its dialog not only with one another, but with all who will listen.

We may summarize the process of Christian education in the early church by saying that teaching and learning occurred within a community context. Learning was multifaceted, including meeting together, ritual, story, singing, interpretation, and dialog. The teaching may not bring God's grace, but it can give shape to re-member God's grace. Preaching, teaching, liturgy, and other activities already mentioned are expressions of the basic covenantal interactions that constitute community.

A word about Jesus' teaching. Apparently, the Gospels depend heavily on the sayings of Jesus, which must have been assembled in the process of preaching and teaching about him. Storytelling and interpretation are therefore at the center of the Gospels. For Matthew, Jesus is a teacher of the intent of the law. In Luke, Jesus speaks and acts on

47

justice issues. In John, Jesus is in dialog with the powers of darkness. In Paul, preaching, debate, letter writing, and friendship reflect a variety of teaching patterns, indicative of the variety of social settings in which the gospel was taught.

Was Jesus an Oriental teacher, as Gilbert Highet suggests?[3] Did he give pronouncements and then wait for them to sink in? Were his discourses punctuated with much silence and meditation? Certainly, his sayings are remembered as aphorisms and stories, but that may reflect the social setting in which they were collected as much as his teaching style. In the New Testament accounts, the teaching of Jesus varies according to the social setting. His teaching was close to the tradition; was memorable; included parable, story, debate, and deeds; and was done in large and small groups, occasional and long-term groups. It certainly presumed God's shaping of a people and a willingness to suffer for his faith. Highet's suggestions seem out of touch with critical scholarship.

THE MEDIEVAL CHURCH AND THE GOSPEL

Both the Hebrew idea of schools of prophets living according to their special understanding of God's Word; congregations preserving, reading, and studying God's Word; and training schools for children; and the New Testament idea of communities studying the Scripture, schools of disciples, and schools of critical commentary (such as that of Matthew), were not at all alien to the Greek idea of schools of philosophy. Early Christianity quickly developed leaders who had philosophical training, but who understood philosophy as a Christian enterprise. This happened principally in Alexandria, but also in Rome. In schools such as those of Justin Martyr and Origen, the Christian faith was taught as a true philosophy. This idea was taken over by the monastic movement, where preparing the Scriptures and studying the tradition were primary disciplines. Still another form of education was a catechetical time for children in some early Christian congregations.

The fall of the Roman Empire meant the dissolution of learning for many people. Life became rude and basic, even cruel. Against this, Charlemagne and Alcuin elevated the goal of education. The monastic movement kept alive the unity of disciplined community, devotion, study, and work. The monastic movement was basically sectarian, and so it had its own separate schools and its own ethos. William the Conqueror, in governing England, attempted to revive the disciplines of worship, study, and debate of Scripture. These were best promoted through the monastic communities. In the Middle Ages the monastic and military ideal combined to form various orders of knights.

Since so few people could read during the Middle Ages, education of the people took the form of public plays, public and private devotion, liturgy, and cathedral art with its sculptured biblical scenes. Mendicant monks became educators of the people. The universities developed under the power of the church and the desire of people to be educated. The greatness of the universities lay in their ability to defend critics such as Peter Abelard, who forthrightly pointed out contradictions in the Christian tradition.

The power of the church became so strong that fear of excommunication caused most people to accept the church's teaching. The Inquisition served to enforce this rule. However, communities of dissent developed around the ideal that all the people could know and interpret the Scripture according to the Spirit's direction, e.g., Waldensians, Hussites, and Lollards. Interestingly, universities anticipated this change. Although the universities continued in the Augustinian tradition, they were sharply challenged by Aristotelianism. Aquinas managed to show that Aristotle did not conflict with the church fathers, but his synthesis broke apart under the criticism of William of Occam and Duns Scotus. Their views gave support to the idea that the truth is within individuals and independent of the church's authority. The third order of Saint Francis also increased hope that everyone could live with the same dedication as the monastic communities. Popular religious devotion joined forces with political restiveness against Rome's control and with radical economic changes in the feudal culture to establish the historical precondition for the Reformation. An important precondition of the Reformation was the invention of the printing press and the vernacular translations of the Scriptures. This meant all who were educated could read the Word of God and could be instructed by their own reading.

Aside from the religious communities, the cathedrals, the mendicant monks, the troubadours, the public plays, and the confessional, court life also shaped the popular religious self-concept. The ideal of the lady and the gentleman combined the courtesy (court-esy) of privileged society with the monastic ideals. Children's literature of the time also reflected these same ideals. The confessional represented an enormously powerful means of education, since it was supported by the threat of excommunication. For this reason, Luther's challenge to the medieval church focused on confession.

THE REFORMATION AND AFTER

The Reformation represented a radical educational shift. The medieval church had emphasized learning to accept and function within one's place in society. Education, through the cathedral, the arts, and drama, was heavily visual. Simple people learned to conform to the teachings of the church, as already described. With Luther, knowledge of God became a matter of the heart. Faith was no longer an objective reality operant upon anyone who did not mentally resist the power of the sacrament. Faith was, rather, experiencing one's will being knowingly drawn to God. Faith required repentance before God, not the priest, and a willingness to acknowledge one's inability to justify oneself. The experience of faith included a proper understanding of justification. Therefore, preaching replaced eucharist, confession, and penance as primary educational methods. The university faculties of religion were to protect the truth of the faith. Pastors were to be rightly taught, and they in turn were to preach correct doctrine. The people learned by being instructed in the Scriptures, but that instruction could not replace the actual experience of confessing one's sin and trusting that one has been forgiven.

Learning began to focus much more on hearing the word of God than on visualizing spiritual reality. Calvin continued Luther's focus on preaching, as did Zwingli. With Zwingli's doctrine of sacrament as a reminder, remembering became paramount. However, in all of these cases the truth of what was taught was enforced by the public authorities. Here, many of the Anabaptist groups took a different stance toward authority. They understood that each believer was to correct the other's vision. For them, the truth came in a consensus of the believing community rather than in the power of the legislature to enforce certain views.

The zeal of the Reformation was replaced by efforts to systematize the doctrines of the reformers. The various groups of the Reformation warred against one another until finally they conceded each other's right to exist in the Treaty of Westphalia. Following Luther's example, catechisms for children were developed. Luther's doctrine of sacrament led to the inevitable conclusion that baptism is not complete without a proper understanding of grace. Baptism is not complete without confirmation.

The formalism of post-Reformation theology, coupled with the rudeness of life during the religious wars, led to the development of Pietism. The Pietists taught that faith was not simply an intellectual consent, but a consent of the whole heart. Such heart-felt devotion would be accompanied by study of the Scriptures, love and service toward one's fellow human beings, and constant worship of and prayer to God. Pietism led to the modern mission movement. It was accompanied by the secular movement to Enlightenment, which is the doctrine that everyone can, to some extent, understand what is true and do what is right, without the assistance of superstition or external compulsion.

The implications for education were enormous. If everyone should rightly understand the Scriptures, everyone must know how to read them. Catechism is important for every child, but so then is a proper sense of God's grace when the child is mature enough to understand. This view lent great impetus to the movement for universal education. Religious education in the Scriptures could then parallel a child's capacity to read. But religious education was divided between catechesis as education in right doctrine, and nurture as education of the heart. In societies with a state church, religious education came to be taught as a subject in the public school, and was matched to the child's growing ability to read.

THE SUNDAY SCHOOL

The Sunday school grew up in England as the convergence of a number of tendencies. First, it was literary and reformist. Robert Raikes wanted to provide literacy and moral training for poor children on the street, many of whom were causing trouble. These unruly children were the result of the industrialism that lured many people to urban areas. Quickly, the Sunday school movement was taken over by the evangelicals, who saw it as an opportunity for religious training and evangelization of children. The Sunday School Union developed to support the extension of Sunday schools.[4]

Sunday schools soon spread to the United States, first to Philadelphia, and then to other communities. The Sunday School Union in the United States set the goal of a Sunday school in every community. A teacher and children were located and books were left by itinerant promoters dedicated to founding Sunday schools. Many Union Sunday schools developed congregations around them. The Sunday school movement was taken into churches in the period from 1830 to the Civil War. In the post–Civil War period Dwight Moody and others gave the Sunday school movement an evangelical thrust. Sunday school conventions on the order of political conventions were set up at local, district, state, and international levels, which became a focus for ecumenical activity. Councils of churches often developed in the wake of the conventions.

In 1903, the Religious Education Association was set up to promote the idea of using the findings of modern psychology and education in religious education. New conceptions of child development, a graded curriculum, and experiential learning were particularly promoted. These ideas gained immediate acceptance in many churches until the 1930s, when the concept of educating into faith was challenged by neo-orthodoxy. The whole "ecology of education" was shifting, and along with it, the religious sensibilities of millions of people. Church colleges were becoming secularized. Working women and popular entertainment such as movies and television led to a decline in Sunday school attendance. The social criticism of the 1960s challenged the "suburban captivity of the church" and the middle-class captivity of the Sunday school.[5] For many, Sunday school came to mean everything trivial about religion. Nevertheless, many evangelical Sunday schools using buses to transport students and stressing students' conversion kept high enrollments.

The decade of the seventies saw the renaissance of a plethora of activities under the aegis of Christian education. Some groups have accepted the challenge of the death of the Sunday school and sought to resurrect the longer tradition of catechesis (Westerhoff). If the birth of the social sciences was felt in 1903, then the radical expansion of the social sciences was felt in the seventies. Almost all the recent ideas of psychology and education are to be found in one church school program or another. While the future of the Sunday school is uncertain, there seems to be a broadening of the selection of ways to nurture Christian faith.

CHURCH AND STATE IN AMERICA

In colonial America, religious education was carried on in the family, the school, the church, and to some extent the public. Again, one should look at the role of education in the community covenant rather than simply examine the methods of educating. Universities founded in colonial America have become the great universities of today (Harvard, Yale, Princeton). Without exception, these schools were founded around schools of theology, in the tradition of the European universities.

The teaching of religion in the public school was not so much a separate subject, but interwoven into the curriculum. This is best illustrated by *The New England Primer*,[6] a book employing biblical quotations and religious stories to teach reading. Children were taught

Aristotle's view that to live well one must constantly meditate upon one's death. Many moral maxims and stories were included in the primer. However, *The New England Primer* presumed a unified religious and political orientation, a situation that would not last long in America.

The many religious groups of colonial America often depended on their common life, worship, and long sermons to do the educating of children and adults alike. Some groups developed their own elementary schools, others did not. Just as the plurality of religious commitment forced the constitutional convention to allow and protect freedom of religion, that is, religious pluralism, so educators sought some way to allow for religious pluralism in public schools. The way ahead was to separate the religious and moral content of education. The specifically religious was left to home and church, while the moral and educational were taught in the school. Robert Lynn, Elliott Wright, and others have suggested that even so, these early public schools were Protestant in fact because of the strong Protestant ethos of that time.[7]

With the growth of America and the increasing pluralism of the society, the problem of a unified moral commitment among citizens continued to assert itself. Leading educators of the time saw public education as a primary source of common moral commitment, and the McGuffey reader was developed to help forge that consensus.[8] It contained stories with a moral or religious tone, which became grist for the educational mills. The readers were very widely used, and they continued the distinctly Protestant tone of the public schools. The many Catholic immigrants who came into the United States in the late nineteenth century felt excluded from what remained predominantly a Protestant school system. Some Lutherans, Catholics, Mennonites, and other groups provided their own private parochial schools.

Pluralism in the United States has grown in the twentieth century, and public schools have been pushed to provide an education that adjusts to it. Specifically, the courts have sought to avoid an established religion in the public schools, while at the same time encouraging appropriate moral teaching. The 1920s saw the growth of released time education for religion. Children on school property and during school hours were released for religious education, which was generally done by cooperating Protestant denominations. However the Supreme Court ruled released time to be unconstitutional. The high court, in the 1963 Schempp decision, has allowed that teaching *about* religion can be done as a part of regular course work. Worship or teaching for conversion is not permitted. As a result, many high schools are now offering courses about religion. Some released time religious teaching is also still carried on.

Religiously neutral moral education continues to be very important in the public schools, either formally or informally. The moral intention found in *The New England Primer* and the McGuffey reader is today found in a variety of courses. In the early 1980s, the National Council of Churches prepared materials for use in public schools that lift up the values of peace.[9] Courses in moral development and moral responsibility are widely taught. At the same time, there has been an increase in private and Christian schools. Even as the number of Roman Catholic private schools has diminished, the number of others has increased. The pattern of moral education in the public schools, religious interpretation within the church and family, and private schools for those bodies most at variance with the common ethos seems to be continuing as it has since the colonial period. The particular issue of prayer in the public schools reflects the doubleness of the values involved. Is non-denominational prayer possible? Would such prayer violate the constitutional safeguard against established religion? These are current questions of public debate.

The discussion so far has traced the highlights of the story of teaching in the faith community from the time of the early Hebrews through the history of Christianity in the West, and especially in the United States. By taking a longer view of the story of teaching, the reader can set the trends of twentieth-century Christian education into a broader perspective. However, one's perspective can be tested even further by contrasting a modern non-Western experience with what has already been given. The purpose of the following case study is for the reader to understand how the content, process, and effects of Christian teaching are related to each other in a non-Western culture. The awareness of teaching in other cultures is very important if the purpose of Christian education is global participation. To this end I have chosen the story of Christian teaching in Nigeria, primarily because of my own personal experience there.

■ ■ ■

CASE STUDY: SOCIAL PRACTICE AND CHRISTIAN TEACHING IN NIGERIA

An Approach

From January to March, 1983, I taught courses in Christian doctrine and education at the Theological College of Northern Nigeria in a position obtained through my affiliation with the Church of the Brethren, one of the eight Protestant denominations cooperatively sponsoring the college. There are perhaps only a half dozen seminaries teaching at the college and postgraduate level in Nigeria. (However, this is balanced by the fact that the public universities have sizable religion departments.) I resided in the school's guest house, and my travel outside the school was limited, although I did travel for about two weeks, primarily in northeastern Nigeria, in the vicinity of Maiduguri and Biu.

Some weeks after I arrived, it occurred to me that the religious situation of Nigeria is uniquely suited to the study of the social effects of Christianity and of Islam. Roughly half the population is Muslim and the other half is Christian. No one knows the exact numbers because the last census was taken a decade ago and was acknowledged to be very approximate at that time. There are also adherents to traditional religion as practiced in the villages, but their numbers are also uncertain.

Nigeria provides a unique test situation in which the effects of Christian and Islamic teaching can be compared to each other and to those of traditional religion. This uniqueness becomes more evident when one remembers that in most countries where Islam is powerful, its adherents have total control. Islam must share its influence in Nigeria, since the constitution protects freedom of religious belief and since the Muslim Sharia courts have not been given authority over all legal decisions. The result is that the power and influence of Islam and Christianity are roughly balanced.

Southern Nigeria, where education and technology are more advanced, is predominantly Christian. Northern Nigeria, the locus of Muslim dominance for a thousand years through the Hausa and Filani tribes, remains largely Muslim. Competition for the loyalty of the people is intense, often public, and sometimes breaks into riots. Local traditions still persist. One of my informants suggested that the Yoruba tribe in the southwest of Nigeria are more Yoruba than Christian. I spent a week visiting the people in the bush outside Biu, which is located in northeastern Nigeria. I found intense loyalty to the traditions of the Bura, Higgi, Chibuck, and other tribes, in spite of the fact that the Muslim Filani tribe had been dominant in the area for hundreds of years. Much local tradition has been lost to either Christianity or Islam, but much also persists.

The division of Nigeria between Islam and Christianity provides what Max Weber called "an historical experiment." Weber used this method to investigate the economic effects of the Protestant Reformation. The main line of Weber's argument is that when social, cultural, and political factors are similar from one region to another, and when at the same time religious belief and practice differ from one region to another, then whatever economic differences are present may in part be due to the difference in religious belief and practice. Weber argues that such conditions prevailed in sixteenth-century Europe. Modern capitalism began to be practiced on a wider scale in just those areas where Protestantism was predominant. Thus Weber argues for the influence of Protestantism by providing a "spirit" that was essential, although not sufficient in itself, for the beginning of modern capitalism.

Nigeria provides a similar historical experiment. Since the religious division is within the same country, social, political, and cultural factors are alike from one place to another. Since given regions are either predominantly Christian or Muslim, the influence of the religion in those regions becomes evident by comparing them to one another. One important exception is that local traditions may vary from one tribe to another. One then becomes especially interested in those tribes where some have become Christian and some Muslim. One can also attend to tribes that have overcome their differences.

The limitations of Weber's method have been hotly debated for a century.[10] Many questions have been raised, but it is not my purpose here to review that discussion. Suffice it to say that in spite of the criticisms, Weber's thesis is still widely respected. More severe than the limitation of Weber's methods were my own circumstantial limitations. I was not able to gain firsthand experience of very much of Nigeria. Rather, I was limited to a few conversations with a few knowledgable people. Therefore what I suggest can only be taken as tentative observations. My findings may be totally in error, but my personal experience leads me to think they have some validity.

After an initial discussion of Christianity and its alternatives in Nigeria, I will offer some suggestions about Christianity's influence on family and gender roles, the state, economics, and finally, educational and service institutions.

Christian Teaching in Nigeria

Christianity first came to Nigeria through the freed slaves from Freetown. Somewhat later, missionaries from European mission societies appeared, and still later came missionaries from America. The Christian influence in Nigeria is therefore about two centuries old. Roman Catholic missions came in the twentieth century, as did the Church of the Brethren mission to which I was related. Christianity in the south is generally acknowledged to be much more advanced than that of the north. The largest Protestant churches in the north are the Evangelical Church of West Africa (ECWA) and the fellowship of evangelical churches in Nigeria (TEKAN). The latter group includes such churches as Anglican, Lutheran, Methodist, English Baptist, and Church of the Brethren.[11]

Basic teaching one hears in the churches includes God's grace and acceptance of all believers in Jesus Christ; the change of heart brought by God's love, through Christ; Christian freedom from pagan traditions; the sanctity of marriage; the fellowship of the church; the power of the Holy Spirit; the importance of the study of the Bible; the love of one another, even including the enemy; and God's ultimate triumph over the evil of this world. While so general a description cannot be completely accurate, it gives the reader an impression. I suspect that all the denominations of America and Europe are active in Nigeria, including the Mormons, Jehovah's Witnesses, and other groups. In addition, Africa has given rise to a unique group of Christian sects reflecting the influence of traditional tribal religions.

Many missionaries are present and active in Nigeria, although their numbers have declined with the mission movement's attempt to indigenize missions. The Nigerian government is also much stricter about allowing only persons with technical training into the country.

Traditional Religion

Traditional religion in Nigeria is based on a tribal system. A tribe is a group with a unity of language and common religious, kinship, economic, and social commitments. There are hundreds of local tribes, and therefore hundreds of local languages. The tribes with which I became most familiar were the Bura, Higgi, Margi, and Chibuk, all of whom originally resided in northeastern Nigeria. At one time tribes must have been restricted to one area, but now tribal members reside throughout Nigeria.

While customs varied from one tribe to another, some generalizations seem to hold. Usually the men were members of a male cult. They handled the sacred artifacts, kept the tribal secrets, and directed the religious rituals. Men who could afford the bride price would have a number

61

of wives. Each wife would farm her own land as well as a share of her husband's land. From her own land she would feed her children, and she would keep any profit she could make. She was also obligated to till her husband's crops. Therefore a man with many wives would usually have considerable wealth. The men protected their wives in warfare, so that women ordinarily outnumbered men.

There were periodic tribal ceremonies with much magic and sacrifice to the spirits. Religious practices were related to the spirits, the ancestors, and the High God. The spirits of the ancestors were thought to return and reside in various family members, and it was important to keep the memory and traditions of the ancestors alive. Different spirits controlled the tribe's day-to-day and seasonal destiny. To satisfy the displeasure of the spirits, it was necesssary to offer a variety of sacrifices. The High God was considered to be above the ancestors and the spirits. When all else failed, one appealed to the High God. Each tribe had its local ancestors and spirits, but the High God was above all tribes.

Islam

Islam came to Nigeria some seven hundred years ago. It was carried by the Filani tribe in the northeast and the Hausa tribe in the northwest. Islam traditionally came to an area either through military occupation or by the conversion of a political leader who in turn required his subjects to be converted. More recently Islam has also used street preaching and conversion techniques more characteristic of Christianity. An Islamic community is under the moral leadership of the Emir, who usually has great influence and wealth. Legal controversies are decided by Muslim law as administered by the Sharia court. Times of prayer begin as early as 4:00 A.M. and run through the day. I often saw a truck driver, worker, or merchant stop whatever he was doing at 4:00 P.M. to prostrate himself in prayer.

Almsgiving is a virtue of all believers, and beggars are therefore thought to bring blessing to the community. There are many beggars at every public meeting place. Generally the positions of greatest power are controlled by Muslims, while Christians tend to have civil service positions. Christians are thought to be more numerous than Muslims in the police force and the army. The basic Islamic virtue is one of submission, which is the root meaning of the word "Islam." Muslims are submissive to their religious superiors, and they expect those whom they control to be submissive to them. There is a strong sense of loyalty to a leader who is thought to be following Muslim law, but that loyalty can shift when the religious law is considered to be violated. The Koran, the Muslim Scripture, permits plunder of enemies. Muslims were considered by my informants to control much of the trade and the business of Nigeria. They also have a strong sense of God's will. To be caught in cheating or fraud must mean that God is against that particular episode.

The Family and the Role of Women

Everyone seems to agree that Christianity brought with it monogamy. Christians were originally called "the one-wifed people." The missionaries were originally quite strict about monogamy, requiring that every wife except the first be put away. That resulted in a group of divorced women and dislocated children who were intensely anti-Christian. The churches today argue that divorce is as much forbidden in the Bible as polygamy. Therefore a man married to several wives before being converted to Christianity can now come into the church without divorcing those wives. Marriages after conversion must be monogamous. However, churches face pressure to allow plural marriages, and a number of Christian sectarian churches allow traditional marriage practices. Although Islam sanctions plural marriages, there are many monogamous marriages among Muslims.

Christianity has considerably changed the lives of women. Unlike traditional customs, Christianity does not regard women as periodically unclean. Women are allowed to participate in the worship service, something forbidden by both traditional religion and Islam. Christian women take an active part in church life and worship. Women are now being admitted into pastoral training programs.

Christianity releases many women and men from local loyalties. They become free to move to urban areas. The new-found freedom is, however, a mixed blessing. Single women in the cities have difficulty finding jobs, and many resort to prostitution. Married women in the cities often must return to the village to farm their land, lest it be assigned to someone else. The husband's job is too tenuous to risk losing farming privileges. As an only wife, a woman may have greater hardship in providing for her husband and less opportunity to accumulate any resources of her own.

Christianity provides an ideal of love and care between family members that is neither traditional nor Muslim. In contrast to the older customs, Christian couples want to love their children. Much conversation at the theological school where I taught was given to overcoming the traditional secrecy and reserve between husband and wife. Still, most Christian women serve meals to their husbands and then retire to a separate room to eat with the children. Christian women from a Muslim area have trouble even looking at a man, something forbidden by Muslim tradition.

The State

British protection of what is now Nigeria began in the nineteenth century when British ships sought to limit the slave trade. By 1900 England established its rule over Nigeria, a rule which lasted until 1960. In that year Nigeria became self-governing under its own constitution. The constitution was amended in 1975, granting a separation of religion and politics.

My informants seemed agreed that Christianity contributed much to the cessation of slavery in Nigeria, whereas the Muslim faith did not discourage the practice. Missionaries fought against it in many ways, often buying slaves at the market in order to free them. The British effort to limit slavery was not entirely successful until the missionaries opposed it. Slavery is now constitutionally forbidden.

I was intrigued by the question of whether Christianity affected attitudes regarding war and peace. All my informants said that Christianity encourages love of all people rather than enmity. Previously, tribal customs often led to constant intertribal warfare. In forging the political unity of Nigeria, the British forbade intertribal warfare, and villages violating this order were leveled to the ground. Some of my informants attributed the relative peacefulness of today to the strictness of the British rule against warfare. In general my informants felt that Christian teaching seems to make people more peaceable. An exception to this observation was seen in the recent civil war, when the predominantly Christian Ibo tribe was slaughtered by other Christians.

The struggle between Christianity and Islam led to freedom of religion under the present constitution. Local governments must provide both Christian and Muslim religious training for those who want it. What is actually provided, however, depends a great deal upon the religious sentiments of local administrators. As already mentioned, the 1975 constitutional revision did not allow the Sharia court system, which would have put all Christians under Muslim law. Today the Sharia courts exist as a parallel system for Muslims, beside the established secular courts.

Economics

There is a great deal of physical labor in Nigeria (of which women seem to carry a large share), but there seems to be very little sense of the work ethic as Max Weber described it, and little effort to expedite commerce. Businesspeople seem lax about helping customers, but that may be a Western bias. Many expect to receive "gifts" for carrying out responsibilities. There are frequent strikes because local governments are often unable to meet the people's expectations.

The elite Christian lawyers and doctors work together under professional standards, while trade unions protect employees from the work ethic. Seldom is anyone fired. Under the tribal system all persons were to be cared for, and the unions perpetuate that attitude. There is little sense of vocation. While Muslims control most of the trading, the more important fact is that trade ethics are related to family obligations. As Max Weber observed, when trade is related to traditional family patterns, modern work attitudes do not develop. Many Nigerian people are not well educated, so the country lacks a substratum of skilled workers.

Christianity releases people from local customs, makes them mobile, and brings them to urban areas. Christianity supports the secular and encourages education. There are radically fewer beggars in Christian areas, the crippled being cared for by their families. But these same tendencies have also led to social problems such as alcoholism, drug addiction, prostitution, and unemployment.

Schools and Hospitals

Nearly everyone I spoke to agreed that schools and hospitals were initiated by the missionaries. Medicine and education added enormous appeal to Christianity. Recently, schools and hospitals were taken over by the state. The state itself recognizes the decline in these institutions since they are no longer run by Christian groups. It has asked the churches to take schools and hospitals back again, but they will not do so—the cost is too forbidding. Universities have now been established by the federal government on the European and American model. There is a tremendous desire for education, students generally feeling that the government owes everyone an education.

Conclusion

Christianity seems to have brought some dramatic social changes to Nigeria; monogamous marriage, abolition of slavery, and modern education and medicine are the most obvious. A wider range of choices for women, peaceful rather than bellicose attitudes, a sense of public justice, economic mobility, and professional groups with ethical standards may be due in part to Christianity, although these latter effects seem less directly related to Christian teaching than the former. I cannot make a strong case for Christianity establishing the work ethic, because of public indifference and laxity of commercial interest. Christianity also seems indirectly to have contributed to such social problems as unemployment and alcholism.

■ ■ ■

A NOTE ON THE USE OF CASE STUDIES

The advantage of a case study is that it gives people an actual account from life for purposes of discussion. Everyone has the same data in front of them. Some educators believe that the case study should be long and involved, to convey something of the complexity of actual life. Cases should present factual data and narrate some of the actual complexities; they may conclude by posing the choice for the reader. Case studies are disadvantaged by being limited to the perspective of the writer. Often the writer's opinion strongly biases what is presented, so that important data may be left out. Case studies also may simplify what are complex problems in actual life.

The teaching of case studies can be instructive when the teacher poses a problem for the students to discuss. While a teacher may want to show how a given problem looks in a live situation, teaching a case study is best done by encouraging students to define for themselves the most basic issue. Inevitably, the case can be interpreted in different ways, and therefore students often do not agree about which issue is prior to all others. The search for a fundamental perspective can be very instructive. Life itself does not identify the questions to be addressed. Case studies reflect life when they stimulate the reader to struggle to find the real problem. In identifying problems and solutions, students should be able to give evidence from the case to support a point of view.

Cases are most instructive when there is a difference of opinion about an issue. The discussion becomes spirited and inquiry becomes stronger. The instructor can help by clearly identifying issues as they emerge in a group discussion.

STUDY SUGGESTIONS
Exercises

1. Develop a time line for your congregation. Let the line represent the total life of the congrega-

tion. Mark the line to represent every decade. In a large meeting of the whole congregation ask people to remember events for each decade. Who were the significant people? Who were the pastors? What were the high and low points in the life of the church? Which were the significant turning points? How did customs and practices change? How did people's commitments and loyalties change? What was happening in the world at the time, and how did it influence the church? What is the current direction of the congregation's story?

2. Conduct a worship service as it would have been conducted in an earlier decade. If persons from that decade are still alive, let them help plan the service. Have people wear clothing of that time. Remind people of world events of the day. Carry out the service as it was done then, using appropriate hymns and worship resources. After the event discuss with one another the changes that have occurred in the congregation's form of worship. What is enduring in the church's story, and what is subject to change?

3. In a large group, or perhaps in individual interviews, ask persons to discuss the reasons for their loyalty to the church. If in a large group, divide into buzz groups of two persons who will discuss with one another the question, What loyalty do I feel to the church and why? After fifteen minutes ask the groups of two to join together in groups of four to discuss the same question. Then ask all the groups to share something of their discussion with the whole assembly. What did you discover about loyalty to the church? How has it changed over the years?

4. Meet with a Jewish congregation. Let each group share the ways in which they teach the tradition to members of the congregation, both older and younger. To what extent does the Jewish congregation follow the procedures listed in this chapter? How different and how similar are the two groups' approaches to education?

5. Divide your group into four subgroups. Let each one of the groups take a different Gospel and examine Jesus' teaching methods. Study a commentary on the Gospel to discover how the biblical account may reflect the circumstances of the Gospel writer and the community for which the Gospel was originally intended. Come together and compare the teaching methods of each Gospel. How are the accounts of those methods influenced by the circumstances of the writing? What do you conclude about teaching in the early church? Are there analogies for today?

6. Let a Roman Catholic and a Protestant group meet together. Compare with one another how teaching is carried out in your congregation. Who decides what will be taught? What curriculum is used? What are the main purposes of the curriculum? What are the main teaching events? How important is worship to teaching? What roles do the pastor and the priest have? To what extent do Roman Catholic congregations use methods similar to those of the medieval period, as described in this chapter?

7. Go to the library to discover materials that were used for Christian teaching in the United States before the twentieth century. Look for Sunday School Union materials, *The New England Primer*, and McGuffey readers. What themes

were being taught? How much content was secular and how much was religious?

8. At the library, get the text of the 1963 Schempp decision of the Supreme Court, which forbids school-sponsored religious ceremonies but allows classes to study about religion. Visit any public school in your area in which there are classes about religion. Interview the teachers, the principal, and several students. Does the Schempp distinction between sponsoring religion and studying about religion hold up in practice?

9. Visit a Muslim community, or at least someone from a Muslim community. Share with one another how religious teaching is done. How does religious teaching affect community customs and practices? Are there differences between Muslim and Christian approaches to religious teaching? If so, what are they?

10. Discuss the case study of Nigeria given in this chapter. What is the interaction between Christian teaching and community practice in Nigeria? How does it compare with traditional religion and Islam? Do you find the same kind of interactions in your own congregation?

Questions for Discussion

1. How do stories make people aware of the change in community practices?

2. To what extent can the Hebrew idea of Torah be the Christian ideal of religious education?

3. What are the characteristics of good teaching as seen in the gospel account?

4. What elements of medieval religious education are appropriate for contemporary religious education?

5. How did the message of the reformers of the sixteenth century change the ideals and methods of religious education in the church?
6. Compare the "ecology of education" in the nineteenth and the late twentieth centuries as it has influenced religious education.
7. What is the value of separating religious and public education? How far ought such separation go?
8. In reviewing the history of Christianity, what are the dominant modes of religious education?
9. To what extent has the effect of religious teaching on the role of women in Nigeria been positive and/or negative?
10. Name some of the changes in Nigerian social practice associated with Christian teaching.

Suggestions for Further Reading

Walter Brueggemann, *The Creative Word: Canon as a Model for Biblical Education.*
Brueggemann shows how Torah, prophets, and wisdom offer different and complementary styles of teaching.

Robert W. Lynn and Elliott Wright, *The Big Little School.*
Traces the origin and continuing influence of the Sunday school.

Jack L. Seymour, *From Sunday School to Church School: Continuities in Protestant Church Education in the United States, 1860–1929.*
Offers an alternative interpretation to Lynn's on the history of the Sunday school.

Lewis Sherrill, *The Rise of Christian Education.*
An older book that traces the same story presented in this chapter.

Chapter Three:

THE GLOBAL COMMUNITY

Briefly stated, the purpose of Christian education both individually and communally is to live in repentance, prayer, and service for the sake of God's kingdom. Christian education should explore and critique the ongoing life and practice of the faith community in view of its biblical heritage; accept and renew the covenant of faithfulness to the Christian story of God's grace and love; and transform and reform the community's life and practice by participating in the global community that God in Christ is bringing into this time and place.

This way of stating the purpose of the church's teaching ministry puts priority on the community context. It locates doctrine within the setting of practice and moves from actual practice toward participation in God's kingdom. In each moment there is both a receiving and a response in one and the same action. Practice is received as it is and critiqued. Faithfulness is accepted and renewed. The new life in Christ is received as transformation and acted out as reformation. In the language of classical theology, the movement is from regeneration to justification to santification. In the expression of piety the movement is from repentance to prayer to service. In all moments the direction is toward global participation.

SEARCH FOR A PURPOSE

When we look to the present and future of education and nurture in the faith community, we are inevitably drawn to a discussion of purpose, which anticipates the new community. To discuss the purpose of Christian education is to be drawn into the ongoing story of that purpose. Therefore we now look to the effort to define or describe the purpose of the educational enterprise within the community of faith.

The Reformation had a passionate concern for right teaching. In the Lutheran phrase, the goal of right teaching was faith active in love. Right teaching does not in itself bring the grace of God; it has the more indirect function of fending off and correcting misunderstandings. Teaching in the church aims at clarifying the proper understanding of faith active in love. The presence and power of God's grace is not dependent on any human activity, certainly not teaching or preaching. However, the church can attempt to correct misunderstandings that stand in the way of perceiving and responding to God's grace. In a general way, Calvin's understanding of teaching in the church was very similar. For both Luther and Calvin, the pastor has a fundamental responsibility to be sure that the gospel is rightly understood in the congregation.

The Pietist revival of the seventeenth and eighteenth centuries brought a new element to the purpose of education. The gospel was not only to be rightly understood, but was also to be genuinely experienced and actively expressed. Schleiermacher suggested that the purpose of teaching in the church is "God-consciousness."

The proper awareness of God is not principally an understanding, but rather a feeling of "absolute dependence" that is expressed in all that one does. Of course, devotion is not to be devoid of right understanding, but neither is devotion necessarily included in a correct conception. Luther had recognized that understanding at best has merely a negative or corrective function. The Pietists attempted to put more directly what Luther allowed to be the reality beyond words. The question, which we will not attempt to answer, is whether the Pietists distorted a right understanding of God's grace by speaking more directly of human affections toward God.[1]

Nineteenth-century American churches aimed at a biblical understanding that affected public practice.[2] By the latter part of the century the purpose of the church school was to enhance maturity of character, biblical understanding, church participation, and civic responsibility.[3] The early twentieth century saw the birth of progressivism in religious education. The focus moved to the development of moral character, graded biblical materials, church participation, and responsibility for the total human community. Progressivist George Albert Coe constantly called for religious education to aim at a broader world awareness.[4] These goals represent a concerted effort to put into wider practice what was already explicit by the latter nineteenth century.[5] In contrast to the progressive education movement, fundamentalism and evangelicalism wanted more stress on the Bible and less on social-psychological theory.

One of the most influential statements of purpose formulated in the early twentieth century was written by Paul Vieth in 1929 and revised by the Division of Christian Education of the National Council of Churches in America. The revised list includes eight comprehensive objectives:

1. God

Christian education seeks to foster in growing persons a consciousness of *God* as a reality in human experience, and a sense of personal relationship to Him.

2. Jesus Christ

Christian education seeks to develop in growing persons such an understanding and application of the personality, life, and teaching of *Jesus* as will lead to experience of Him as Savior and Lord, loyalty to Him and His cause, and will manifest itself in daily life and conduct.

3. Christ-like character

Christian education seeks to foster in growing persons a progressive and continuous development of *Christ-like character.*

4. Christian social order

Christian education seeks to develop in growing persons the ability and disposition to participate in and contribute constructively to the building of a *social order* throughout the world, embodying the ideal of the Fatherhood of God and the brotherhood of man.

5. Churchmanship

Christian education seeks to develop in growing persons the ability and disposition to participate in the organized society of Christians—the *Church.*

6. Christian Family

Christian education seeks to develop in growing persons an appreciation of the meaning and importance of the *Christian family,* and the ability and disposition to participate in and contribute constructively to the life of this primary social group.

7. Christian life philosophy

Christian education seeks to lead growing persons into a Christian interpretation of life and the universe; the ability to see in it God's purpose and plan; a *life philosophy* built on this interpretation.

8. Bible and other materials

Christian education seeks to effect in growing persons the assimilation of the best religious experience of the race, preeminently that recorded in the *Bible,* as effective guidance to present experience.[6]

The mid-twentieth century saw strong criticism of the progressivist movement in religious education. Neo-orthodoxy questioned whether faith can ever be a product of instruction. The call was for a return to the study of the central Christian doctrines and to right instruction. Neo-orthodoxy was very much influenced by Kierkegaard, who wrote of the Christ, "He is the sign, the sign of contradiction, and so all direct communication is impossible."[7] Under the influence of neo-orthodoxy, religious education became more sceptical of social science, more concerned about sin, revelation, and grace.

The objectives formulated in the mid-twentieth century show increasing theological influence, as shown in the following statement by Lawrence Little et al.:

> The supreme purpose of Christian education is to enable persons to become aware of the seeking love of God as revealed in Jesus Christ and to respond in faith to this love in ways that will help them grow as children of God, live in accordance with the will of God, and sustain a vital relationship to the Christian Community.

Little then proceeded to give this further specification, that Christian education under the guidance of the Holy Spirit endeavors

> To assist persons, at each state of development, to realize the highest potentialities of the self as divinely created, to commit themselves to Christ, and to grow toward maturity as persons;
> To help persons establish and maintain Christian relationships with their families, their churches, and with other individuals and groups, taking responsible roles in society, and seeing in every human being an object of the love of God;
> To aid persons in gaining a better understanding and awareness of the natural world as God's creation and accepting responsibility for conserving its values and using them in the service of God and of mankind;

To lead persons to an increasing understanding and appreciation of the Bible, whereby they may hear and obey the Word of God; to help them appreciate and use effectively other elements in the historical Christian heritage;

To enable persons to discover and fulfill responsible roles in the Christian fellowship through faithful participation in the local and world mission of the church.[8]

The statement of objectives just given was very influential in forming the cooperative curriculum project of the National Council of Churches. The outlines of the cooperative curriculum project were used by many Protestant denominations to develop their own study materials.

During the same period, H. Richard Niebuhr wrote a statement of "the purpose of the church and its ministry." He concluded that the purpose is "the increase of the love of God and neighbor."[9] His concern was to state the goal directly and simply enough to help release churches from the nationalistic and denominational idolatries in which they are caught.

CURRENT OPTIONS

A recent publication suggests that there are currently five major approaches to religious education.[10] These approaches continue the tendencies of the earlier part of the century. Nevertheless, several new emphases are present. Liberation theology and hermeneutical theory have been introduced, the radical critique of the church school is evident, and new theories of faith development are being proposed. The five options suggested by Seymour and Miller are: religious instruction, faith community, spiritual development, liberation, and interpretation. Let us consider each in turn.

The goal of *religious instruction* is to transmit Christian understanding and practice. Sara Little distinguishes instruction, in which the learner has the freedom to choose, from indoctrination, in which the learner is in some way compelled to adopt a certain understanding.[11] The freedom to understand and choose means that conversion can be at the center of instruction.

The goal of the *faith community* approach is "to build a congregation into a community where persons can encounter the faith and learn its lifestyle."[12] There is an increased focus on the community nature of the Christian church and its educational settings. The life of the congregation becomes the setting within which Christian learning takes place.

The goal of *spiritual development* is to grow in faith to spiritual maturity. The growth of the whole person includes emotional, moral, and spiritual development. The various stages of development can be more or less identified, and these stages serve to guide the church in its educational task. Differences between individuals are accounted important, and each is encouraged to grow in her or his own way and at her or his own rate.

The goal of *liberation* is to transform both the church and people for liberation and humanization. People are to become critically aware of oppressive structures, especially those that are racist, sexist, economic, political, and cultural. They learn to understand the ways in which their private and corporate, secular and religious life patterns contribute to the oppression of other people. The goal is increasing justice for all people.

The goal of *interpretation* is to connect Christian perspectives and practices to contemporary experiences. People are engaged in exploring and seeking meaning from surrounding reality in terms of the ongoing Christian story. The emphasis is on uncovering God's activity in the events of the day.

What is evident from these five contemporary approaches to Christian education is the strong continuity with Paul Vieth's eight goals. The understanding of God and Christ is picked up by the instructional model, although each of the other models includes a focus on God and Christ. Christ-like character is picked up in the developmental model. The Christian social order is seen in liberation theology. The Christian philosophy of life is continued in the hermeneutic model, although also in the others. Biblical understanding is especially central to instruction and hermeneutic. The focus on family is missing, except perhaps in the congregational model, but in fact, this was a later addition to Vieth's original list.

The five contemporary approaches also show the effect of contemporary issues. Religious instruction has been shaped by half a century of learning theory and a new orthodoxy in theology. The congregational model is influenced by anthropology and sociology as well as a renewed theology of the church. Human development has been an expanding field of study for decades, and this is now coupled with interest in spirituality. Liberation shows the influence of Third World self-awareness. Hermeneutic has grown out an interest in the science of interpretation and a century of critical study of Scripture. So the current statement of the purposes of Christian education reflects current trends as well as strong continuity with the earlier statements.

EMERGING OPTIONS

In addition to the five models and purposes suggested by Seymour and Miller, a number of other purposes are emerging. To some extent they are variants upon the above themes, but in other ways they are not. For example, Mary Elizabeth Moore offers a *traditioning model* of education. She suggests that "the primary goals of

Christian religious education . . . are knowledge with understanding and the transformation of person's actions, beliefs, and values."[13] The "knowledge with understanding" is of the past events of the tradition, Scripture, and church history. The "transformation" comes in present beliefs and values, as persons anticipate the future. Moore's traditioning model has much in common with the hermeneutical and the congregational models given above.

Another new way of speaking of the purpose of Christian education is in terms of *shalom,* God's peace. The popular idea of peace is that of quietness, meditation, absence of inward tension, and absence of overt conflict. But the biblical concept of shalom is much more dynamic, active, outgoing, and energizing. Shalom is a fullness and completeness in which one and all feel the depth of life within ongoing activity. Shalom overcomes the powers by which life tears itself apart. Shalom is to live life richly, to have one's place in nature, to be related to a community and a community of communities, to experience life as God intends it.

	Value of Persons		Creative Change	
God's Power and Love		**SHALOM**		Value of Conflict
	Human Network		Care for Resources	

There are several elements in the vision of shalom. First, shalom includes the idea that all people are of value. The many ways in which people are discriminated against and oppressed are to be overcome. Second, shalom includes

81

participation and creative change. Change in life is to be accepted as full of possibilities for creativity, even when change is potentially destructive. Third is a positive understanding of conflict. David Augsberger encourages "carefrontation," the challenging of other people because you care for them.[14] Like change, conflict offers possibilities for renewal and creativity.

A fourth element of shalom is care for the world's resources. Humankind is nourished by the creation. The technological revolution cannot change the fact that humankind lives by the river of waters and the tree of life. To pollute nature is to destroy the human umbilical cord. Fifth, shalom is participation in the network of human community. Human societies are interdependent, and the network of interdependence must be cared for and strengthened. Finally, shalom is a vision of God's love and power. Genuine love is full of power, and creative power is an expression of love. So love, power, and justice are joined in the biblical vision of shalom.

Turning from shalom to still another formulation of the purpose of Christian education, some groups are calling for the goal of *discipleship.* Christian education is to provide a context within the congregation in which persons can discuss the problems facing them, commit their lives to Jesus Christ as Savior and Lord and to the church as the people of God, and participate as a body of disciples in the mission of God in the world.[15]

A number of writers are calling Christians to *educate the public.*[16] This purpose is to be engaged in corporately by a community of faith. The stories of what God has done for humanity are reenacted in word and sacrament, reshaping those who participate. They in turn reshape the human environment in the direction of peace and justice.

Religious education must accept its actual role in shaping public attitudes. This involves an exploration of the function of religious experience and faith in the practice of individuals and communities. Religious education should find ways by which the religious faith of persons and groups can affect their everyday experience. Education should be a part of larger congregational events rather than only a private experience or small group discussion. Church education should make connections with other agencies in the wider community so as to shape the emerging vision of the common life. Religious educators should therefore give attention to "mobilizing networks of community agencies, with the intention of negotiating educational programs and strategies for incorporating successive generations into the visions, attitudes, and values of the emerging paideia."[17]

Evangelism continues to be a goal for Christian education. The goal of evangelism is "to persuade men and women to become disciples of Jesus Christ and to serve him in the fellowship of his church."[18] The church growth movement has emphasized the incorporation of persons into the fellowship of the church rather than simply the individual experience of conversion. Such incorporation puts a priority on education both before and after conversion. Education informs so that people might be persuaded, and it better informs those who have already been persuaded. The relationship of evangelism and religious education was foremost throughout the nineteenth century in America, so the church growth movement picks up a long-standing historical trend.[19]

The goal of education for *transformation* parallels the evangelistic concern for conversion.[20] James Loder finds that much religious education is concerned only about social and psychological issues. Loder calls for a deeper penetration into the soul, to the point where the living God engages persons. There, the social veneer is broken through and persons find a new vision to sustain life.

These are the transforming moments, the instances of transition. They are a time of the negation of both past meanings and present doubts. In transforming moments the grace of God in Christ engages human life. Religious education ought therefore to have primary concern about the many transition moments of life.

Another emerging purpose is that of *spiritual growth.* Rediscovery of the spiritual resources of Christianity is currently widespread.[21] Centuries of discipline and resources in meditation and prayer are being rediscovered. Spiritual education seeks to discover a spirit-filled relationship with God that is beyond anxiety and hostility. It seeks constantly to discover the image of God in all other persons. All of the creation becomes the arena of God's love, the place where the Spirit of God will instruct anyone who is receptive.[22]

Emerging Options for Educational Purposes

Traditioning:	Knowledge with understanding and transformation of actions, beliefs, and values.
Shalom:	To live life richly, have a place in nature, participate in life's wholeness, be related to God's power and love.
Discipleship:	To participate as a body of believers in God's mission in the world.
Educating the Public:	To move from religious participation to the shaping of public opinion.
Evangelism:	To persuade persons to become disciples of Christ and serve him in the fellowship of the church.

84

Transformation: To be in touch with the tranform-
ing moments of persons.

Spiritual Growth: To discover that knowing is not
control but rather love.

Education for spiritual growth rests on knowing that is
not control, but rather love.[23] To teach is to become open
to the truth, "to create a space in which obedience to truth
is practiced." Therefore teaching and learning require a
discipline of the spirit, an awareness of the truth beyond
all management, of love beyond all effort. Education for
spiritual growth is much more than a rephrasing of secular
methods of education; it is a recovery of the centuries-old
spiritual traditions of Christianity.

THE GLOBAL CONTEXT

The story of the purpose of Christian education shows
that the purpose is constantly being reformulated according to the circumstances and the new vision of the time.
The circumstances include social, economic, political,
and cultural trends that move history toward the next
epoch. In the late twentieth century pluralism, urbanism,
technology, poverty, militarism, and global interdependence are some of the primary factors affecting the
purposes of religious education.

Pluralism seems to be continually increasing,[24] in part
as the result of the migration of different cultural groups.
Actually, the sixteenth-century Reformation legitimized
secular culture, and secular institutions have been
multiplying since that time. The United States Constitution guarantees the freedom of differing belief, and so
pluralism is a legally established policy.

Countries like the Soviet Union and China as well as
isolated tribes in Africa and South America also experi-

ence the pressures of multiple cultures. These pressures are augmented by the continuing increase in world population and the continuing growth of great metropolitan centers. Economic forces, political conflict, and in some cases famine are causing large migrations. Many Latins and Asians are coming to the United States, as did south Europeans earlier in the century. Famine is forcing thousands of people in Africa to migrate. Mexico City is expected to grow to a city of twenty-five or thirty million people by the turn of the century. Urbanism, awareness of ethnicity, and migration are worldwide trends.

Some discussions of pluralism and secularization have suggested that religion is disappearing in the twentieth century.[25] Recent discussions seem to concede that not only is religion here to stay, but also that the world is becoming more overtly religious.[26] Whether it's Hinduism in India, Protestantism in Ireland, Islam in Iran, Catholicism in Europe, or fundamentalism in the United States, the resurgence of religion is powerful. People all over the world are becoming more self-conscious about their religious and cultural identities. The paradoxical result is that increasing secularization and pluralism are accompanied by increasing religious self-consciousness and commitment.

Economically, many people around the world are in poverty. Though poverty may be a state of mind, poverty for many goes beyond psychology to actual starvation. Paradoxically, international corporations are wealthier and more powerful than ever before, while poverty is more severe. For many people economic deprivation is enforced with political oppression. Many governments resort to the violation of human rights to maintain political control of the poor, and oppressed people turn to terror to break political control.

The migration already mentioned often gives people low status in the host community. For instance, the people of Ghana have low status in Nigeria. Latins, Asians, and blacks generally have low status in the United States. Those from Hong Kong have low status in China. Rural peoples are forced into urban areas where they have little status. Migrant workers in many countries do the least desirable work in order to eke out a meager existence, to the benefit of the majority population. Whether migrant Mexicans in Chicago or migrant Indians in Mexico City, they wash dishes or sell trinkets for survival. Blacks, Latins, and Asians are greatly underrepresented in the job market in the United States in proportion to their numbers in the total population.

There has been a worldwide revolution in customs, roles, and expectations. The Bushmen of southern Africa are being radically changed by pressures from the government of South Africa. The Samoans are much more acculturated than when Margaret Mead conducted her study.[27] Women around the world have a new self-consciousness, and role relationships between males and females are being radically restructured. Women in many places are struggling for economic independence and for inclusive language that is not dominated by masculine metaphors. Paradoxically, the challenge to established customs provokes strong efforts to preserve old traditions. Changed customs bring a magnified pluralism.

Politically, the world is divided between two superpowers, with many smaller powers struggling for greater autonomy. The armaments race continues to pose the possibility of world destruction. The superpower stalemate leads to brushwars, usually in places where political and religious differences reinforce one another. As was already mentioned, the political situation leads to the violation of human rights on one hand, and acts of terrorism, often with religious sanction, on the other hand.

The world's growing population is sustained by an increasingly complex technology. The fundamental character of Western technology is to control and restructure the environment. The result has been pollution, depletion of natural resources, and continuing extinction of animal species. Agricultural engineering has led to super-pest insects, and medical technology has led to complex ethical dilemmas. The world is bound to a technology that seems ever more difficult to control.

As in all generations, religious education takes place within the trends and the vision of the times. Even when education or the church ignores such trends, they have their effect, for such trends are woven into the everyday customs and practices of all people in a myriad of ways. World trends call for a conscious vision to meet them.

EDUCATION FOR GLOBAL PARTICIPATION

Our proposal is that the goal of Christian education be global participation—education for a global community. Religious education occurs in the juxtaposition of the local community and the global community. In the New Testament the church is a sign of the coming kingdom of God, which is a global community of faith. The church, though, is an ambiguous sign, fraught with weakness. The world is a mixture of good and evil; the kingdom of God can be viewed only by anticipating its coming, that is, in an act of faith and hope. In biblical terms, the goal is that all might grow into the maturity of the headship of Jesus Christ, that every knee might bow and every tongue confess that Jesus Christ is Lord, that the reign of God might come on earth as it is in heaven (Ephesians 4:11-16; Philippians 2:20; Matthew 7:10).

In the New Testament, salvation includes liberation. To be in Christ is to be liberated from the principalities and powers of the age. In the cross and the resurrection Christ has overcome the powers. The powers of this age are despair, oppression, poverty, starvation, minority status, violation of human rights, threat of annihilation, terror, and environmental pollution. These are evidences of dehumanization and death in the twentieth century. At their center is a secret urge of humanity to create and sustain itself without accepting the originating and nourishing power of God.[28]

Liberation means examining interactive patterns to discover how they are a part of patterns and interests that keep men and women subjugated. Liberation means participating in the church celebrations and renewals of covenant by which people sustain faith, hope, and love in the midst of the overwhelming powers of the age. Liberation is not simply "coming out from under"; rather, it is the co-creation of a new way. Liberation is a fuller understanding coupled with the creation of new, non-subjugating customs. To celebrate the body of Christ is to begin to live in the way of liberation.

Therefore the first mark of global participation is to recover the power and meaning of the Christian story for these times. The first mark is a joining of study and celebration of the grace of God in Jesus Christ. The interpretation of Scripture privately, in small groups, as a congregation, as groups of congregations, and ecumenically is fundamental to global awareness. Interpretation cannot be separated from repentance, commitment, celebration, and service. Unless the depths of human resistance are overcome in celebration and service, then the power and meaning of the Christian story has not yet been recovered. The sense of God's power, presence and providence, grace, love, and joy are the first mark.

The second mark of global participation is the experience of being joined in the body of Christ. It is the community's support of one another as they live, celebrate, and seek the mind of Christ day by day. Such a community cares for one another enough to support, encourage, grieve with, correct, and be reconciled to one another. Community practices spring from the love of God and from care for one another. Such care must reach beyond the immediate group to the wider community, and finally to the whole human family, for whom Christ died and now lives.

A third mark is global awareness, an awareness of the interpenetration of the community's way of life with the global network of life-patterns. Global awareness means not only study, but actual cross-cultural experiences by which a sharper sense of life-patterns is achieved. Global awareness includes sociopolitical analysis. Mere awareness of difference is not sufficient. People must have insight into ways in which their common patterns relate with those of others. Global awareness is also an awareness of and preservation of the creation and its resources.

Engagement in mission is a fourth mark of global participation. The church at every level is a missionary activity. In all its functions the church celebrates and anticipates the formation and transformation of persons. People are called by God to become part of the relationships and activities by which the kingdom of God becomes a reality. The church is called to be a part of the growth by which the kingdom of God becomes a human reality.

Finally, the fifth mark of global participation is public witness. "Public" in this instance includes both religious and secular elements. In times of tranquility public witness may take the form of letting the Christian faith affect the public consensus. At other times public witness must stand against the wider consensus. When the nations contemplate injustice, the church is called to protest even though there is consensus about injustice. Such witness is a part of educating the public. In times of persecution the church will find ways to continue to celebrate, which even in secrecy is a public witness to the gathered group and to later generations. The church is to be willing to join other churches to form an ecumenical consensus, and willing to join with secular groups to form a moral consensus.

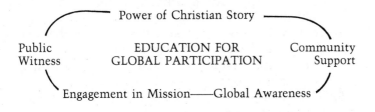

Power of Christian Story

Public Witness
EDUCATION FOR GLOBAL PARTICIPATION
Community Support

Engagement in Mission——Global Awareness

The purpose of religious education is global participation, that is, participation in the coming of the kingdom of God. It begins with study, the renewal of worship, and commitment to the power of the Christian story. It proceeds to mutual support, global awareness, engagement in mission, and public witness. It includes spirituality, imagination, transformation, shalom, and discipleship. It also includes traditioning, church growth, and educating the public. It moves through spiritual discipline and congregational renewal and growth; however, discipline, renewal, and growth are always in relation to global awareness and a transformed way of life. It refers God's power to historical trends without identifying them. So global participation is closely connected to the emerging goals we have identified above.

HUNGER WORKSHOP

The Nurture Commission of one congregation decided early in summer to attempt an intergenerational learning center approach to church school education during the first three weeks in September. The influence of a nearby congregation and the annual denominational conference led them to focus upon the problem of world hunger.

The objectives were stated as follows:

1. To gain identification with and feeling for the problem of hunger facing the world;
2. To give an opportunity for various kinds of expression of identification with and feeling for the problem;
3. To provide an occasion for everyone from the first grade up to have an occasion to interact;
4. To allow great self-initiative and choice in arriving at the means of expression and interaction;
5. To find ways in which families and others might continue to work on the problem of world hunger;
6. To celebrate the creativity and lament the discovery that comes from such a study, in a Sunday morning worship service.

An initial visit to a neighboring congregation experienced in intergenerational events assisted the committee to establish a plan, which had three elements. During the initial church school hour people were to assemble in small groups to find some symbol to express their current understanding and feeling about the world hunger problem. This was to be done in a room in which people were seated so as to symbolize the crowded conditions of the have-not peoples and the freedom of those who are not impoverished. Next, people were to be divided into various interest groups, including music, dance, Bible, arts and crafts, cooking and nutrition, legislative action, and denominational policy. Each interest group was to develop its own form of expression. Interest groups were to include persons of different ages insofar as persons wanted to be in those groups.

The committee decided to have at least one leader, and in some instances two or three leaders for each group. The *resource* leaders were responsible for materials and technical skills. The *enabling* leaders were to encourage and assist the group process. All leaders were brought together for a pre-planning session. They introduced a number of innovations to the plan: (a) the first session should begin with a film delivering a strong visual stimulus about the problem; (b) each family should be encouraged to participate between sessions by fasting, collecting money, living on a welfare budget, etc.; (c) each interest group leader should give thought to the group's focus and bring some illustrative object; (d) the concluding worship service should be designed around the creative efforts of the various groups. The presence at this meeting of people from the neighboring congregation was decisive in helping the leaders understand what their responsibilities were to be. Leaders grasped the idea of helping and encouraging students rather than directing them.

Saturday morning, before the initial church school session, a number of persons gathered in the church to make preparations. The room was divided so that the majority of those representing the poor could be crowded into one area. This was done simply by putting masking tape on the floor. Name tags were made, the color of the tag indicating whether individuals were poor, moderately poor, or wealthy. Patterns were provided to allow early arrivers to cut out their name tags in the shapes of various nations; late arrivers simply pinned on the tags as they were. Tables were set up for the initial interest group displays, pictures and posters with data about the hungry were mounted on the walls and hung from the ceilings, and equipment for the film was set up.

On the first Sunday morning, some one hundred and twenty persons of all ages arrived and began preparing name tags. When finished, they were free to go to the interest group tables and sign up for a group. Everyone was then asked to be seated, and the film was shown. Next, people were sent to a section of the room according to the color of their name tags; the poor crowded into one small corner, and the rich were given the rest of the space in the room. They were instructed to recall impressions from the film in groups of four to six. The adults were asked to encourage the children, and the children were asked not to be bashful. While they were doing this, refreshments were served. The rich received lavish helpings of rolls and beverages, the moderately poor received only a doughnut, and the poor were given water and crackers.

Following the discussion and "refreshments," everyone listened to comments from the various small groups. Then each of the resource leaders briefly described the activity of her or his interest group, and people were told they could sign up for any group. Leaders were available to answer questions. Before being dismissed, families were told how they could participate through the week in preparation for the coming Sunday morning session.

In the following two sessions the interest groups developed hymns, dance, and crafts related to hunger. A nutrition group practiced cooking more nutritious meals for less expense. A Bible group studied passages related to hunger. A legislative group developed letters to be sent to congresspersons, which they sent after getting signatures from other participants. A denominational group studied denominational statements, formulated suggestions for what the denomination should be doing, and forwarded these to the denominational offices. A worship committee developed a final worship service incorporating something from each of the interest groups. A number of families fasted and contributed the money they saved on their food budget. Responses from all of these groups were included in the final worship service.

In evaluating its work, the planning committee decided that the goals were moderately well achieved. People needed more instruction for the events to work better. There was interaction between age groups, but children had a difficult time expressing themselves. Children were represented in various interest groups, but most assembled in two particular groups. The work of the interest groups showed that all participants gained insight into some facet of the world hunger problem. The families who took on a daily spiritual discipline were the most enthusiastic about the whole event.

STORY AND CONTEXT

Education for global participation is a way of furthering the purposes of Christian education over the past century. Global participation attempts to be in touch with historical global trends while at the same time intensifying Bible study and spiritual discipline. Recently emergent statements of purpose for Christian education have been included within the concept of education for global participation.

Global participation is closely related, but not identical, to the kingdom of God. The kingdom of God is the center of all human relationships, but it also infinitely transcends them all. Therefore, Jesus spoke of the kingdom as both present and coming; such will continue to be the case. The coming of the kingdom is both powerful and actual, touching the intersection of local communities of faith and the global community. The kingdom is both local and global, in spite of the contradictions between these two, just as it is both present and coming. Christian education is to encourage people to live in repentance, prayer, and service for the sake of God's kingdom.

STUDY SUGGESTIONS

Exercises

1. After reading this chapter, set down your own statement of the goal of Christian education. In what ways does your statement agree or disagree with the one in this chapter?

2. Hold a debate regarding the five current definitions of the purpose of religious education. Appoint one or two persons to a team and let each team represent one of the five positions. Give each team's main speaker five minutes to defend her or his point of view. Give secondary speakers two minutes of rebuttal time. Vote to decide which team presented the best case. You may also want to vote on which of the five purposes the entire group considers most valid.

3. Hold a simulation of a church council meeting attempting to decide the purpose of its educational program. Assign each one of the emerging purposes to one, two, or three persons who are especially interested in that purpose. Give the groups some time (perhaps a week) to research their topics. Instruct each group that during the council discussion the group is to hold to its point of view until it is convinced that everyone has understood its main point. Then they may begin to compromise. Choose a chairperson who will direct the council meeting to attempt to agree on a statement of purpose for the church's

education program. If they do not agree, select several persons from differing points of view to work out a compromise statement to be discussed at the next meeting.

4. Hold a discussion in which you develop two lists. One list will be entitled "Direct Communication." Under that title write down what part of the Christian faith can be communicated directly and how that is best done. Entitle the other list "Indirect Communication." Under that title write down what part of the Christian faith can be communicated only indirectly and how that is best done.

5. Compare the statements of purpose by Paul Vieth and Lawrence Little. How similar and how different do you find them to be? Which of Vieth's eight objectives have been continued through the twentieth century? Which have been dropped? What has been added?

6. Working in small groups, let each group prepare a lesson plan according to one of the current or emerging options. Let each group conduct its lesson for the whole group. Then list the strengths and weaknesses of each approach.

7. Set up a plan for a summer camping program around the concept of shalom. Let each of the six elements of the concept be represented in some way. Take special care to see that the fifth element, participation in the network of the human community, is represented, as it will be more difficult than some of the others represent in the camping setting.

8. Discuss some of the ways the total education program of a congregation with which you are familiar would change if its primary goal were

educating the public. Discuss what changes would be made for each age level.

9. Visit a congregation in which the membership is growing. Discuss with the pastor or the nurture commission how the education program fits into the growth pattern of the church. What part of their program can be used in other churches, and what part is unique to that congregation?

10. Let each person in your group identify one significant transformation that has taken place in her or his life. In groups of two share with one another a significant transformation in your life. Allow time for those who want to share with the whole group. Now discuss the question, How important are major transitions in one's life? To what extent should the purpose of education be training for and learning from the times of transition? Are some transitions common to everyone in the group?

11. Let your group take on a spiritual discipline of prayer meditation or silence. Invite the pastor or someone else to help you form a common discipline. Carry on the discipline for some time, perhaps several weeks. Consider the value of spiritual discipline to you. Is it a primary goal of Christian education?

12. Study together a book about historical trends such as *Megatrends*.[29] List the ways in which these trends affect your church program, your denominational program, your life in general. Should church education be aware of such trends?

Questions for Discussion

1. What are the reasons for and against having a formulated goal for Christian education?

2. Did Pietism distort Luther's understanding of God's grace?
3. Compare and contrast the statements of purpose by Paul Vieth and Lawrence Little given above.
4. Which of the five contemporary approaches of Seymour and Miller may be joined together and which may not?
5. How does the goal of shalom change the practice of religious education?
6. Compare and contrast the various emerging options listed above. Which are contradictory and which are not?
7. Which elements listed in the global context are the most significant for Christian education?
8. How adequate is global participation as a goal for Christian education?

Suggestions for Further Reading

Parker J. Palmer, *To Know As We Are Known: A Spirituality of Education.*
Presents a call for spirituality as the foundation and aim of education.
Jack L. Seymour and Donald E. Miller, *Contemporary Approaches to Christian Education.*
Brief summaries of five alternative approaches to Christian education by six different religious educators.
Jack L. Seymour, Robert T. O'Gorman, and Charles Foster, *The Church in the Education of the Public.*
Argues for the recovery of the education of the public as the legitimate aim of religious education.
C. Peter Wagner, *Church Growth and the Whole Gospel: A Biblical Mandate.*
A defense of church growth against those who say that it limits the gospel.

II
STORY

Chapter Four:

SHARING THE STORY

THE BIBLE AND RELIGIOUS EDUCATION

The purpose of this chapter is to look at the Bible and religious education. All "peoples of the book" believe that a knowledge of the Scriptures is important for understanding God's will. Our point of view is that to discover the meaning of the Bible for the faith community of the present requires studying the meaning of the Bible for the faith communities that produced it. To find God's Word for today, the people of faith must study the way God spoke to people in the past.

The importance of the Bible to religious education is something on which Catholic, Protestant, and Jewish people agree. At the time of the Reformation, Catholics and Protestants disagreed vehemently about the place of Scripture and tradition in the church's teaching. Luther, and other reformers with him, argued for Scripture alone (*sola scriptura*). Luther brought the whole force of his criticism against such accumulated traditions as confession, indulgences, and the authority of the papacy. The Roman Catholic Church in turn insisted upon both

Scripture and tradition. In the eighteenth and nineteenth centuries, Protestant scholarship gave rise to the application of historical and literary methods to the study of Scriptures. Roman Catholic scholars again objected to a method that seemed to undercut the authority of tradition and doctrine.

The twentieth century has seen a radical change of opinion on the question of Scripture and tradition. Protestant scholars have come to view the Scriptures as a tradition in process, and most insist that the whole history of interpretation is important to the study of a passage. Twentieth-century Roman Catholic and Jewish scholars seem more willing to accept the methods of historical criticism. Biblical scholars of various faiths often agree that the study of Scripture should include a study of the history of the traditions of interpretation.

The importance of Scripture to religious education can be illustrated by the Sunday school movement's adoption of the Uniform Lesson Plan. According to the plan, all participating denominations agreed to use the same scriptural passages, the same outline of lessons for writers, and the same calendar in developing their Sunday school lessons. Even so, the twentieth century has seen a continuing debate about whether churches have kept the Bible central in their teaching. One such critic is James D. Smart, who says that the church's failure to teach the Scriptures is the result of a breakdown in communication between scholars and teachers, preachers and people, and between separate departments of theological seminaries.[1] Though Protestant, Catholic, and Jewish commentators seem to agree about the importance of studying the Scriptures, the debate goes on about how that is best done.

THE BIBLE AND LIFE

During the twentieth century, religious education has been divided over the issue of the Bible and life experience.

Is the biblical message prior, or is present lived experience prior? The modern religious education movement is often dated from 1903 with the founding of the Religious Education Association. This group was dedicated to promoting a focus on religious experience and the use of the social sciences in the study of religion. During the same decade the fundamentalist movement was born, with its focus upon the inerrancy of Scriptures and the inability of (social) science to comprehend the meaning of faith. The two movements pointed religious education in seemingly opposite directions.

This concern about religious experience had a heavy impact on churches during the next several decades. Graded lessons were introduced in the early 1920s. At the same time, neo-orthodoxy was being shaped by such theologians as Karl Barth, Dietrich Bonhoeffer, and Emil Brunner. These writers spoke of the transcendence of God and the sinfulness of human experience. The neo-orthodox criticism of any educational method in religion was taken up by Harrison Elliott in 1940.[2] The criticism of religious experience grew. In the decade of the sixties it was voiced by Peter Berger,[3] who argued that religious educational methods generally promote common religious values rather than the faith of the Scriptures.[4]

Three Typical Approaches to Scripture and Experience

	Propositional	*Existential*	*Experiential*
Knowledge	Propositional knowledge	Existential encounter	Scripture illustrates religious experience
Method	Memorize and consent	Hear and encounter	Express and act
Learning	Learn by reproducing	Learn by confronting	Learn by doing

| Activity | Memorize and apply | Study and worship | Game and drama |
| Aim | Datable conversion | Continual conversion | Growth and development |

The accompanying chart summarizes three typical approaches to Scripture. In the propositional and existential approaches the focus is on the content of Scripture, albeit in quite different ways. The propositional approach allows for religious experience, e.g., conversion, that is constantly judged by willingness to consent to certain propositions. The existential approach features existential experience, but always in relation to the scriptural account. The third approach, "religious experience," features lived experience and activity, but then searches for illustration in Scripture.

Sara Little makes a distinction between *content* and *process* which runs parallel to the above distinction between existential and experiential approaches.[5] She suggests James Smart as the typical example of a content approach and Randolph Miller as the typical example of a process approach. In the content approach, (1) the living Word confronts, (2) the teacher clears the way, (3) the Holy Spirit brings the Word, (4) fellowship is a result of the gift of grace, (5) the Bible is the beginning point, and (6) the Bible has commanding authority. In the process approach, (1) revelation is experienced in growth, (2) the teacher helps the student interpret experience, (3) the Spirit brings saving relationships, (4) participation in fellowship is prior to all learning, (5) the Bible illustrates, and (6) the Bible has teaching authority.

INTERPRETING THE BIBLE

Biblical scholars have tended to get beyond the separation of biblical message and present experience by seeing

106

both within the ongoing process of history. Some writers are beginning to relate scholarly methods of biblical interpretation to religious education. A number of recent attempts have been made to bring together the Bible and life experience.[6] A few Bible scholars and religious educators are agreed that scholarly exegesis and religious education both have to do with the discovery of meaning (hermeneutic), and that the two disciplines ought to inform one another.[7]

Documentary criticism was the beginning of the modern historical study of the Scriptures. Wellhausen's study of the book of Genesis led him to the conclusion that there are at least four different documentary sources for the book as it was canonized.[8] Documentary criticism is a part of *source* criticism, an attempt to reconstruct the authors' intentions and the hearers' expectations within that cultural setting. Some scholars then turned to *form* criticism, the attempt to reconstruct the social setting in which smaller units (pericopes) of Scripture arose. For example, some of the psalms may have arisen as a part of ordination festivals, and the basis for I Corinthians 13 may have been a hymn.

Having identified larger and smaller units of narrative behind a text, the next problem was that of how the units were put together and of the influence of their editors on the final text. The technical name for such an editor is "redactor," and study of how the smaller units were brought together is called *redaction* criticism. Such criticism focuses on different layers of tradition in the text and the shift that takes place in meaning as the final text takes shape.

Canon critics look for the meaning of the text to the community that gave it canonical authority. Historical criticism is faulted by canon critics because it reduces the Bible to a set of historical facts in which the Word of God is not present. Canon critics study how the Bible was given canonical authority by communities who believed it to be the Word of God. They try to discover what those communities considered God's Word to be. The text as it developed, was put together, edited, and finally canonized is equally as important as what an original author wrote or may have intended. Canon is a given historical community's way of understanding God's Word at a given time. Both the history behind the text and the theological understanding of the text are held together.

Structural analysis attempts to recover the meaning of a text beyond the historical circumstances of its origin. The structuralists argue that a text has a meaning that transcends the circumstances in which it was written. This transcending or classic meaning is best found by analyzing the structure and logic of the text itself. A classic text is one whose meaning has significance for many situations beyond the one in which it was first written.[9]

A Summary of Contemporary Scholarly Methods of Bible Study

Method	*Typical Questions*
Documentary	What are the documents behind the text?
Source	What were the author's intentions and the reader's expectations?
Form	What was the social setting of the smaller units behind the documents?
Redaction	How were the units and documents reshaped as they were put together?

Canon	What was the meaning of the text for the community that collected and canonized it?
Structural	What is the more universal meaning of the final text, viewed as a structure?

Canon criticism is especially helpful in a study of the faith community as an educational model. Of all the methods in the diagram, canon criticism focuses most directly on the believing community. Neither a religious nor a literary history, the history of canon is a study of the features of a particular set of biblical texts in relation to their use within the faith community.[10]

THE ANALOGY OF COMMUNITY

There is an analogy between the original community's faith and the present community's faith. This we shall refer to as the *analogy of community*. The relationship between what is present and what is not present may be spoken of in various ways. Aquinas spoke of the analogy of being; Barth, of the analogy of faith. The "analogy of community" brings out its community dimension. Interpretation theory attempts to explain how a past event can become a present living reality. How does the faith of a past community become a living faith for a present community? Putting the question in this way may allow us to get beyond the separation of the Bible and life.

There is both a continuity and a discontinuity between the understanding of the Bible by an original community of faith and the understanding of the Bible by contemporary community. The belief and practice of a modern community has continuity with the tradition that was given the status of Scripture by an earlier community. There is also discontinuity, for contemporary circumstances and modern conditions are different from those of an earlier time. Brueggemann believes that church education has not kept either the continuity with the tradition or openness to new situations in view. Liberal education has "largely abandoned the tradition for the sake of experiential learning," and conservative education has "presented the canonical story as though it were closed."[11]

The most basic structure of the canon is the separation of the Hebrew Bible from the New Testament. In that separation one also finds both continuity and discontinuity. The New Testament community understands itself to be a continuity of the faith of Israel. The faith that God revealed to Abraham, Moses, David, and the prophets is presupposed in all New Testament writings. What Christ teaches is continuous with Moses. However, the coming of Christ as a new Moses with new authority also marks a break with the old canon. The universalism of faith in God, hinted at in books like Jonah and Ruth, is very explicit in the New Testament. New circumstances allow for a reinterpretation of the past community of faith.

As the New Testament is both continuous and discontinuous with the Hebrew Bible, so also is the present community's interpretation of Scripture. The present community can attempt to be aware of the assumptions it brings to the Bible. What are its present interests and social status? Why is one interpretation preferred rather than another? What are its expectations, and where do we feel tension with the text?

When we are aware of our own preconceptions, we can look to the meaning of the biblical text for the earlier faith community. What traditions are behind the text? What was the author's intent and how did the author's readers hear what was written? How was the culture of that time

different from our own? What social position did the writer
and hearers have? What was the point of tension between
the writer and the hearers? How did the text change and how
was it shaped by later editors? Why was the text given its
final shape? What meaning did it have for the community
then? What did they understand the Word of God to be?
How does that world view challenge our own? How does the
passage speak to our own circumstances? What is its
meaning for us now? What is God's Word to us now?

In the analogy of community, the present community of
faith gets closer to understanding the meaning of the
passage for an earlier community by being more aware of
itself. The present community has the freedom to
reinterpret the Scripture for its own circumstance, just as
the earlier community that canonized the Scripture
reinterpreted the sacred writings it had at hand. The
present community is joined with an earlier community's
understanding and commitments, but the present community remains acutely aware of how things have
changed. So the continuity and discontinuity is main-
tained in the analogy of community.[12]

Analogy of Community

Past Community	Present Community
Documents	Various translations
Author's intent	Our intentions and interests
Culture then	Culture now
Social location	Social location
Hearer's expectations	Our expectations
Hearer's point of tension in the text	Our point of tension with the text
Growth of the tradition	Various interpretations and commentaries

111

Meaning then   Meaning now
Wider meaning   Wider meaning
God's Word to them   God's Word to us

THE PAST COMMUNITY

The Hebrew Bible canon is divided into Torah, Prophets, and Writings. Walter Brueggemann has suggested that conservative educators tend to prefer the Torah, social critics prefer the Prophets, and humanistic psychologists prefer the wisdom literature. Brueggemann emphasizes that all three are in the canon, and none of the three must be lost.[13] Torah is a statement of *ethos*, of what is given and is not negotiable by future generations. The Prophets are a statement of *pathos*. They agonize over the contradiction between what was promised and what presently prevails. The Writings are a statement of *logos*. In them one finds a continuing search for deeper levels of meaning that pertain to new situations.[14]

The interpreting community can look at Scriptures in terms of both process and content. The content of the Torah is the story of God, who covenants with the creation and who constantly creates anew. The process of the Torah is that of telling a story. While the story is "not negotiable," it is told in various ways in order to meet new circumstances. One dramatic example is the retelling of the Exodus story in the book of Deuteronomy (which literally means the second law, or the second telling of the law). The story is illustrated by drama and worship, such as the piling of stones where a special event occurred, or by placing the words of the law on the doorposts of the house. The stories and the drama are calculated to arouse the curiosity of children, whose questions are answered as they ask them. The stories have an enduring urgency, but neither question nor answer can be forced until the hearer is ready.

Brueggemann calls story the primal mode of Israel's knowing.[15] The Torah is a story that has authority without being authoritarian. Story is concrete, open-ended, imaginative, experiential, individual, temporal, and accessible to all. It intends to build a community that will understand itself differently from other communities of the time.[16]

The content of the prophetic literature relates to challenging existing social structures in the name of the promises of the Torah. The process of the prophets is to experience the pain of the situation and create a poetic discourse. The prophets endure, express their pain, and call people to return to the promise. While the authority of the Torah is greater, the authority of the prophets rests directly upon it. Contemporary learning communities are also called to identify the pain of our time and to look at that pain in terms of the biblical promises. Like the prophets, communities of today can be encouraged to express themselves creatively, perhaps in poetry. Such creation can help give expression to both pain and hope. Sensitivity to pain and joy in relation to God's promise is the source of a community's social action.

The wisdom literature attests to the depths of faith in all the circumstances of life. Faith in God is the beginning of all wisdom. All times and circumstances of life are vain and unsatisfying unless faith is there. The process of wisdom is to discuss and search out the truth for every new situation. The effort is to develop proverbs, sayings, or conversations that plumb the enduring truths of life. The Writings did not have the same authority in the Hebrew community as the Torah or the Prophets, but they were clearly included within the canon. Conversations, conjecture, observations, and search for truth in the faith community do not have the same authority as the story of

God's love, but the search for truth is also clearly an important part of the learning process.

The New Testament canon is also divided into three parts: the Gospels, the apostle, and the writings.[17] Though the Pauline letters (the apostle) represent the oldest sources, the Gospels were the first to win general use among the churches as Scripture. The Pauline letters were added to the Gospels, and gradually the other writings were added.

The Gospels all speak of the life, death, and resurrection of Jesus Christ. Their primary mode is story. The fact that the story is told in different ways and with different emphases indicates how storytelling can vary according to its setting. The message of the Pauline letters is that all who will believe are reconciled to God in Jesus Christ. Like the prophets, Paul suffers under the tension between God's grace and the actual weakness of the congregations. He writes creatively in his joy and pain. The writings of the New Testament search out the meaning of the gospel for different situations, but their inclusion in the canon affirms the constant search for the meaning of the gospel in various circumstances of life.

THE PRESENT COMMUNITY

Contemporary communities come to the Bible with feelings, preconceptions, and expectations. No one ever comes to an experience absolutely blank. The concerns of a present community are embedded in interactions, relationships, and a shared story. Understanding the past story as recounted in the Bible in relation to the ongoing story here and now is the heart of spiritual guidance. That process of interpreting a sacred story is already evident in both the Hebrew Bible and the New Testament, as we have already seen.

While present experience is always most immediate, it is not always easily identified. Important feelings, relationships, and commitment may be only half remembered, or perhaps they have never been spoken of before. On the other hand, every group assembles with certain concerns uppermost in mind. Present action and present involvement are often the most effective way to focus interest upon a topic.

Questions or conversations about today's feelings, desires, decisions, commitments, beliefs, values, and perceptions can be the entrance to genuine inquiry about the past biblical story. Such perceptions are more intense if they are about oneself, one's own group, or one's own faith community. Good questions actually engage persons. For example, if the biblical passage to be studied is that of Joseph and his brothers, a teacher might ask, "Is anyone in your family treated with more favor than the others?" For any of Jesus' healing miracles the teacher might ask, "Have you ever been really sick? How does it feel?" A story can be opened up by locating a theme that most people can identify in their present lives. Tom Groome asks questions that elicit present commitments.[18] Paulo Freire evokes people's experiences around the theme of oppression.[19] Ross Snyder seeks to find a "lived moment."[20]

Many different questions can touch on the interactions in groups and lead to an inquiry into the biblical story. What in the wider culture influences us most? What values are expressed in television and advertising? Who are we in terms of social class, race, sex, age? What are the individual differences among us? What are our ongoing stories as individuals, as a group, as a faith community? Who cares about us most? What is expected of us? How does our church's belief affect us? What interests us in the biblical story? What translation of the story do we prefer? How would we retell the story? What tension or problem does the story raise for us? What difference does knowing the meaning of the story make for us? What is the meaning of the story for us today? What questions does the story bring to mind? Can we do something together to express or act out what we have discovered? What can we celebrate? Can we create something? Can we contribute something to the larger community of faith?

In the analogy of community we have spoken of the link between a present and a past community. However both present and past are moving toward a future. This constant movement toward the future is a part of the analogy of community. As a present community of faith is limited and enlarged by touching a past community's understanding of God's Word, the present community will be drawn toward some future act or process of obedience and hope. Hearing the story is not complete until one is drawn to express its truth, i.e., until one is drawn into a new future.[21]

Does one begin with present interaction or the past story? One can begin with either, whichever quickens interest. All study requires interest, readiness, and a teachable moment. Present concerns can quicken interest, but the story may focus issues more quickly. The movement may be from our relationship to the biblical story to the connection between them. The movement may also go from the story to present relationships. In either case the interaction of biblical story and present story is the heart of sharing the story with one another.

TELLING THE STORY

The fundamental mode of Scripture is story. Both Torah and gospel are stories to tell and they aim at the formation

116

of alternative communities.[22] The fundamental mode of history is also story. Every individual, every group, and every community of faith has its own story. Story and identity are very close to one another.

In telling a story the storyteller stands in the framework of the story. Questioning is suspended for the moment. The narrative becomes an expression of the teller. The interest of the story depends more upon the teller's total identification with the story than upon the story's being totally comprehensible. Gestures, objects, and drama help to bring the story to life.

At the same time, the storyteller has a certain distance from the story. The storyteller knows that this is a special time, "storytime."[23] The storyteller is responsive to signals from the listeners, and anticipates their point of view. She or he phrases the story so listeners can participate more fully and develops it so that the interests of the hearers are touched. Without losing its fundamental structure or message, it stretches to include the listener. Deuteronomy illustrates how the Torah stretches to meet new listeners. Similarly, the Gospel of John varies from the other Gospels, in order to reach the listeners.

Story is in narrative form, a form that has a number of special characteristics. Narrative joins together the concrete and the abstract. The concepts of the story unfold in particular events. Narrative keeps cognition, volition, and feeling together. Stories are not merely perceptual; they are full of emotive clues. The narrative also has an intentional framework, a plot, that holds the story together. It begins, develops, and comes to a conclusion.

A story is dramatic. Tension or conflict inevitably develops, for without tension there is no drama, and without drama, no story. The tension is resolved in some manner in the course of the story. The resolution is comic if it can rise above the tension, but tragic if tension endures.

A story offers a point of view on the world. It gives the listeners an "onlook," a perspective. To hear the story is to have one's own perspective broadened. When Jesus was asked who one's neighbor is, he answered through the story of the Good Samaritan. The hearers of that story view came to the world differently. Perhaps this is the reason for his repeated admonition, "Let those who have ears, hear."

A story is a narrative event. The person of the teller and the persons of the listeners are joined together in the unfolding of a narrative. This unity of teller, listener, and narrative is an event. The narrative transcends the event and joins one to earlier communities who heard the same story. The story touches the identity of both teller and listener, for otherwise it cannot really be told or heard. Story is therefore community-forming and is fundamental to other community activities.[24]

HEARING THE STORY

To hear a story the audience must listen. While the example below refers to children, the principle applies to adults as well. People can be encouraged to listen by both direct and indirect suggestion. Indirectly, one can have a storytime, a story place, and a ritual of beginning: "It is time for our story. Let's all put our things away and go to the story circle. As soon as everyone is quiet, we will begin." To bring out special props for the story, or to arrive in special dress, calls attention to the story.

More directly, the storyteller can say, "I want everyone to listen carefully." The listener can be told what to look for: "In this story someone helps someone else. I want you to find out how she does it." The listeners can be encouraged to give stylized responses: "Whenever I mention the wind, I want all of you to say 'Whooooo.' "

The teller can refer directly to the listeners: "I think Peter felt just like you do when you are afraid." The storyteller can also anticipate what will happen after the story: "When the story is finished, I want you to tell me what part you liked best."

One can seldom hear a story deeply without questioning it, and the questions of the hearers are far more important than the questions of the storyteller. Of course, the storyteller may pose questions to draw listeners out: "Which of the three was neighbor to him who fell among thieves?" There are many kinds of questions, e.g., fact, opinion, value, or identity. Of them all, faith is most closely related to questions of identity: "Why is this important? What should we do about it? How does it affect us?" To question a story is to learn to be critical. A six-year-old can ask if the story really happened. A twenty-year-old can ask about the author's intentions. A twenty-year-old can ask whether it is possible to live like that today. Even a three-year-old can ask, "Is it time to stop?"

Questioning may lead to a kind of searching that is appropriate to wisdom, if it moves between the story and personal experience. "Do we have idols in our own lives today? Does this story have anything to say about the Atomic Age?" The search for wisdom, which is a part of the biblical canon, is also a part of the life of every group and every person.

To participate in a story deeply, a group not only listens and questions, but also begins to live within the framework of the story and recreate it. They share the story with others who will listen. In recreating the story the whole group becomes storytellers too, as well as listeners. As storytellers, they do not mimic someone else—they create something new. A group can create through dramatizations, painting pictures, or writing

119

prayers. These expressions can become great and pro-phetic when they really catch the tension between their own points of view and that of the story.

READINESS FOR THE BIBLE

It is often said that the Bible is not a children's book.[25] Much of the Bible, it is claimed, was not written for children, cannot be understood by children, and is of no interest to children. Ronald Goldman has taken this position further by asserting that introducing biblical concepts before children are ready for them can be harmful. Later, when such children have developed the capacity to understand biblical faith, they might resist it because of earlier misconceptions.[26]

The research of James Fowler and of Ana-Maria Rizzuto offers an answer to Goldman's claim.[27] From interviews of youth and adults, Fowler traced the development of faith through several stages. Earlier stages are egocentric and literal, while later stages are genuinely symbolic. As a child's cognitive abilities mature, the child reconstructs the previous, less mature image of God. Fowler believes that reconstructed earlier images of faith lend power to later symbolic images. The less mature faith perceptions of younger children should not be used as an argument against teaching religion to them. Rather than depriving them of religious teaching, children should be encouraged to grow and construct more mature views.

Ana-Maria Rizzuto, from a psychoanalytic perspective, arrives at a similar conclusion. Rizzuto objects to the Freudian view that faith in God is an "illusion" to be outgrown and discarded. Rizzuto distinguishes between an illusion and a hallucination. Unlike a hallucination, an illusion can help a person orient to reality. Belief in truth, beauty, goodness, and science have the character of illusion, but they give people a perspective on reality. The experience of God arises with the earliest relationships to parents. By age three, most children have a strong sense of God's reality, which is closely related to their own sense of identity. For most persons of Western culture, this early belief in God is a basis for reality orientation. Belief in God comes from the way in which a child is affirmed by parents and teachers. Children know the true character of their parents and teachers, and with this they must deal, no matter what they are taught. Rizzuto's research, like Fowler's, suggests that children's immature perceptions of God are very important to them even though such perceptions change as children grow toward adulthood.

Mary Wilcox suggests that a teacher should prepare to tell Bible stories by working out the normal developmental sequence of understanding. For example, in the story of the prodigal son, children of seven to ten years of age may believe that the prodigal ought to be punished by the father, whereas children eleven years of age and older may believe that the son has been punished sufficiently. This is a part of the pre-understanding that children may bring to the story. An awareness of the normal development of understanding may help a teacher be more sensitive to children's questions.[28]

The process of reconstructing faith continues throughout life, for adults as well as children. Discovering the pre-understanding of a group and their readiness to learn is at the heart of teaching at any age level.

THE BIBLE AND PUBLIC EDUCATION

The Supreme Court has ruled that schools may teach "about" religion, but may not teach for conversion, belief, or worship. Since the faith community model of education refers to a religious community, how can it be used in public schools?

The answer is that a public school class can objectively study the way in which the Scriptures were formed and canonized by a faith community.[29] They can also study the way the Scriptures have been interpreted in faith communities throughout history, and they can study the way those passages are currently understood and practiced by various communities of faith. They can discuss and perhaps dramatize the stories. However, one cannot move to belief, conversion, or worship on the basis of the stories. The public school class is not a confessing community, but it can study the way communities of faith understand and believe in the Scriptures. The community model is therefore amenable to public school education as defined by the courts.

VERSIONS OF THE BIBLE

There are many versions of the Bible available for study. Which is to be used? Versions such as Phillips and *The Living Bible* are actually paraphrases, which means that great liberty was used in rendering the text into English. Some translations are done by single individuals rather than groups. Of the group translations, some are authorized by church bodies and some are not. The Revised Standard Version is an authorized version in America, as is the New English Bible in England. Using many versions adds to the richness of understanding. In the same way the use of original versions written in Greek and Hebrew may add even greater depth to understanding. However, an authorized version represents a faith community's decision about what is authoritative. It is therefore appropriate to let authorized versions be the center of study and worship, employing other translations to augment understanding. Historically, decisions about canon have been based on wide usage, and so use continues to influence translation.

122

STUDY SUGGESTIONS

Exercises

1. Collect lesson materials from two or three different denominations that use the same uniform lesson plan. Compare lessons based upon the same outline. What similarities and differences do you notice?

2. Have someone in your group review Harrison Elliott's book, *Can Religious Education Be Christian?*[30] Ask someone else to review H. Shelton Smith's book, *Faith and Nurture.*[31] Let your group discuss which point of view seems more plausible.

3. Ask teachers in your church to prepare lessons using three different approaches to Scripture and experience described in this chapter. Bring the teachers together and have them compare the approaches to Scripture and experience they have used.

4. Find a teacher who puts primary emphasis on process in teaching, and another who puts more emphasis on content. Let each of them explain why they do what they do, and then let the whole group discuss the relative importance of content and process.

5. Choose a small passage of Scripture, such as one of the parables. Spend some time analyzing it, using each of the methods of Bible study given in the chapter: documentary, source, form, redaction, canon, and structural. If you are a group, go through this process together. What does the passage mean for you as a result of your study?

6. Use the same passage of Scripture as in the previous exercise. In light of your reading of the

passage make an analysis of your present community according to the "analogy of community." How do your analysis of the present community and your reading of the passage interact with one another?

7. Choose a passage from the Torah, another from the Prophets, and a third from the wisdom Writings. Study each of the passages in terms of both its content and its process. Try to find examples of Torah, prophecy, and wisdom in your own community. Develop a method of expressing the process of each of these three modes of biblical teaching. For example, on the basis of human violation of God's love described in the Torah, develop some artistic expression from your group.

8. Try your hand at writing to another group of Christians using the form that Paul used in his letters. Begin with a salutation of grace from God in Christ. Proceed to a statement of the gospel. Discuss whatever issues you like. Give personal greetings. End with a benediction.

9. With a passage of scripture of your own choosing before you, ask the group questions posed in the section of this chapter entitled "the present community."

10. In your group, practice the suggestions given on telling a story. Listen to one another and make suggestions. Offer to go to other groups in the church to tell the stories you have been rehearsing. For example, you might offer to tell the children's story in the worship service or to take a story to another church school class.

Questions for Discussion

1. What do you understand to be the relationship between Scripture and tradition in the church's teaching?
2. How are the Bible and life experience related to one another? How does this relationship affect teaching in the church?
3. What are the strengths and limitations of a critical historical study of the Bible in encountering God's Word?
4. How can one get from the "then" of the biblical time to the "now" of our time?
5. In what way is the New Testament continuous with the Old, and in what way discontinuous?
6. Is it possible to use different types of biblical literature as a clue to ways of teaching today?
7. How does one move from a study of the Scripture to decisions about living?
8. What are the characteristics of good storytelling?
9. Is the Bible a book for adults, not children?
10. What version(s) of the Bible should be used in teaching and worship?

Suggestions for Further Reading

Robert Alter, *The Art of Biblical Narrative.*
A discussion of the place of narrative and story in the formation of the Bible.
Robert M. Grant and David Tracey, *A Short History of the Interpretation of the Bible.*
Reviews the various ways the Bible has been interpreted.
Patricia Griggs, *Using Storytelling in Christian Education.*
A brief and readable account of using stories with children.
John H. Hayes and Carl R. Holladay, *Biblical Exegesis: A Beginner's Handbook.*
This book has a fuller discussion of the methods mentioned in this chapter.

Chapter Five:

EXPRESSING THE STORY

Prior to all other considerations, the community of faith lives the story of faith. Living the story inevitably includes giving verbal expression to it. Theology is the community's effort to question and research the story; to give a faithful, devotional, and coherent account of the story; and to otherwise guide the community of faith in the story's many modes of expression. Theology interacts with the norms, practices, customs, loyalties, commitments, experiences, and circumstances of people within the congregation and the wider community. Theology is therefore a fundamental and basic expression of community life.

Because it seeks to orient people toward a life of faith and to encourage them in discovering the mind and way of Christ, Christian education cannot avoid being a theological expression. Researching the story, giving a faithful account, and guiding community life—the basic theological functions—are very appropriate to the educational ideal of pursuing the truth. Christian education as theology is an expression of a community that is already living the story before, during, and after the effort to educate.

THE STORY OF THEOLOGY

The Bible has few if any formal theological treatises as such. Perhaps the book of Romans comes as close to being a theological treatise as any. But even Romans must not be read as simply an abstract propositional statement of truth. The book is best understood within the story of Paul's missionary journeys and his impending visit to the Christian church in Rome. It is a letter addressed to a group of people with problems and concerns, and to these people Paul writes.

The other books of the Bible are even less theological treatises than is Romans. They include worship, wisdom, law, apocalyptic vision, prophetic utterances, teaching, and many other modes of speech embedded within the narrative. They are part of a living community, were written for and received by a community, and have been preserved and passed on by the community of faith.[1]

The various functions of the community of faith inevitably gave rise to theology. The community is constantly called on to summarize what it believes. In the Torah one finds a summary of the Exodus story as it might be told to children (Deuteronomy 6). The preaching of the apostles in the early chapters of Acts is a summary of the gospel story.[2] The post-apostolic church was also called on to give summaries of what it believed. Though such summaries could take the form of a set of doctrines, they belonged to an ongoing narrative and were validated by referring back to the narrative of the originating events.

Biblical communities created a language of worship that can be found throughout Scripture. Various administrative, counseling, evangelistic, and ethical questions are addressed in the Scripture in reference to the community's actual problems. For example, the problem of including Gentiles in the church gave rise to much of what Paul wrote. Theology cannot be separated from expressions of worship, administrative, counseling, evangelism, and other functions.

All such expressions attempt to be true to the story, coherent, and pertinent to given circumstances. Indeed, a faith community's verbal expression must incorporate all three characteristics, if it is not to be handicapped. Current practice therefore tends to follow Schleiermacher in dividing theology into historical and biblical, systematic, and practical areas, according to these three theological functions.

True to story	*Coherent*	*Pertinent*
biblical and historical theology	systematic theology	practical theology

The importance of teaching in the development of theology is seen in the ancient terms Torah, doctrine, and orthodoxy. Torah means teaching or instruction, doctrine is from a Latin root that also means teaching, and orthodoxy means the right, proper, or authoritative teaching. The question of doctrine and orthodoxy in the early church was a question of the proper way to interpret the story. The canon of the Scripture and the creeds arose as a way of trying to assure that the story would be properly interpreted.

Doctrines of the church arose to counter particular difficulties. To the Gnostic claim that the creation originates from an inferior urge (demiurge) from which one may be delivered by secret knowledge (gnosis), Clement of Rome answered that the will of the One Living God is the demiurge.[3] Similarly, Justin Martyr's theology addressed a series of questions: how is Christianity related to Israel, to Greek philosophy, to popular superstition, and to the Roman empire? Justin's answers are focused around four themes: (1) Jesus is the true Messiah, the Christ; (2) Christianity is the true philosophy; (3) Christianity opposes all superstition; and (4) the devotion of the Christians preserves the Roman empire. In the same way, Augustine's argument against Pelagius' doctrine of free will was an answer to a particular issue. Theology arises as it searches the Christian story to address particular issues.

The concern for proper teaching very early raised the question of authority. Where does teaching authority lie? Whose interpretation is authoritative? An early tradition answered that the authoritative teaching is vested in the ordained clergy. By the time of the Middle Ages, the church, i.e., the clergy, had the power to decide whether beliefs and practices were correct or not. Furthermore, the church enforced its decisions by the threat of excommunication, inquisition, and physical torture. Much medieval theology arose out of devotional and spiritual practices. New ways of life were accompanied by new way of looking at truth. The influence of the Muslims was accompanied by the rediscovery of the Aristotelian texts. Thomas Aquinas produced a great synthesis in which he tried to remain faithful to the story of the early church fathers and at the same time incorporate the newly discovered Aristotelian ideas.

The radical empiricism of people like Duns Scotus and Roger Bacon broke the Thomistic synthesis apart during the time that secular modes of life were prevailing. New ways of life, new trade, new explorations, the discovery of the new world, new inventions, the printing of the Bible, all set the tone for understanding the story in a new way. Luther appealed to careful study of the Scripture to show that the faith of the church is not mediated by ecclesial authority. Rather, he believed that the grace and love of God come to one and all directly through Christ, and that the function of right teaching is to keep that doctrinal clarity before people.

One result of the Reformation was to strengthen suspicion of clerical teaching. Pietism was a movement encouraging the people to interpret the Scriptures for themselves, without benefit of clerical assistance. Carrying forward this outlook, the Sunday school movement was also predominantly a lay movement that encouraged people to read, memorize, and interpret the Scripture directly. Theology was reduced to simple and easily remembered propositions such as God loves you, Christ has died for your forgiveness, obey the Ten Commandments, and live like Jesus.

The modern lay theological movement has its own inherent difficulties. Individual lay teachers may lose touch with the community of faith. Pastors tend to lose their teaching responsibility. Sustained, disciplined efforts to remain true to the whole story and to find coherence are abandoned for the sake of simple and direct teaching. At the same time it is very important that theology be a genuine expression of the faith and practice of the people. The lay theological movement is to be encouraged. Formal, authoritative, and disciplined theology has its place as it contributes to and is enriched by the living story of the people. Otherwise the split between clerical doctrinal authority and the faith of the people, uncovered in earlier centuries, will continue.

In the congregational polity that arose from the left wing of the Reformation, authority for teaching came from the consensus of believers rather than from the declaration of the authoritative head. In congregational polity, the searching of every member for the meaning and coherence of the story is part of the authority of the consensus. Authoritative doctrine and lay teaching depend on one another in a congregational polity, but lay teaching must conform to clerical authority in an episcopal polity.

NARRATIVE MEANING

Reviewing the story of theology even so briefly shows that theology grows out of the living story of the people of faith. Everyday experience, feelings, preconceptions, and common practices are the continuing context of theology. While theology aims at coherent expression of the meaning of the story, faithfulness to the whole story and guidance for such functions as worship, care, teaching, evangelism, and administration are equally important.

The narrative structure of a story is constituted by the causal, intentional, and analogical relationships between various events. The various events interpret one another by a movement from beginning to end. The relationship of past moments in the story to the present and anticipation of future moments are seen by analogy. Therefore analogy is the primary principle of coherence for a story. The analogy not only allows the hearer to understand the continuity of the original story, but also to discover a similar sequence in other events. For example, Jesus' parable of the Good Samaritan illustrates a meaningful sequence of events that could very likely have happened. Hearing the parable allows the hearer to discover a similarly patterned sequence of events in her or his own life.

When formulated around propositions rather than narrative, theology tends to overlook events. Without events in interrelationship there can be no narrative and no story. The story does not eliminate propositional understanding;

rather, the story illuminates propositions. Narrative is selective, focusing attention on some events and not on others.

Seeing the relationship between events and the relationship between one story and another is an exercise in imagination. The imagination called for is not simply the analytical sort that sees technical relationships. Rather, the need is for an imagination that perceives the context, meaning, and purpose of life in general and of our lives together in particular. It is the kind of imagination used in telling one's own story.

Narrative imagination is at the center of revelation and of theology. Religious education can have theological depth only to the extent that it encourages and enriches the analogical imagination.[4] A number of educators have revolted against the technical approach to education in which everything is reduced to objectives and procedures. They are calling for the exercise of imagination, of analogy and metaphor. Therein is the spiritual dimension of education recovered and therein does the relationship between the story of this community and the story of God's saving grace become visible.[5]

These comments are intended to make clear that the verbal story arises from and returns to the living of the story. The meaning of the story is not simply in the words of the teller but also in the interrelationship of the teller and hearer. The customs, practices, and commitments of a people give a certain functional meaning to a story and so the narrative structure of the story is influenced by this functional meaning for the group.

THE CONTEMPORARY DEBATE

The modern religious education movement has arisen from the coming together of the age-old concern of the community for right teaching and modern educational theory. The Sunday school movement paralleled that for popular education. The advent of graded curricula paralleled the discovery of developmental differences in ability. Religious education is therefore affected by changes in educational theory as well as by changes in theology.

Both theology and education are also affected by other disciplines. Theology is affected by changes in philosophy, biblical studies, society, culture, political events, and religious practice. Education is affected by changes in education philosophy, psychology, sociology, administration, and educational practice. Thus religious education is affected by all of the above.

Current debate focuses on the relative importance of theology and education in religious education. James Michael Lee and Charles Melchert both call for much more attention to educational theory. Lee's primary point is that theology can give no guidance at all to good teaching in the church.[6] Good teaching comes from a careful consideration of what is known by the social sciences about teaching and learning. Theology can give authoritative concepts, while only the social sciences can give an informed account of how people learn. What is most needed by religious education, says Lee, is a vision of learning and teaching that is informed by research. Only in that way will people learn in a manner that affects their deeper commitments. Theology stands in the way because its authoritative structure contradicts what is scientifically known about learning.

Melchert's argument is similar, except he comes at the question from an analysis of language rather than from social psychology. Melchert argues that religious education must be education or it is nothing.[7] Too much religious education, he says, is poor education. What is needed is a theory of religious education that pays very careful attention to education. Religious education must attend to clarity of concepts and to wisdom that is deeper than technical knowledge.

In contrast, Don Browning and David Tracy are calling for religious education to be understood as practical theology.[8] Practical theology is guided by both historical and systematic theology, but the ethics of practice are most important. They feel religious education must pay careful attention to questions of ethics. The practical disciplines have tended to neglect ethics or to assume that everything is within God's grace. Educators must instead become adept at seeing the ethical structure of their educational arguments. They should know that the use of objectives, an almost universal educational practice, often implies a pragmatic or even utilitarian ethic. But of this we shall say more later.

A number of educators argue for the importance of theology in religious education. Westerhoff feels that the pastor's traditional teaching authority as it was exercised for hundreds of years should be revived. He sees the turn to Sunday school occurring over the past two hundred years as a deviation from the much longer tradition of the pastor as teacher. The pastoral teacher is to train the people in theological understanding. Theology is therefore central to Westerhoff's view.[9]

Larry Richards also contends for the primacy of theology, but from a much different tradition.[10] According to Richards, the center of Christian education, as of all things in the church, is the experience of God's presence. With no experience of God's presence, all educational effort is in vain. This experience is expressed principally in the living covenant between persons. Those who know

135

God should express their care for others before all else. Teaching is first of all a matter of friendship and only then a matter of articulation. Education depends upon getting a correct doctrine of revelation. In that sense Christian education is first of all a theological discipline.

The current debate about the relative place of theology and education in the discipline of religious education cannot be resolved. If not pushed too far, the debate is actually productive of new ideas, and therefore useful. From our point of view all ministries within the church are theological expressions. This does not mean that every expression must fit a statement that has been authoritatively established. Rather, it means that all expressions of the church that seek to be faithful to the story, coherent, and pertinent are theology in the deepest functional sense even when those expressions do not have authoritative status.

Religious education is certainly theology in the functional sense just given. In fact, the arguments of Lee and Melchert calling for more emphasis on educational theory are precisely arguments of coherence and pertinence. They insist that unless something is really learned, the theology doesn't matter. Furthermore, unless something is really meaningful to the students, theology doesn't matter. But these are the fundamental requirements of functional theology. Pointedly stated, to be good theology, religious education must be good education.

The problem is that in a structure where theology refers to authoritative statements, what we are calling functional theology may not be legitimate theology. In a structure that invites dialog, functional theology is certainly theology. In fact, authoritative theology and functional theology constantly guide and shape each other.[11]

To say that religious education must be good education to be good theology means equally well that it should be good theology to be good education. Richards and Westerhoff are right in calling for the theological, and Browning in calling for the ethical, grounding of educational practice. However, the formula we have given does not resolve the issue. The actual debate between education and theology must continue in order to clarify the relationship as the disciplines change.

SCHOOLS OF THEOLOGY

Another approach to uncovering the relationship of theology and education is to look at various schools of theology and their emphases. One influential approach is *process theology*, whose primary spokespersons in the United States are perhaps John Cobb and Bernard Meland.[12] Taking their stance in the process philosophy of Alfred North Whitehead, process theologians emphasize the interrelatedness of all events in the cosmos. Whatever enhances awareness of creativity enhances God's creative process, and conversely whatever blocks awareness of creativity blocks the creative process. The proponents of process theology have called attention to the doctrines of God, creation, preservation of world resources, the global community, and the dialog between world religions.

Liberation theology is another very influential theological movement. Speaking out on the economic and political struggles of Latin America, liberation theologians call for a new economic and political order. They call for a transformed consciousness that is not bound by an attitude of hopelessness and despair. They also call for believing and acting on the belief that the conditions of poverty, hunger, and political oppression can be changed. Liberation theologians are much influenced by Marxist analysis of social and economic conditions. Their approach is opening up new ways of understanding the gospel story.

Liberation theology has had a strong impact upon North America and Europe. The impact takes a different form from that in the South American setting since North Americans and Europeans are more the oppressors than the oppressed. However, many groups in the United States are oppressed minorities. Black theology calls attention to the situation of black people in the United States. It relates the suffering of blacks over the years to the suffering of God's people in the Scriptures. According to adherents of this school, God is on the side of the oppressed, and one must be black to be liberated.

Another liberation voice is that of feminist theology. Theologians like Rosemary Reuther give special attention to the male assumptions of traditional theology.[13] They question male images of God, and they search for the role of women in the gospel story. They are also rewriting church history using inclusive language and making explicit the contributions of women, most of whom have been ignored by male historians.

European theology is also much influenced by social and economic questions. Moltmann's *theology of hope* has recast traditional Christian doctrines in terms of future possibility rather than past event.[14] Eschatology rather than origins becomes the principle question. The doctrines of Christ, Spirit, salvation, church, and history are all seen as within the possibilities that God is opening for the creation and for human kind. Theology of hope calls for justice as a principle theme, and it attempts to transcend the political cold war in which the world has been locked since World War II.

Historicism is an approach to theology that understands doctrine and practice in terms of their historical context.

The church and culture both are part of an ongoing history. Propositions and biblical materials must also be set within their historical context to be properly understood. Revelation comes to humankind as a historical experience.

Roman Catholic theology is as varied as Protestant theology, and so a variety of points of view are represented. The Scriptures are to be understood within their social and historical setting. Sacrament and authority are being reinterpreted in terms of modern historical thought instead of the older concepts of eternal essences. The voice of the people has been taken into theological formulations, and modern social, economic, and political issues are addressed.

Evangelical theology is showing increasing strength. Evangelicalism is concerned with preserving the authority of Scripture without necessarily adopting a literal, fundamentalist view. The individual experience of conversion and salvation remains central. The focus on church growth takes sociological factors of congregational life into account. Evangelicalism shows a new readiness to express its political opinions in the public arena, with some evangelicals joining justice issues with the good news.

A *theology of discipleship* has arisen from widespread concern about justice and international peace. Discipleship theology reinterprets Jesus and the Gospels to show their political relevance for their day. Political relevance is understood in terms of community processes and movements rather than the political control of social structures. Discipleship encourages decisive, committed, and continuing non-violent action for justice and peace, always in relationship to dedicated communities. Worship and covenantal renewal are at the center of discipleship.

Ecumenical theology, sponsored by the World Council of Churches, i.e., the conciliar movement, is concerned with the structures of community life undergirding the various expressions of Christian faith. Conciliar theology also contextualizes theology according to the cultural setting. This concern moves toward a Latin American theology, an African theology, an Asian theology, and a North American theology. The contextualization may become even more local in an attempt to incorporate the living belief of local people all over the world.

The World Council of Churches has adopted a statement on baptism, eucharist, and the ministry that allows for the variety of traditions, but is able to find enough communality that all can adopt it. The statement attempts to reconcile those who understand the continuity of the church to be in the succession of persons ordained from the time of the apostles and those who understand this continuity to be faithfulness to the apostolic tradition, calling them to be open to the interpretations and practice of one another's point of view.[15]

THEOLOGICAL DOCTRINES

Doctrines are the teachings of the different theological positions. The doctrines have obvious power for Christian education because they represent the central issues around which teaching will be done. Traditionally, Christian doctrine has been organized around the Trinity, with the doctrine of revelation as prologue and the doctrine of the kingdom of God as postlogue. Let us consider each of these doctrines briefly in terms of its impact on religious education.

The doctrine of revelation is being discussed in terms of whether there is general revelation in the wider culture and in nature, or whether revelation comes only through the relationship to Jesus Christ. Does religious experience mediate revelation, or is revelation paradoxically beyond experience? Does the critical study of Scripture enhance or restrict revelation? Is revelation best expressed by propositional statements or by narrative accounts?

In this book we take the position that general revelation has an ambiguity that is clarified and deepened only by referring to our relationship to Christ. Even religious experience is paradoxical, mediating a revelation that is present and at the same time beyond itself. The critical study of Scripture may enhance revelation, which is best expressed as story. Revelation needs constantly to be tested against the scriptural story, cultural experience, personal experience, and the opinion of the community of faith. Revelation comes primarily within a living community of devotion and discourse that celebrates, questions, and extends the story.

The doctrine of God is open to new ways of understanding the meaning of Trinity. The presence and absence of God is discussed, especially in view of the Holocaust of World War II. The doctrine of God raises the question of how God can be both all-powerful and all-loving in view of the pervasiveness of evil. Is God in some ways limited? Can the images of God be made more inclusive, to include female images or minority images?

The doctrine of Christ focuses on the atonement. How does one describe the way in which the human separation from God has been overcome in the Christ? How can the paradoxical doctrine of the humanity and divinity of Christ be expressed in the twentieth century? Is atonement primarily an individual experience, or is atonement with God at the same time a reconciliation between persons? What does it mean to be "in Christ"? Does the life of Jesus have meaning for contemporary justice questions?

The doctrine of the Holy Spirit raises the question of the marks of the Holy Spirit. How is the power of the Holy

Spirit related to the community of faithful believers? How is sanctification to be described, and how is it related to faith development? How are Christians to regard the twentieth-century shift in public morality? How are justice and love related to one another? How is the Holy Spirit related to the larger world? What are the marks of healing?

The doctrine of the kingdom of God raises the question of the social character of the kingdom. How is the kingdom of God related to the psychological, social, and political issues of this generation? What is the direction of purpose in history, and how is the ambiguity of history to be understood? What is the meaning of and Christian response to the threat of global annihilation?

Each of these questions has a dramatic effect upon teaching. If common experience is not revelational, then religious teaching ought not attend to it. If the images of God ought to be more inclusive, then teaching should reflect the more inclusive language. If atonement always involves reconciliation, then God's forgiveness is to be taught in a reconciling way. If the kingdom of God is liberating, then it should be taught as liberation.

These doctrinal questions should not hide the fact that doctrines and questions are set within a social context. Any doctrine or question can hide as much as it reveals. The question of evil may hide the pain that a person feels. The question of justice may become detached from the actual practice of the community. The doctrine of the kingdom of God may be locked into middle-class morality. The meaning of a doctrine may not be properly considered outside the practices that give rise to the doctrine.

Consider how the teaching about Christ may interact with community practice. In a group in which the emphasis is on imitating the human perfection of Christ, there may be certain implicit rules according to which each person is expected to act. Perhaps no one is expected to express anger because Christ taught that anger toward another person is tantamount to murder (Matthew 5:22). The presence of any anger in such a group may be very disturbing and disruptive. Or again, perhaps Christ is thought to be the embodiment of self-giving. Every group member may be expected to give credence to the ideal of self-giving, even though the actual practice is predominantly self-preservation.

Another group may understand Christ as the one who justifies and forgives humankind. In such a group, trusting and accepting one another may become primary. Spontaneous expression and the receiving of whatever is offered may be paramount. When tensions arise and conflicts develop, forgiving, accepting, or otherwise moving through the conflicts may become most important. In the Lutheran and Augustinian traditions, people are sinners and justified saints at one and the same time. A group could go in the direction of logical understanding of the principle of justification, or it could move to embody a kind of deep-level acceptance of all persons.

Another way to view Christ is as the one who sanctifies humankind. The Spirit of Christ moves people to grow in Godliness. Under such an image, growth assumes primary importance. A teacher, pastor, or parent following the doctrine of sanctification might give the greatest attention to how each person is growing. Again the image may be one that is taught merely as a doctrine, or one that is embodied as a value by a group.

Christ may also be thought of as mutuality within the community. The Pauline image of the body of Christ refers not only to Jesus, but also to the community of faith. Collectively the church is the body of Christ and individually members of it (I Corinthians 12). In the body of Christ the life of each can be mutually fulfilling to those

143

of the others. The pain and hopes of each become the pain and hopes of all. With such a view of Christ a family or group may be principally concerned with how persons interact with one another. Responsibility to one another and complimentary abilities may receive the attention of parent, pastor, or teacher.

Of course, there are other ways to view Christ. This account is given simply to show how the doctrine of Christ may interact strongly with the way the story is lived. The images do not entirely exclude one another. A fuller view of Christ may include elements of each, and the story may be lived out in view of justice, trust, growth, and mutuality of all participants.

Educational practice, like every other practice, is not simply an expression of official belief, or even of deeply held beliefs. Practice stands between doctrines, deeply held promises and commitments, and the movement of events. The interplay of belief, leadership, and commonly accepted norms gives form and direction to Christian practice. It is therefore also decisive for educational practice.

NARRATIVE AND METHOD

We have suggested that according to its functions, theology is faithful to the story, coherent, and pertinent to the situation at one and the same time. Theology is an expression of devotion, guidance, and inquiry, varying according to the situation and the mode of expression. The wholeness of theology tends to be divided by its above named functions into historical, systematic, and practical theology. If we speak of practical theology as that which is pertinent to a situation, we mean also to include faithfulness to the story and narrative coherence.

This suggestion is very close to that of Edward Farley, who insists that practical theology is first of all theology, but theology that must be related to situations of preaching, evangelicalism, teaching, administration, care, and the like.[16] Practical theology must develop a way of understanding the different situations and suggest an appropriate mode of action. Since ethics deals with the question of what we are to do, practical theology certainly includes ethical considerations. Practical theology is both an interpretation of the tradition and an interpretation of the specific situation. It is concerned about how the world comes to greater wholeness and how the faith community is related to that healing process.

In what way does Christian education share a method with other branches of practical theology? Likely, there cannot be a strictly scientific method for practical theology. John Dewey was able to develop a scientific educational method by presuming agreement about behaviorally defined objectives.[17] When objectives are clearly stated, then methods can be scientifically tested. By way of contrast, a narrative approach takes into account the ongoing debate about which problems to give attention to, but therein a narrative approach loses its strictly scientific method.

Steven Toulmin has suggested that some subject matter is non-disciplinable because it cannot be shaped into an ideal that is abstract, isolable, and single-valued.[18] It may have disciplinable elements, but may lose all value when narrowed enough to become a tight discipline. It may nevertheless be reasonable. For that matter, the recognized sciences have value only insofar as they contribute to non-disciplinable enterprises. Living the story is non-disciplinable in Toulmin's terms.

Poling and Miller have suggested a method for practical theology that includes the following elements: (1) description of lived experience, (2) critical awareness of perspectives and interests, (3) correlation of perspectives from culture and the Christian tradition, (4) interpretation of meaning and value, (5) critique of interpretation, and (6) guidelines and specific plans for a particular community.[19] Such a sequence of steps does not constitute a strict scientific method. Practical theology moves between a reading of the specific situation and a reading of the longer tradition of the ongoing stories of living communities of faith. This back and forth (i.e. dialectical) relationship between the situation as it is coming to be and the longer heritage is picked up in the six steps just given.

We may rephrase the steps to be more in keeping with the language of education, narrative, and community. So rephrased, the steps are:

1. Describe and set some practice within a narrative;
2. Question and challenge the practice as narrated;
3. Correlate the Christian story and current cultural perspectives;
4. Develop an evaluative description and consider reform or renewal of the practice;
5. Critically review the story, description, and proposed practice;
6. Renew or reform the practice while renarrating the story within the community.

The method begins with the actual practice of a community, whether it be a small group, a congregation, a school, a voluntary association, a nation, or a group of nations. The method moves to set the practice within the narrative of the community in order to find its current meaning. In the first step, the process is pre-reflective, which is to say that the experience is simply narrated the way it feels. Everyday experience, lived moments, feelings, preconceptions, thoughts, customs, common practice, and cultural significance are all quite acceptable. However, the effort is to situate fragmentary experience in a longer, ongoing narrative.

The story as developed is then challenged and questioned. This second step is a move to a more disciplined, even scientific inquiry. The analysis may be from the point of view of a discipline such as psychology, sociology, or literature, to name only a few. The attempt is to get beneath the surface behavior to some deeper understanding. A theory of cause, purpose, and relationship will take shape.

The practice in question is then reviewed in terms of the Scripture and the tradition. In the third step, analogies between the present practice and the heritage of faith are explored. A similar scriptural practice in its community setting and story is likened to the present practice in its community setting and story. This is the "analogy of community" spoken of in chapter 4.

The discussion of the Bible and the tradition naturally leads to the fourth step, an evaluative description of the practice and its meaning. The narrative account and the evaluation belong to one another. One cannot describe what is happening in the longer story of the community without at the same time making an evaluation. That evaluation springs out of three earlier steps.[20] It may lead to the intention of renewing or reforming the practice. Perhaps the underlying covenant will be renewed and the practice itself will be revised in some way.

The fifth step is a critical review of story, description, and projected practice. A self-critical community will be aware of faithfulness, health, power, and justice issues.[21] Are the meaning and practice neurotic, that is, destructive of health in some way? Does the practice hide an attempt to give pseudo-power from a motive of resentment? Is there a recognition of actual power? Is the newly reformed practice just? Is it as fair to minorities, the poor, third world persons, women, and other oppressed groups as it is to the majority? Is the newly proposed narrated practice faithful? Does it truly represent the power of the ongoing story of salvation and the new creation of God's kingdom? Here is where ethical analysis is critical.

Finally, in the sixth step, the method leads to a renewed or reformed practice within the ongoing story as renarrated. The community does not experimentally abstract itself from the situation "for purposes of learning." The purposes of learning are also a part of the story and are to be considered so. The community takes seriously its story and its ways of life. Such an educational procedure is part of the method of theology in the latter's relationship to teaching and learning.

This educational method has some similarity to Dewey's, but here the continuing relationship with the tradition is fundamental, whereas for Dewey it is not. Dewey attempts to be value-free and experimental; this method lives deeply within values and commitment while calling communities to be oriented toward the global community, God's kingdom. The method is similar to Groome's shared praxis, which is discussed in the next chapter. However the relation to narrative is sharper. Groome seems to limit his approach to the classroom, whereas this method is a part of the larger discipline of theology. This method is further developed in the latter steps, giving more attention to ethical evaluation and analysis than does Groome.[22]

STORY AND CONTEXT

Theology is the expression of the community as it lives the story. In being faithful to the story, coherent, and pertinent, theology incorporates remembering, questioning, celebrating, evaluating, and anticipating. In this sense all verbal expressions of the community, in their attempt to be faithful, coherent, and pertinent, are theology. Theology is the community in dialog with one another, seeking the mind of Christ.

The problem of right teaching (orthodoxy) is the problem of the continuity of the community in its ongoing story. Teaching is located between the confessional and searching modes of theology. Functionally there is no contradiction between theology and disciplined study. However, the community gives authority to certain teachings, which then are in tension with the spirit of free inquiry. The church lives and is renewed in that tension. Confessing assures continuity and searching assures truthfulness and integrity. Orthodoxy is always subject to question and questioning always threatens orthodoxy. Neither can be given up. The community seeks to be both faithful and truthful as it reaches to participate in the global community.

STUDY SUGGESTIONS

Exercises

1. Write out your own statement of belief and share it with others in your group. As each of you gives your statement, include a description of turning points that led to the particular beliefs you espouse. Allow enough time for each person so that each can share something genuinely important.

2. Choose any book (or chapter) in the Bible and characterize the theology of that book. What are

the basic doctrines of the book and how are they related to one another? Does the book give you any clues to how the doctrines are related to common practices and customs of the time?

3. Interview members of the congregation to find out the approved teaching (orthodoxy) and the approved practice (orthopraxis) of the congregation. In what way does your congregation's approved teaching vary from the approved teaching for the whole denomination? How is the teaching related to common practice? What pressures are put on persons who do not follow the approved teaching and the approved practice?

4. Search out sermons, newsletter statements, and other statements that were made about a serious problem confronting the congregation. The problem may be one of stewardship, care, evangelism, or something else. Is there any common theology coming through these statements? Do they give indications of the functional theology of the congregation?

5. Does the teaching in the congregation have some coherent authority? Is the authority of teaching due to official appointment? Is the authority due to a common spirit in the congregation? Does the pastor give authority to the teaching? May teachers teach whatever they prefer? What gives continuity to the congregation's story?

6. Share your favorite story with one another. What do you like about the story? What does the story do for you? What power does story have that other forms of expression do not?

7. Set up a debate in your group over the question, Should religious education be first of all good education or good theology? Let each position

give at least one five-minute statement and a two-minute rebuttal to the other side. If you have enough persons, have two five-minute statements and two rebuttals of two minutes from each side. Vote on which side argued most persuasively. What does your group conclude about the issue?

8. Choose a theme from at least one of the current theological schools to study and discuss. Read a statement or invite someone to speak to you about the issues. For example, study the World Council of Churches document, *Baptism, Eucharist and Ministry.* Have your pastor or someone else lead a discussion. In what way is your belief about these doctrines challenged by the World Council document?

9. Study how the doctrine of Christ interacts with the practice of teaching in your congregation. Ask several teachers about their belief in Christ, and how their belief affects their teaching. Possibly, visit a group being taught to observe the teaching practice. If several of you do this, compare notes about the relationship of the doctrine of Christ and the actual teaching practice.

10. Carry out a discussion in your group in which you work through the steps of the theological method given above. Let the method inform your work on a church committee. Try to include each step in the work of your committee. How helpful do you find the method to be?

Questions for Discussion

1. In what way is theology a fundamental expression of community life?

2. What are the alternatives to considering theology as a faithful, coherent, pertinent expression of community life?

3. How have theology and teaching been related to one another in the Christian tradition?

4. What is the proper relationship between individual belief and authoritative doctrine?

5. In what ways is the narrative form appropriate to revelation? In what ways are other literary forms appropriate to revelation?

6. What is the role of imagination in theology? What are the educational implications?

7. How should the debate about the priority of education and of theology in religious education be resolved?

8. How is Christian education to proceed in view of the variety of theologies mentioned above?

9. How is theology affected by the practice of a community?

10. What are the strengths and weaknesses of the method of practical theology of education described above?

Suggestions for Further Reading

Don S. Browning, ed., *Practical Theology.*
A series of essays that attempt to establish practical theology as a discipline joining Christian education with other practical areas.

Sallie McFague, *Metaphorical Theology: Model of God in Religious Language.*
A study of metaphor in theology with special reference to feminine metaphors.

James N. Poling and Donald E. Miller, *Foundations for a Practical Theology of Ministry.*

Explains the method of practical theology in this chapter in greater detail.

Norma Thompson, ed., *Religious Education and Theology.*

Articles by various religious educators regarding the relationship of religious education and theology.

Chapter Six:

LIVING THE STORY

We are already living and interacting long before we find the symbolic expression to interpret the story we are living. So the story is an interpretation of life as we live it. Living the story is not the same as talking about it or studying it. Instead, it changes as we find ways of studying and expressing it. Living the story includes hearing, perceiving, intending, interacting, promising, experiencing, and worshiping. To paraphrase a famous maxim, to live without having a story is to be blind, and to have a story without living it is to be empty.[1]

RELIGION AS PRACTICAL

The story has not been heard until the hearer also lives within the story. Let us put this otherwise to include both children and adults. The story is not received until the receiver begins to interact with the person and community who bear the story. Thus children interact with their parents long before they become aware of the story within which they are interacting. In like manner they interact with school and community before becoming aware of the story borne by that school or community. The child interacts with the faith community before knowing the story that shapes that interaction.

Youth and adults also interact with a community bearing a story, which they hear expressed in multiple ways, from informal conversation through study to worship. They respond both to the community and to the story. To the extent that they find themselves related to the story and to the community, they have begun to receive the story. To the extent that they acknowledge this relationship and publicly commit themselves to it, they are responding to the story. To the extent that they search for ways to give further expression to those relationships and the story, they are being transformed by and extending the story. So the story becomes to some degree their own source of identity and their own community. This receiving, responding to, and extending the story in relation to the community that bears it, we speak of as living the story.

However, the faith community is part of a wider complex of communities which finally includes the whole human community. While in the past some populations could ignore others, the interrelatedness of the entire human community is becoming increasingly evident. Modern transportation and communication have made the human community a global village, albeit one fraught with radical and multiple differences. Everyone is in the situation of discovering a story within the world community that was being shaped before she or he was born and that exerted its influence before she or he was aware of it. The conjunction of the local community's story and the global community's story is at the heart of the meaning of the faith community's story. To live in the story of the faith community is to be exposed to the global community's story and to have the way one relates to other communities transformed. The faith community's story is a bond between its people, between people of different languages and traditions, and between the past and the future.

The gospel story is never simply and equally accepted by everyone. In fact, each person, each community, and each tradition has a different version. Denominational bodies prescribe boundaries (orthodoxy) for telling and living the gospel story. The continual struggle to clarify and to reinterpret the story is itself a part of the story. Consequently, the story lives in the effort to clarify it as well as in the daily activities of those who have heard the story.

Sociologists have shown that societies develop layers of meaning which justify customary activity. In this way religion becomes the ultimate justification for interlocking social patterns constituting a way of life. A rural church may teach that farming is a special vocation given by God, which serves as the ultimate justification for an agricultural way of life. An academic community may teach that truth is the ultimate gift of God, thereby justifying an academic way of life. A lower-class church may advocate humble service as the most Christ-like attitude, thereby justifying their underprivileged, everyday way of life. Youth may understand vitality as God-given, and age may teach restraint and responsibility as required by God. In each case the faith story justifies a given custom, practice, or way of life.

While the faith story may at times serve to justify everyday customs and practices, it may also bring change or innovation. Every slave-owning culture has justified its way of life by claiming that slavery was instituted by God. However, the faith story may convince some that slavery is evil. The abolitionists of nineteenth-century America

157

taught that the Scripture is opposed to human slavery, and the power of the reinterpreted story began to reshape many local communities. The civil rights movement of the twentieth century was born in the black church and was led largely by churches and synagogues across the country.

Some noted historians consider the teachings of the reformers essential to the economic changes of the sixteenth century.[2] Until that time Europe was largely organized as a feudal society. Luther, Calvin, the Anabaptists, and other reformers taught the sanctity of secular vocations, the direct relation of each individual to God, and the importance of constantly working for the coming of the kingdom of God. Luther himself left the monastery and married. Quickly, new patterns of relationships were taught, accepted, and adopted. Many other significant events were also occurring then, including exploration of the new world, inventions, and expansion of the monetary system. The teaching of the church seems to have encouraged the social, economic, and political changes that followed the Reformation. We see, then, that the story not only justifies given customs and practices, but sometimes encourages reform, innovation, and change.

Religious belief has reportedly been linked to prejudice. Some Nazis claimed to be good churchmen, and Ku Klux Klansmen frequently justify their practice by Scripture. The worst human slaughter is often justified in the name of faith, be it God's blessing on a war, or God commanding a sniper to kill innocent bystanders. These are extreme examples, but those who have studied the authoritarian personality conclude that authoritarianism is linked to religious belief.[3]

More recent researches have led to more refined conclusions. If one does not depend simply on what people *say* their beliefs are, then the picture changes. If regular and committed church attenders are separated from others who say they are believers, the regular church attenders do not turn out to be more authoritarian than the average population. Therefore Gordon Allport suggested that religious beliefs may be either intrinsic or extrinsic. Intrinsic belief leads to behavior that is more affirming and tolerant of other people; intrinsic belief is, in a word, less authoritarian. Extrinsic belief tends to be more authoritarian.[4]

Religious belief is often affected by the interplay of local and translocal practices. By translocal practices, we mean those carried by regions or institutions considerably more extensive than local communities. For a congregation, denominational and ecumenical expectations are translocal. As mentioned above, local practices governing ethnic, sexual, marriage, age, and work patterns tend to be justified by local religious traditions. The teaching of such translocal bodies as denominations or ecumenical groups may be at great variance with local teaching. In fact, in nearly every local church there is considerable tension with translocal teaching.

Some local people distrust both modern reason and modern technology, and may justify these attitudes through religious conservatism or fundamentalism. The official translocal stance regarding reason and technology may be positive (liberalism), but local churches may reject this position if a negative evaluation of these two predominates.

Local belief may consider that a person is appointed by God to teach, preach, and baptize simply through the gift of the Holy Spirit. Every denomination has rules and procedures by which ordination is conferred. Tension between local belief and denominational teaching is inevitable. This struggle is particularly poignant in the case of women seeking ordination. The discussion occurs in local communities about whether the Scriptures allow for the ordination of women. The argument is sometimes solved locally by having a woman serve as a temporary pastor for a period of time. Eventually, actual practice begins to affect the belief.

The same struggle can be seen in the teachings of various denominations about economics. Some denominations have called for criticism of the international practices of American corporations, or of American economic support for South Africa. Local practice tends to continue local investments that sustain such corporations without criticism. A similar pattern can be seen in the struggle between the official Roman Catholic teaching about birth control and abortion and the widespread acceptance of such practices at the local level.

The result of this struggle is that congregations stand between local customs and attitudes on one hand and translocal denominational teaching on the other. The battle line between denominational belief and the ethos of the world runs through the congregations. Conversely, the denomination stands between various local pressures and ecumenical opinion.

The story of the faith community is eminently practical in that the interaction of teaching and practice is intense and continuous. Teaching may move in the direction of legitimating local practice or innovating new practice. The way congregations live the story determines what their own, unique versions will be, and cannot be known except by being closely acquainted with their everyday belief and practice.

THE EVERYDAY LIFE OF THE CONGREGATION

Certain functions are basic to all communities, but they take on a special form in communities of faith. *All communities give their members a basic perspective on the world.* In the Christian church that perspective is shaped by the Christian tradition and doctrine as they are interpreted and reinterpreted. The Holy Scripture is the foremost document shaping the community's perspective, although Scripture can be perceived and interpreted in radically different ways. The various denominational doctrines shape a community's perspective. At the same time, the public media of print and television, as well as daily conversation, shape public opinion. The extent to which local public opinion interacts with the church's perspective is critical to the everyday life of the congregation. The influence inevitably goes in both directions.

All communities give their members a basic emotional orientation. Certain enduring emotional attitudes are constantly lifted up in the Scripture, and these attitudinal virtues have been marks of discipleship throughout the years. They include faith, hope, love, humility, perseverence, courage, truthfulness, integrity, reverence, generosity, and gratitude. Such attitudes are rooted in the more fundamental orientation of reverence to God—creator, redeemer, and sustainer of all life. The New Testament warns against attitudes of superior knowledge, fatedness, cynicism, despair, hopelessness, false trust, hatred, and greed. The Christian struggle is not against flesh and blood, but against the emotional attitudes just mentioned. To continue to stand for a new moral order in the face of the intransigency of the present order requires patience and distance, and at the same time courageous engagement and assertiveness. The Christian virtues therefore underlie social ethics.

All communities give their members a basic expressive language. The Christian church uses language shaped by the history of the tradition. Rooted in Hebrew and Greek, it has developed through Latin and other languages. The church is influenced by the biblical languages, which continually require new translation. The stories, phrases, metaphors, and images of the Scripture shape the language of the community of faith: "the body of Christ," "the communion of saints," "the people of God," "the kingdom of God," to name a few. The early apostolic preaching and teaching and the life and teaching of Jesus are also central to the church's language.

All communities give their members certain common values. The values of the Christian church cluster around the event of Jesus Christ. They feature the love of God and of all persons, combined with concern about justice. Human justice is rooted in the divine activity by which humankind is made just by God. The human propensity for injustice is borne by God so that people may start afresh. In Christ, the community dies to the old and is born to the new, all of which is symbolized in worship and teaching. Various other values such as power, wealth, prestige, and glory are overcome in Christ: the power of God includes the powerless; the wealth of God includes the poor; the prestige of God includes the disinherited; the glory of God includes the common and everyday. This transforming of human values by the divine is what H. Richard Niebuhr calls radical monotheism.[5] The doctrine of one God means one value transcends all others. Radical monotheism means that all of our values are being transformed by the one value. At no point can that one value be replaced by another value, for the one value is superior.

All communities give their members certain modes of thinking which represent the popular philosophies of the time. These include atheism, materialism, hedonism, egoism, pragmatism, idealism, and many, many others. The Christian church teaches its members to think of their lives in relation to the meaning of Christ's kingdom, power, and presence. Sometimes this is formalized into a network of doctrine. Most recently, it is being discussed as an ongoing story. In practical terms, the members of a community of faith ask, What are we to do in view of what God is enabling and demanding? What are we to do as believers in Jesus Christ and members of his church? The competing questions are, What are we to do to save our lives, our families, our possessions, and our privileges? The struggle between these competing questions occurs in local communities.

All communities give their members a certain way of relating to people which stands between trust and mistrust, generosity and rejection, respect and control. The Christian church teaches people to consider each other as brothers and sisters in Christ, sons and daughters of one God. They are to serve one another and to be friends. They are to be persons for others, to paraphrase Bonhoeffer.[6] They are neighbors to all, even to the most despised, even to the Samaritan. The struggle between these attitudes and separation or apartheid, marks the place where the human community is being formed.

Collectively, these basic perspectives, virtues, language, values, thinking, and relationships are the *living covenant* of a community. The living covenant cannot be described in formal terms. One must participate in a particular community and observe and interact with it to know its living covenant. We can suggest various patterns, as we have done; we can also refer to biblical images. But the living covenant is discovered in actual participation in a given community. To the extent that the living covenant embodies biblical images, it is the living spirit and power of Christ. The living covenant is a dynamic relationship between stated beliefs, worship practices, and larger community patterns. Formal teaching and the living covenant intersect in an actual faith community.[7]

THEORY AND PRACTICE

The current discussion about living the story can be traced in the debate about theory and practice brought to the fore by liberation theology. Among religious educators, Thomas Groome has called for a reexamination of the relationship of theory and praxis. According to Groome, a wide separation now exists between the theory or story and actual practice. He believes this separation to be deadly for religious education and calls for Christian religious education built on integration of story and practice.

Groome calls his approach by the original term "shared praxis." Praxis is not to be considered as practice in the ordinary sense. It is not the application of given theory or ideals, nor simply ongoing activity. Praxis begins rather with what is actually being done and proceeds to reflect and theorize upon what is being done. The theory has the function of influencing practice. The influence of theory is not so much by application as by a continual attempt to become aware of what is being practiced and what the implications are. In designating this interaction of theory and practice by the term *praxis*, Groome is in touch with much liberation theology.

Educational Conceptions of Theory and Practice

Theory	*Practice*	*Praxis*
To know the truth is to do it.	To do the truth is to know it.	To know the truth is to reflect upon the continuing story of what we are doing.

164

Socrates and his disciples assumed that if we really know something we will do it. Perhaps he would have suggested that the gulf between knowing and doing is the result of shallow understanding. Those who stress the learning of content often assume that when persons know the meaning of something, they will act according to their knowledge. In religious education it is therefore important to learn the basic religious doctrines and ideas. To know that God loves each person is basic to living in relation to God's love.

John Dewey challenged the classical theoretical approach to practice. He argued that genuine knowledge comes in the reverse order. As we experience something and act upon it in thoughtful ways, we experience the truth. He therefore believed all learning requires the interested attention and activity of the learner. We are constantly learning through our activity, but learning can be sharpened by choosing what we will do and by becoming aware of the consequences of our choices.

What Dewey gained in a practical approach to learning, he lost in relation to the tradition. If one attends only to immediate choices and their consequences, one loses the longer story of the community. Therefore the praxis approach attempts to retain the basis of learning in what is actually being done, but the learners are also kept aware of the continuing story. Praxis attempts thereby to integrate both the theory and the practice approaches to education.

THE ETHIC OF PRACTICE

Ethicists have also paid much attention to the relationship of thought and action. Many contemporary ethicists suggest that there are three types of such a relationship. The first is that of living according to the most universal rules that one can imagine. Immanuel Kant is surely the foremost modern spokesperson for this view. According to Kant we are to give voice to the rules by which we live and act (maxims). Then we are to imagine that everyone lives according to those same rules. If we can wholeheartedly will such rules to become universal for everyone in similar circumstances, then we may indeed adopt them. Rawls gives contemporary expression to this idea; he says that we should choose rules under a "veil of ignorance," i.e., without knowing what role we will have to play in the practice that is established by the rule.[8]

Ethical Conceptions of Theory and Practice

Rule	*Consequence*	*Virtue*
Act according to rules under which you would be willing to live in whatever circumstance.	Act so as to bring the greatest benefit to the greatest number of persons.	Live out of a narrative of the good life and of a character that embodies it.

An alternate approach to action comes from utilitarians such as John Stuart Mill.[9] According to this view we should consider the needs of every concerned person, and then choose so as to gain the greatest benefit for everyone concerned. A parent is often in the position of deciding whether a young person shall be allowed to remain out late, or a teacher may have to decide when to terminate a discussion. The utilitarian suggestion is to give attention to the consequences for all of the persons concerned. Whichever action brings more benefit to most persons is the one to follow.

Still a third approach to the ethics of practice is that of virtue. Although some ethicists will not allow this approach, others are vigorously attempting to defend it.[10] According to this third view, the rules by which we act take meaning only in actual situations, so the underlying narrative is basic to every rule of practice. Furthermore, the character of a person is shaped more by the ongoing narrative of the person's life than by the rules that he or she follows. Only a full account of a situation in its continuity with the past and the future allows a person to discern what to do.

As with the educational view of practice, the third approach here also attempts to hold together elements of the other two views. Ethical discernment attempts to judge what would be a fair rule for everyone, and it attempts to consider the benefit to all persons. This is done within an effort to recount the ongoing narrative. So there is a close parallel between the three ethical views and the three educational views of practice.

Theory and Practice

Education	To know the truth is to do it.	We learn by doing.	To know the truth is to reflect upon the continuing story.
Ethics	Act according to rules under which you would be willing to live in whatever circumstances.	Act so as to bring the greatest benefit to the greatest number of persons.	Live out of a narrative of the good life and a character that embodies it.

In summary, Christian ethicists differ in their analysis of theory and practice. Some call for living by the most universal principles possible, others call for attending to consequences, and still others appeal to a kind of intuitional grasp of the total situation. The latter group includes H. Richard Niebuhr, Karl Barth, James Gustafson, and Paul Lehmann, who are not willing to rest either with universal principles or with consequences alone. Paul Lehmann, for example, feels that a sense of God's humanizing activity in the world, Christ's forgiveness, and the awareness of conscience within the Christian community should be joined together to give ethical insight.[11]

While agreeing with Lehmann's appeal for an intuition of the total situation, Gustafson is critical of Lehmann for dismissing principles and consequences too quickly. Gustafson insists that while one must be aware of both principles and consequences, they are insufficient without moral discernment. For Gustafson, moral discernment is more than following a checklist, acting spontaneously, applying a set of principles, or responding to information. Discernment includes an awareness of all of the following: an evaluative description of the occasion, relevant information, power available, overall perspective, causes, human values, moral principles, world views and beliefs, affections, dispositions, motives, desires, consequences, purposes, and relation to the larger context. This is all considered within God's creating, judging, and redeeming governance. Discernment requires study of the Scripture, prayer, and worship within the ongoing community of faith.

Gustafson's account of discernment goes beyond the educator's dictum to know the student and know the tradition. It offers many suggestions about what the story is to include. Discussion of principles, rules, values, feelings, desires, and consequences is important. But in the end, the community of faith makes an intuitive judgment. The context for any small group judgment is the larger community of faith, prayer, and worship. An ethic of discernment seems not to exclude the valuable contributions of both rules and consequences. Gustafson's account of discernment includes oral discussion with the community of faith.[12] However, Paul Lehmann clarifies that discernment or conscience is worked out in the give-and-take of interaction within the community of faith, the body of Christ.

Christian education as practical theology does well to attend to such ethical considerations. Christian educators have been very concerned about purposes, goals, and objectives. To some extent there is a similar concern about the gospel message and respect for all persons. The first set of concerns parallels the ethic of consequences, while the second set of concerns parallels the ethic of universal principles. An appeal to discernment and conscience puts concern for goals as well as principles into the context of the ongoing narrative of the community of faith. Purposes are to be clarified and the principles of justice to be identified, but they are always part of a community whose ongoing narrative, within the gospel narrative, is the fundamental reality.

EDUCATION FOR JUSTICE

Discussion about practice leads directly into questions of social ethics and justice. Social ethics has to do with providing a guiding vision for human institutions in order that life might be more livable for everyone. A basic issue of social ethics is that of justice. What is the fairest way to organize human institutions, and what are the fairest rules for such organization? Ever since Plato, educators throughout Western history have been concerned about the link between education and justice.[13]

In Brian Wren's view, justice education begins with a realization that genuine learning requires a total change of awareness, a change that is perceptual, volitional, and emotional. Such changes come as people explore issues that deeply concern them in their everyday lives. In the case of justice, as people learn about the ways in which they are being unfairly taken advantage of, and about ways to combat their oppression, they begin to have a total change of awareness. This change cannot be separated from beginning to live in ways that bring about justice.

Justice can never be the absolute equality of all in terms of privileges and responsibilities. A just society does not give children and adults the same privileges and responsibilities, nor those with moderate and those with greater talents. Some allowance must be made for those who serve the greater benefit of others. So parents have responsibilities and privileges that children do not, and leaders have responsibilities and privileges that followers do not. John Rawls has suggested that the principle of justice requires that where social and economic inequalities are allowed, they be arranged so that they are of greatest benefit to the least advantaged.[14]

Wren points out that the powerful seldom if ever voluntarily give up their privileges. Furthermore, the powerful tend to control cultural symbols so that the underprivileged are depicted as of less worth. They "lack initiative," "are not dependable," "are not responsible," and generally "are not worthy of respect." Unfortunately, the underprivileged tend to think of themselves in the same terms. Many women, for example, find it nearly impossible to believe they are of as much worth and ability as men. Minority groups similarly find their self-image turned against themselves.

Education for justice therefore begins with reclaiming self-images that are affirming rather than depreciating. For this reason the slogans "Black is Beautiful" and "I am somebody" became popular in the black community, and "Hispanic is Beautiful" and "Red is Beautiful" in the Latin and Native American communities. Since language is so close to self-image and self-worth, the struggle for non-depreciating and globally inclusive language is an important element in education for justice.

Wren further argues that injustice is held in place by various kinds of power. To change an unjust relationship will nearly always involve a confrontation. Education for justice makes people aware of the inevitability of confrontation. Not only language, but also customary practice and role expectations are enforced by power. For example, Martin Luther King, Jr., challenged the practice of forcing blacks to sit in the back of buses, which led to an open and dramatic conflict. Conflicts may be resolved by dialog, negotiation, and spiritual discipline, but education for justice includes an awareness of the inevitability of challenge.

Over against Wren's point of view is that of Stanley Hauerwas.[15] In the opinion of Hauerwas, the foremost expression of justice is worship. Biblical justice is not principally located in one or another set of rules, in one or another action. Rather, social justice is located primarily in the story of God's justifying grace in Jesus Christ as the story is embodied in particular communities of faith. Justice is located at the intersection of a community's being justified in God's grace and living in justifying relationships with one another, including those outside the community. Hauerwas thus puts a high priority on worship and study of the story.

A missing element in Wren's account is the congregation. For a congregation to take on a different practice means that it encounters and challenges the everyday practice of the wider community. Congregations can establish sanctuary for oppressed and illegal refugees. Congregations can encourage one another not to use products manufactured by companies engaged in unjust practices. Congregations can decide that stewardship means to cease wasting natural resources. They can send their members into places of open hostility, to protest violence. In a less confrontive style, they can make their views known to a congress and meet with like-minded community groups. In so many ways congregations can encourage a life-pattern that challenges injustice and reaches out evangelistically to others.

The congregation can become an island of justice in the culture. Different congregations will of course come to different moral conclusions, which in itself is not so important. More important is that the congregation seeks to embody a faithful way of life that becomes a living covenant for them. Congregations can be self-critical centers of life-style education. They can together seek ways of living that challenge the oppression around them. Being together as a congregation is the primary social ethic of the church. The primary ethical witness of the church is to accept God's grace, live as an ethical community within God's love, and find ways to give community expression to a transformed lifestyle.

Hauerwas correctly points to the fact that the church celebrates God's grace in Christ through spiritual discipline and ceremonies of worship. Therein the congregation nourishes the virtues that allow people to continue to live a life-style at odds with surrounding injustice. The congregation lives as those who are justified and are a part of the gospel story. Their life together is more than deeds of justice and mercy. They simply try to be at one with who they know themselves genuinely to be. In the words of

172

Paul, "If anyone is in Christ, he is a new creation" (2 Corinthians 5:17 RSV).

Life-style education within the enduring covenant is quite different from attempting to motivate people to do deeds of justice that are alien to their normal activity. Life-style education involves an in-depth concern for who a group is and how to live and worship with integrity. It is a search for a covenantal relationship expressed in a life-style rather than in heroic attempts to correct an overwhelming problem. Worship, dialog, and customary practice and role expectations become wed to one another. Careful ethical analysis of life-style choices is always appropriate, but always within the ongoing narrative.

Justice and life-style education are a part of global awareness. At a time when United States citizens are most likely to vote for their own personal economic well-being, with little or no consideration for the well-being of the other peoples around the world, congregations can be islands of global awareness. At a time when the human rights of persons in other countries are not so important as the continuing affluence of ruling elites, life-style education can contribute to greater public awareness of the global community. Congregations are to be the place where there are signs and signals that collective egoism is being overcome by the kingdom of God.

GLOBAL PARTICIPATION

Several educational strategies can be used to encourage global participation. Issue groups can study such problems as poverty, single parenthood, sexual abuse, drug addiction, and alcoholism. Meeting with people who cope with these problems can be much more than a class discussion; it may become an opportunity to make life-style changes. For example, it may mean being careful to include single parents in social gatherings, or perhaps imposing a luxury tax upon oneself in order to contribute more resources to the poor.

Intercultural learning experiences can engage congregations directly in the lives of people from another culture. A non-participatory approach simply studies cultural contrasts for the sake of comparison, while a participatory approach involves face-to-face contact. Such programs as student exchange or refugee resettlement can bring people from other lands to live with the congregation.

Indigenous education is a procedure adapting education to local circumstances. Classical education removes people from their local context; often youth who leave for schooling never return to their home communities again. The older practice of apprenticeship allowed people to learn within a living community. But education can be adapted to each local community circumstance rather than requiring every community to conform to a centralized norm. This requires studying the local situation, the factors that influence it, and the ways people live within that setting.

An example of indigenous education is the people's theology project of the World Council of Churches, which is collecting the stories of people's faith in many places around the world. Instead of telling people what to believe, they are listening to what people actually do believe. These stories, often utterly inspiring, can inform the beliefs of many other people.

STORY AND CONTEXT

The community of faith shares the ongoing story of the Bible and of church history. It reflects on that story and its own practice as it seeks a renewed covenant and commitment. But faith is both practical and meaningful; therefore the congregation may not move only from idea to application. The congregation is already engaged in an ongoing way of life. Their worship, study, and moral discussion constantly challenge and question their way of life. In this ongoing discussion its ways are reinterpreted, renewed, and reformed. The congregation is a community of persons seeking to be faithful to God's creation of a new community in Jesus Christ.

Such a description of the congregation can easily become idealized. Discussion must take into account actual practice. Where common practice hides prejudice, abuse, injustice, neurosis, or where it contributes to such sins nationally and internationally, it ought to be challenged. But the transformation of common practice rests first of all on worship, celebration, and ritual. Living the story is a process of seeking to be deeply in touch with who the congregation really is and with the story of God's power to reconcile and nourish a global community. Educational activities are not a temporary neutralizing of the story. They are in fact one way of living within the story. So the method of practical theology, including Christian education, is part of the story in its context.

STUDY SUGGESTIONS

Exercises

1. Choose some of the common practices of your congregation. Interview a number of people to find out what those practices mean to them. In their view, what would happen if those practices were discontinued? You may want to choose some worship, evangelism, or stewardship practice. Compare notes from your interviews and attempt to reconstruct what the actual function

and meaning of that practice is in the congregation.

2. Visit members of the church who seldom attend, if ever. Explain that you are interested in their relationship to the church. (In fact, the pastor may be well pleased to send you to visit them.) Find out which of the beliefs of your church they consider most important. Which beliefs do they consider of less importance? What are their reasons? After the interviews compare notes to see whether non-attenders have different beliefs from those who attend. Compare your conclusions with those in the present chapter.

3. Carry out a debate on the question, Which has more influence on this congregation—denominational beliefs, local traditions, or individual talents and leadership? Let each of three groups choose one of the positions and study it for a week. Then have a public discussion or debate between the three.

4. The present chapter suggests that every group gives its members the following: a perspective on the world, a basic emotional orientation, an expressive language, common values, a mode of thinking, and a way of relating to others. Describe the way in which your congregation shapes its members with regard to each of the six elements.

5. Hold a debate between the two positions: (1) to know the truth is to do it (Socrates), and (2) to do the truth is to know it (Dewey). This could be done as a formal debate with five minute presentations followed by two minute rebuttals. Following the debate, discuss which argument was stronger.

6. Find someone who is poor or underprivileged in your community. Invite them to your church, or

176

go into their situation. Share life stories with one another. What is the meaning and impact of being underprivileged? In what ways do day by day routines contribute to keeping persons underprivileged?

7. Separate the women from the men in your group. Have the women discuss the advantages and disadvantages of women's role in the church. Have the men discuss the advantages and disadvantages of men's role in the church. Come together and compare notes.

8. Try to locate one way in which your congregation is "an island of justice in the culture." How did this come about? Find out why people continue that practice.

9. Plan a trip, an exchange, or a service project in a community of a much different culture than your own. If you are a middle-class white American group, then visit a black, a Native American, or an Appalachian community. Try to visit a Latin American, African, or Asian community, if possible. Make a special point of exchanging faith stories. Return home with your own collection of "people's theology."

10. For any of the exercises above, pledge yourself to a regular discipline of Bible study and worship, at the weekly service, in your own group, and as a private discipline. Study the Scripture in relation to your daily activity, and seek the relationship between your practice and God's ongoing story in Jesus Christ.

Questions for Discussion

1. What is the relationship between community practice and the prevailing story in a commu-

nity? Do stories change practices or do practices change stories?

2. What is the relationship between religious belief and prejudice? And privilege?
3. In what way should teaching in a congregation be related to local and to translocal religious belief?
4. In what ways are the everyday functions of a community of faith like those of other communities, and in what ways not?
5. What is a living covenant in a congregation?
6. What is the analogy between the educational theory of practice and the ethical theory of practice?
7. Which of the theories of practice in this chapter (rule, consequence, virtue) is most persuasive?
8. To what extent can a congregation inform an individual's ethical discernment?
9. Do the powerful ever willingly give up privilege? What are the implications for justice education?
10. What is life-style education? Indigenous education?

Suggestions for Further Reading

Stanley Hauerwas, *A Community of Character: Toward a Constructive Christian Social Ethic.*
Hauerwas shows how social ethics and congregational life are related.

James Michael Lee, *The Content of Religious Instruction.*
Chapter 9, "Lifestyle Content," is directly relevant to this chapter.

Ernst Troeltsch, *The Social Teaching of the Christian Churches.*

This extensive two-volume study is the classic presentation of the churches' teachings about living the story.
Brian Wren, *Education for Justice.*
Wren brings together liberation pedagogy and Reinhold Niebuhr's ethics, but does not pay sufficient attention to the congregation.

III
FAITH

Chapter Seven:

FAITH AND MORAL DEVELOPMENT

DEFINITIONS

Almost all religious education in whatever tradition aims at moral development. A study of church youth across the United States shows that very liberal and very conservative parents may disagree about many things, but they agree that they want their youth to be encouraged toward morality by their religious education.[1] The ongoing debate about religious instruction and prayer in the public school is fueled by the hope of many that religious instruction and prayer will strengthen the morality of children and youth. The point is that morality is almost always a central purpose of religious education.

In this chapter we shall look at current discussions of faith development and moral development and the relationship between the two. One of the difficult problems of discussing faith and moral development is finding acceptable definitions. One suspects that conservatives and liberals agree so much about a focus on morality because the meaning of morality is not carefully defined and commonly understood.

Lawrence Kohlberg's study of moral development has been very influential on religious educators, but critics have pointed out that Kohlberg defines morality to be fairness, which is a narrow definition in the long history of Western culture. Not only is it narrow; it is also male-oriented, according to Carol Gilligan.[2]

Similarly, James Fowler has given a most influential account of the development of faith. He has defined faith to be a person's attitude toward the ultimate environment.[3] Using this definition anyone can and does have faith. Faith is then not uniquely Christian or Jewish, or even religious. In later writings Fowler seems to reach for a more specifically Christian concept, i.e., vocation, on which to ground his description of faith development.[4]

Our perspective is that both faith and morality are evident in social interaction. Faith is trust and confidence in the story, the relationships, and the way of life that binds a religious community together. Such is the formal statement. Specifically Christian faith is trust in Christ's power to mediate the forgiveness, acceptance, and love of God. Christian faith is to believe in the transforming power of God and to live in the transformed way of God—the kingdom of God.

Descriptively morality is whatever people do. Our perspective is that morality is whatever a people's story, pattern of interactions, and way of life are. The special focus of morality is on what is desirable, valuable, good, or right. Specifically Christian morality is a morality of love, a love that is able to bind all persons together into a story and way of life in which their inmost desires are fulfilled in a self-giving for other persons. Christian faith is trust in the love of God, and Christian love is expression of faith in God. So faith and morality do belong to one another.

From this perspective, we shall review various discussions of faith and moral development. Our purpose is to seek a comprehensive description that can ground educational practice. The critical debate is between cognitive and emotive theories of morality and of faith. The cognitive approach features the perceptual process and is advocated by Jean Piaget, Ronald Goldman, Mary Wilcox, Lawrence Kohlberg, and James Fowler, among others. The emotive approach features feelings and motivation and is advocated by Sigmund Freud, Erik Erikson, and to some extent, by James Fowler.

An interactive hemeneutical approach accounts for the relationship between symbol and social process, individual and community. Religious educators whose views tend in this direction are C. Ellis Nelson, Sara Little, Thomas Groome, Craig Dykstra, and John Westerhoff.[5] This approach attempts to solve problems raised by the other two approaches. The discussion that follows will give examples of each of the three types.

MORAL JUDGMENT

The classical statement of a cognitive view of morality is given in Jean Piaget's *The Moral Judgment of the Child.* Piaget's ground-breaking work is the foundation for much of the discussion of the development of morality by twentieth-century religious educators. On the basis of many interviews with children, Piaget contended that children's perception of morality changes as they mature. Prior to learning to speak, children have no morality as such. During the years three to six, children have an attitude of "unilateral respect," in which moral rules are thought to be absolute and exceptionless. Breaking the rules results in the severest punishment. Piaget calls this period *egocentric* because the child has difficulty distinguishing what goes on outside and inside the imagination. There is a weak understanding of the difference between inward experience and outer reality.

185

A second stage occurs between the years seven and eleven. Morality is in transition between unilateral and mutual respect, the latter representing a social covenant between consenting persons. The transition period is one of mixed morality. School age children keep many of their ideas about absolute, exceptionless rules. At the same time, in their play with other children they are learning to live by "fair" agreements made between themselves. Piaget calls this the period of *concrete operations* because children think literally and specifically about immediate problems.

The third and final stage is called the period of *formal operations*. It includes children of twelve years and above and is characterized by an ability to think hypothetically and abstractly. Youth in this stage have achieved a morality of mutual respect. They realize that moral rules require a covenant between persons, that most rules have their exceptions, and that rules must be modified according to circumstances.

Piaget's Stages of Moral Development

Stage	Age	Judgment	Characteristic
Egocentric	3-6	Unilateral respect	Absolute rules
Concrete	7-11	Mixed respect	Fair procedures
Formal	12-adult	Mutual respect	Covenants of consent

One can see the power of Piaget's analysis by looking more closely at his method. He told children of different ages stories in which they were to choose the better of alternative actions. For example, he would tell children a pair of stories like the following:

A. A little boy who is called John is in his room. He is called to dinner. He goes into the dining room. But behind the door there was a chair, and on the chair there was a tray with fifteen cups on it. John couldn't have known that

there was all this behind the door. He goes in, the door
knocks against the tray, bang go the fifteen cups and they
all get broken!
B. Once there was a little boy whose name was Henry. One
day when his mother was out he tried to get some jam out
of the cupboard. He climbed up on to a chair and stretched
out his arm. But the jam was too high up and he couldn't
reach it and have any. But while he was trying to get it he
knocked over a cup. The cup fell down and broke.[6]

These stories are calculated to set the amount of damage
done against the intentions of the child. John was
innocent, but his clumsiness led to great damage. Henry
was doing what he should not, but his clumsiness led to
small damage. To decide which deed should be punished
requires a choice between intentions and degree of
damage. Given this alternative, preschool children (egocentric) choose to punish the child who caused the greatest
damage. School age children (concrete operations) are
uncertain and give mixed responses. Youth (formal
operations) choose to punish the child with questionable
intentions. Apparently children must be eleven or twelve
years old before they come to a strong understanding of
motives and their importance in moral judgment.

The accompanying table shows some of the other
conclusions Piaget arrived at in his study. Younger
children do not understand what a lie is. They think of it as
something that an adult doesn't like. Older children
(concrete) are confused by the difference between a story
that misstates the facts and a lie. Youth understand that a
lie must include the intention to deceive.

Younger children call for strong punishment for any
infraction. Older children call for a strict balance of the
punishment and the misdeed. Youth allow for difference
of circumstance and age. Younger children believe that
punishment is necessary and should be severe, at least so
they say. Older children believe punishment is always

necessary for a misdeed, but should be proportionate to the deed. Youth feel that punishment should help prevent further misdeeds, so helping to rehabilitate the person. Young children seem to have a mythical belief in punishment. Older children believe that each individual is responsible for himself or herself. Youth tend to accept responsibility as a group.

Young children believe that the bad will always suffer. Older children are not certain about this. Youth believe that the suffering in a person's life is not necessarily related to being either good or bad. For young children morality rests on fear and approval. Older children are mixed in their moral perceptions, but tend to believe in strict fairness. Youth believe in equality tempered by equity. So teenage youth are able to take circumstances and motives into account, while children are not able to do so with assurance. On the other hand, children will try to please adults, and so they will say what they are expected to say, even when they are unable to understand it.

The power of Piaget's research is to show that children are not little adults. Teachers and parents often assume that children understand as adults do, and adults have long since forgotten how they perceived reality as children. Piaget's studies are classic in calling attention to changes in children's perceptions of morality.

The Moral Judgment of Children According to Piaget

	Egocentric (ages 3–7)	Concrete Operations (ages 7–12)	Formal Operations (age 12 & older)
Clumsiness vs. stealing	Magnitude of damage most important	Mixed Reaction	Motive most important

Lying	Does not understand the definition	Confused by motive versus magnitude	Motive most important
Punishment	Expiation	Retribution	Reciprocity
Effect of punishment	Severe and necessary	Proportionate and necessary	Preventive and secondary to rehabilitation
Collective responsibility	Mythical belief in punishment	Individual responsibility	Collective responsibility
Immanent justice	Belief in immanent justice	Mixed belief	No belief in immanent justice
Criteria of justice	Authority, fear and approval	Equality above all else	Equality tempered by equity
Love and justice	Reciprocity as an ideal begins to affect reciprocity as a fact (retributive justice)	Distributive justice replaces retributive	Forgiveness and understanding, reciprocity of retaliation (equity)

Distributive: apportionment of benefits according to merits of individual or in best interest of the community

Equality: condition of being exactly the same

Equity: fairness according to circumstances

Expiation: making complete satisfaction for; atonement

Immanent: remaining or operating within the subject considered; indwelling; inherent

Reciprocity: mutual dependence; cooperation; a return in kind

Retributive: rewarding or punishing

READINESS FOR RELIGION

Building on the work of Piaget, Ronald Goldman, a British religious educator, set forth a view that he called "readiness for religion." Goldman questioned children of different ages about biblical events such as the Exodus. He found that preschool children gave wildly distorted answers to the questions. For example, to the question, Why was Moses afraid to look at God? younger children said such things as, "He didn't like God's face. . . . It's old and frightening"; "Moses loved God and didn't like to see him burn"; "He was frightened of God's voice. It is loud.'"[7] Such answers were characteristic of children in Piaget's egocentric stage, ages five and six. Goldman characterized this stage as "pre-religious thought."

Children of ages seven to eleven, Piaget's period of concrete operations, gave answers that showed awareness of causality, but their answers missed the biblical meaning of the text: "He hadn't been going to church, or anything like that"; "God was stronger than other persons. He was afraid God might hurt him.'"[8] Goldman called this the age of "sub-religious thought." School age children can study life themes such as light, bread, water, and kingship, to give a few of the many possibilities. They can study a simple life of Jesus and background facts about the Bible. But they cannot understand the Bible or the church as the human response to God's call. Their vision of God is too distorted and sub-religious.

By the age of eleven or twelve children begin to show genuine religious understanding. This is Piaget's period of formal operations, and is considered by Goldman to be a time of "personal religious thought." Thirteen-year-old youth said, "There was something over-awing about it. . . . God was great and Moses was like a worm in importance. . . . The sight of God is too much for human eyes. It is too tremendous a vision.'"[9] Goldman concluded

190

that most children must be age thirteen before they genuinely begin to understand what the Bible is about.

Tabular Diagram of Goldman Readiness for Religion[10]

Age	Stage	Understanding
5–7	Pre-religious thought	Enriching experience Spontaneous questions Spontaneous worship
7–11	Sub-religious thought	Life themes, projects, and activities Simple life of Jesus Background Bible facts
11–13	Beginning personal religious thought	Advanced life of Jesus, Acts Advanced life themes
13 plus	Established personal religious thought	O.T. and N.T. chronology Acts and church history Biblical themes of faith

Goldman's account of readiness for religion has had a dramatic impact on the teaching of religion in England, where religious instruction in the public schools is required. The impact on religious education in America was significant, but never so great as in England, possibly because many church schools were simply unwilling to give up teaching from the Bible for the teaching of life themes.

JUSTICE IS FAIRNESS

The American student of Piaget who has had the most dramatic impact on religious education is Lawrence

Kohlberg. Kohlberg was not interested in religious belief as was Goldman; rather, he picked up Piaget's concern about moral judgment. His original research was done with a group of boys whom he interviewed over a period of a decade or more. Kohlberg posed a series of moral dilemmas to these boys to get their responses. Basically, it is a variant of Piaget's method. The boys' answers were then grouped according to a series of stages.

Here is the best known of the dilemmas posed by Kohlberg.[11] This story is usually referred to as the Heinz dilemma. In the story Heinz has a wife who is dying of cancer. A druggist has a medicine which Heinz believes will cure the cancer. The druggist is charging several thousand dollars for the medicine, much more than Heinz is able to pay. He attempts to borrow the sum, but is refused by everyone he asks. He can think of no other way to raise the money. Heinz appeals to the druggist to reduce the cost of the medicine to the point that Heinz can afford it, or to let Heinz owe him the money. The druggist rejects every suggestion. Finally Heinz breaks into the druggist's store and steals the medicine. On the basis of this account Kohlberg asked a number of questions.

1. Should Heinz have done that? Was it actually wrong or right? Why?
2. Is it husband's duty to steal the drug for his wife if he can get it no other way? Would a good husband do it?
3. Did the druggist have the right to charge that much when there was no law actually setting a limit to the price? Why?[12]

[If you think he should steal the drug, answer these:]

4a. If the husband does not feel very close or affectionate to his wife, should he still steal the drug?
4b. Suppose it wasn't Heinz's wife who was dying of cancer, but Heinz's best friend. His friend didn't have any money and there was no one in his family willing

to steal the drug. Should Heinz steal the drug for his friend in that case? Why?[13]

[If you think Heinz should not steal it, answer these:]

5a. Would you steal the drug to save your wife's life?
5b. If you were dying of cancer but were strong enough, would you steal the drug to save your own life?
6. Heinz broke in the store and stole the drug and gave it to his wife. He was caught and brought before the judge. Should the judge send Heinz to jail for stealing, or should he let him go free? Why?[14]

Kohlberg determined that the boys' responses generally followed Piaget's account of moral development. But Kohlberg added three more stages to those of Piaget, bringing the number of stages to six.

Kohlberg's Stages of Moral Development

Preconventional level

Stage One (ages 3–6)*: *Punishment and Obedience*
   If asked whether or not to "tell on" a playmate, a child of this age is likely to say, "I'd better tell or I'll be spanked."

Stage Two (ages 6–10)*: *Naive Instrumental Hedonism*
   To the same question, the child is more likely to answer, "I'll not tell so I will get along better with others." Children of this stage have a highly developed sense that fairness requires everyone to receive an equal portion, whatever the circumstances.

Conventional Level

Stage Three (ages 10-15)*: *Interpersonal Concordance*
   A youth is able to understand and take into

account the perspectives and intentions of other persons. Justice usually involves what is right, including the avoidance of disapproval and of hurting others. Youth in this stage ordinarily have a group of peers to whom they may turn for support for their moral ideas.

Stage Four (ages 15-20)*: *Law and Order*

Whether one should tell about a friend's misdeed now depends upon whether the deed violates the law or seriously disturbs the public order. Justice is established by the maintenance of the values of one's own society, and by doing one's duty.

Postconventional Level

Stage Five (age 20 and up)*: *Social Contract*

Society becomes an agreement among people of differing convictions, for mutual benefit. Therefore it is in the interest of all that the right of all individuals, including minorities, be respected. Whether one should tell about the misdeed of a friend will now depend upon the reason for the action as well as consideration of the effects each possible action will have on the friend and the wider community. Justice therefore is defined in terms of the protection of individual rights.

Stage Six: *Universal Moral Principles*

No age level is given because so few attain this level. Reverence is paramount, not for social order, but for the moral principles that are binding upon all societies and all people. Justice in a situation consists of the equal consideration of all claims, with all persons being considered as ends and never exclusively as means.[15]

*Ages given are only approximate.

Kohlberg's theory of six stages of moral development, as we have already said, has had a dramatic effect upon religious education in North America.

CONFLUENT EDUCATION

Mary Wilcox has taken the concepts of Piaget and Kohlberg and has added a social perspective. Her stages follow Kohlberg's exactly, except as she elaborates the development of the way persons perceive one another.[16]

Wilcox's Stages of Moral Development

Age	Stage	Social Perspective	Characteristics
0–2	0	Egocentric	Self is center of all
3–7	1	Authority	"Big people are the goodest."
8–10	2	Dyadic-Instrumental	Useful exchange without understanding other points of view
11–15	3	Dyadic-Empathetic	Meaningful relationships with understanding of others' motives
16 plus	4	Triadic	One's own society is paramount
			Critical of one's own society
			Societies viewed in terms of universal principles

Willcox's approach proposes that a teacher be keenly aware of the stages of development of children in a class, even charting where the children stand intellectually, morally, and socially. For example, a session on justice for eighth graders may call for a focus on universal justice for all, political representation, and individual responsibility. A teacher should ask her- or himself where these eighth graders are in their moral reasoning. Most should be moving out of stage two into stage three.

In terms of social perspective, stage two persons are dyadic-instrumental. There is limited ability to understand the situation of others. Governments are to prevent destructive behavior. Useful people are more important. Stage three persons are dyadic-empathetic. There is more understanding of other people's situations, and the positive functions of government are better understood. Good people and those less fortunate should receive attention. Intellectually, eighth graders can reason abstractly and hypothetically. Eighth graders may have a limited view of universal justice and responsibility. A lesson and discussion can strengthen stage three thinking.

Religious teachers should consider the intellectual, social, and moral perspectives of their students and adapt their teaching to the students. The reader will see that Wilcox's view is similar to that of Goldman except that Wilcox allows for teaching of religion at the appropriate level. She does not believe that religious teaching should be delayed until the age of formal thinking.

FAITH DEVELOPMENT

The six moral stages of Kohlberg led James Fowler to suggest that there may be parallel stages in the development of faith. Defining faith as one's attitude toward the ultimate environment, Fowler argued that everyone has some kind of faith, including even those who are not religious. Fowler's research approach was to use a series of questions that elicit a person's attitude toward the ultimate environment:[17]

Part I: Life Review

Divide life into chapters: (major) segments created by changes or experiences–"turning points" or general circumstances.

Thinking about yourself at present: What gives your life meaning? What makes life worth living for you?

Part II: Life-shaping Experiences and Relationships

Have your perceptions of your parents changed since you were a child? How?

Are there other persons who at earlier times or at present have been significant in the shaping of your outlook on life?

Have you experienced losses, crises or suffering that have changed or "colored" your life in special ways?

Have you had moments of joy, ecstasy, peak experience or breakthrough that have shaped or changed your life?

Part III: Present Values and Commitments

Can you describe the beliefs and values or attitudes that are most important in guiding your own life?

What is the purpose of human life?

Do you feel that some approaches to life are more "true" or right than others?

Part IV: Religion

Do you have or have you had important religious experiences?

What feelings do you have when you think about God?

Do you consider yourself a religious person?

If you pray, what do you feel is going on when you pray?

Do you feel that your religious outlook is "true"? In what sense? Are religious traditions other than your own "true"?

On the basis of his interviews Fowler did in fact distinguish six stages that parallel Kohlberg's six stages of moral development. In terms of transition from one stage to another, the faith stages tend to lag behind the moral stages.

Fowler's Stages of Faith Development

Prior to age three, faith is undifferentiated, while behavior is sensorimotor and language is still rudimentary.

Stage One (ages 3–7): *Intuitive-Projective*
    Behavior is preoperational and episodic. Empathy is rudimentary. Measured by size and power, authority is primarily family oriented. Religious symbols are magical and numinous. Child is influenced by the manifestations of visible faith of primary adults.

Stage Two (ages 7–11): *Mythic-Literal*
    Child is capable of narrative drama and simple perspective-taking. Authority is still within the family and those immediately related to it. Religious symbols are in one-dimensional and literal terms. Child takes in the stories, beliefs, and practices of the community.

Stage Three (ages 12–18): *Synthetic-Conventional*
    Youth can use symbols, often without being explicit about the meaning. Religious symbols are multidimensional, often conventional, and oriented to tradition. Multiple role-taking makes complex drama possible. With a wide range of social involvements, faith offers help in providing a "meaningful synthesis" within the complexities of life.

Stage Four (ages 18–30): *Individuative-Reflexive*
    Authority is pragmatic or ideological. Social class norms are self-chosen. Morality tends to be law-and-order oriented, coupled with a reflective relativism and a criticism of ideas. Take responsibility for their

commitments, and recognize and try to deal with polar tensions: individuality/community, subjectivity/objectivity, self-fulfillment/service to others, relative/absolute.

Stage Five (ages 30–40): *Conjunctive*
Understand the dialectical interplay between symbolic and conceptual meaning. Understand mutuality between their community and others, grasp the existence and interaction of multiple belief-patterns. Able to transcend social-class norms. Possess a drive to find a unity of symbolic, conceptual, and other belief elements. Affirm own truth without denying that of others and are willing to take the risk of living in anticipation of the coming of a more universal community.

Stage Six (age 40 and up): *Universalizing*
Possess a sense of interrelatedness of all reality. Authority more upon "what is" than upon any person or group. Morality is both universal and critical. Willingness to relate without pretense to all people. Religious symbols point to the wider inclusive reality in which we all live, referred to by Christians as the realm of God.[18]

Fowler's developmental account has had a dramatic impact on North American religious education. It gives genuine guidance to religious instruction and answers the problem raised by Goldman, whether children can study religion prior to when they can think abstractly (circa thirteen years of age). The answer focuses on Fowler's definition of faith as a person's attitude toward the ultimate environment. The question is no longer whether the concept of God is correct. Rather, the question is whether the attitude to whatever is considered to be ultimate is positive. A child's positive attitude toward the ultimate is a step toward the next stage of faith, even when the concept of ultimacy is very limited.

Fowler emphasizes that a preschool child is developing the capacity for imagination, and imagination is essential to mature faith. Therefore play, story, and drama are basic to the later development of mature faith. So also the mythic-literal faith of the school age child allows her or him to take on the stories, beliefs, and observances of her or his community. The new sense of belonging, and narrative and meaning are critical to the development of mature faith. By focusing on imagination and attitude Fowler avoids identifying faith with a correct adult concept of God. The problem of the absence of childhood faith in Goldman's account is thereby overcome by Fowler.

PSYCHOSOCIAL ATTITUDES

Fundamentally, all of the theories discussed so far are cognitive accounts of faith and moral development. An alternate approach to moral development is emotive, and the primary example is the work of Erik Erikson. Working with Sigmund Freud's account of the development of the emotions, Erikson added a social modality that has had a great impact not only on psychotherapy, but also on religious education's concept of moral development.[19]

Stage One (ages 0–1): *Trust versus Mistrust.*
The relationship between the infant and the primary caretaker (mother) will have a quality that the infant resolves into an enduring attitude toward life that is balanced somewhere between trust and mistrust. When trust predominates, then the ego-strength or virtue of hope is establishes.

200

Stage Two (ages 2–3): *Autonomy versus Shame and Doubt.*

In the relationship with the parents the young child learns and adopts a mode of giving and receiving, holding and letting go. When the attitude of autonomy predominates over shame and doubt, then the virtue of will is established.

Stage Three (ages 3–6): *Initiative versus Guilt.*

During these years the conscience is internalized as a self-regulating monitor of all activity. If the child is not oppressed by a guilty conscience, then she or he can take initiative. The resulting virtue is called purpose.

Stage Four (ages 6–11): *Industry versus Inferiority.*

Primary relationships are extended to teachers and age-mates, and the child learns the basic cultural skills, both formal and informal. To the extent that a child develops a sense of accomplishment for some skills, the attitude of industry will prevail over inferiority. The resulting virtue is called competency.

Stage Five (ages 12–18): *Identity versus Identity Confusion.*

Primary relationships shift to include the opinions and attitudes of age-mates. As family values and traditions are called into question, the teenager develops an enduring sense of identity, mixed with confusion. To the extent that a coherent, functional identity prevails over confusion, the resulting virtue is called fidelity.

Stage Six (ages 19–30): *Intimacy versus Isolation.*

Whether or not a person marries, she or he develops an enduring pattern of intimacy which more or less successfully counteracts the sense of isolation. To the extent that a satisfying sense of intimacy develops, a person lives with the virtue of love.

Stage Seven (ages 30–65): *Generativity versus Stagnation.*

The middle adult years may include rearing children, being employed at a job, and otherwise contributing to the community's way of life. To the extent a person feels that something significant is being passed to other persons and to the next generation, an enduring sense of generativity predominates over a sense of stagnation and worthlessness. The resulting virtue is care.

Stage Eight (age 66 and up): *Integrity versus Despair.*

As persons in later adulthood review their lives to determine whether their lives have meaning, they develop a more or less permanent sense of integrity or wholeness mixed with a dimension of despair. To the extent that the attitude of integrity prevails, the virtue of wisdom is present.

Erikson's approach to moral development is based on a concept of a healthy personality. Every person meets a series of crises and resolves them with relative degrees of emotional gain or loss. Each gain or loss becomes more or less enduring according to its proper time and sequence. For example, early support and care for an infant is necessary for the infant to develop a sense of trust. That sense of trust becomes relatively stable in the personality and is not easily shaken by later threats.

The "sense of health" is a combination of conscious feelings, outward behavior, and deep inner states accessible only to therapy. The ego of each person constantly functions to give a sense of continuity and integration to experience. For the ego to function without pain or neurosis requires inward and outer awareness, deep intentionality, coherence of total experience, and mutuality with other egos. When the various crises of development are negotiated with these qualities, then the person lives with a sense of health.

Don Browning suggests that the seventh stage, generativity, is most descriptive of what Erikson means by a healthy personality. The generative person can contribute to other persons, to the community, and to the culture and the historic epoch with relative absence of inner stress, loss of intentionality, or painful experience. Such a generative person is marked not so much by activity, but by a functional sense of giving and receiving within the communities of which she or he is a part. Being able to contribute to one's children as a parent is the primary example.[20]

There is a fundamental difference between these emotive stages of Erikson and the cognitive stages of Piaget and his successors. The emotive stages are based on emotional responses to biological changes, and therefore everyone moves through each stage. There can be emotional gains or losses at each succeeding stage. By contrast, the cognitive stages represent changes in the structure of what people perceive and in how they understand. The sequence from one cognitive stage to the next is invariant; no one can skip a stage. However one need not move to the next stage. A stage three person may remain at that stage all his or her life. Nor can a person move backward unless there is brain damage. Fowler's theory strains from the effort to hold the two together, but finally, Fowler's is a cognitive theory.

THE CRITIQUE OF COGNITIVISM

The cognitive theories of religious and moral development spawned by Piaget's research have come under severe criticism. Craig Dykstra is one such critic, who argues that the cognitive approach to morality focuses on the claims and obligations that bear upon particular hypothetical decisions.[21] The hypothetical dilemmas posed by Piaget and Kohlberg require the hearer to choose between various public obligations. In the example of Kohlberg's story about Heinz and his ailing wife, the listener must choose between Heinz's obligation not to steal and the obligation to save his wife's life, as these two bear upon an imaginary situation.

Dykstra's objection is that morality is much more than making hypothetical choices or being able to reason consistently. Morality has to do with the whole texture of a person's life in relation to actual situations. It has to do with language, with one's perspective on life, and with ongoing loyalties. Furthermore, when religious faith is seen as a relationship "to a transcendent center of power and reality" that acts upon persons "to convert their patterns of thinking and ways of living," then religious faith and morality are intimately connected to one another.

Dykstra develops his own "visional" approach to ethics, wherein a person's larger perspective and intuition, a person's life story and ongoing character are the fundamental indicators of a person's ethics. The metaphors and stories by which a person interprets her or his life give shape to that person's morality. Therefore the biblical stories by which the believer interprets life are decisive for morality. Repentance, prayer, and service are central to morality because they are expressions of a person's basic intuitions about life.

Dykstra's analysis is supported by that of James Loder.[22] Loder believes that in times of great stress and transition the mind searches for a perspective or image or metaphor by which reality may be reconstituted. Persons are transformed as their basic metaphors and images of reality shift.

Religious educators should pay more attention to the shifts in meaning, to the transforming moments. The cognitive stages of Piaget and Kohlberg are not as important as the actual metaphors by which persons see reality.

Dykstra is critical of both Kohlberg's theory or morality and Fowler's stages of faith development. He feels the concept of stage is too structured, too formal, too separated from actual individuals. The transformations in a person's perceptions are actual, particular, individual, and subject to infinite variation. Religious educators should be less concerned about stages and more concerned about the actual stories and perceptual changes of experience.

Another writer who strongly supports such a point of view is Stanley Hauerwas.[23] The writings of Hauerwas attack an approach to religion and ethics that seeks to make universal and wholly objective decisions. Hauerwas therefore works against Kantianism in ethics. Kant had advised that we always ought to act according to those principles that we will to be universal obligations for everyone in similar circumstances.[24] Against such an attempt to be universal, Hauerwas argues for the narrative of a life story as the real context for decision. We decide by trying to be consistent with our own life stories and with our own character.[25] Life stories are built around such ongoing virtues as love, gratitude, hope, and humility.

A different critical approach comes from Carol Gilligan.[26] A student of Kohlberg, Gilligan finds his stages of moral development to be too severely bound to male experience. Practically all of Kohlberg's research was done with young men. Gilligan conducted a series of interviews with young women describing actual decisions about whether or not to have an abortion. On the basis of their responses she developed stages of moral development for women.

Gilligan found an original self-centered level, somewhat parallel to the preconventional level that Kohlberg

205

described for school age boys. Girls then move into a level of self-giving in which they learn to give whatever they must in order to maintain relationships, parallel to Kohlberg's conventional level. However, Gilligan suggests that a more mature third level for women is to modify self-giving so as to be more assertive about personal needs. This runs counter to Kohlberg's post-conventional level. The moral development of boys and girls, therefore, finally moves in opposite directions.

In a critique of Fowler, Gabriel Moran attacks stage six, the stage of universal morality. Moran finds that stage entirely too detached, too infrequent, and too unattainable to be a proper goal for religious education. Moran suggests that Fowler's stage five, conjunctive faith, is much more attainable and thus a much more appropriate goal for religious education. Stage five faith is critical of its own society and is consciously aware of the paradoxes of life. Fowler seems to have accepted the legitimacy of Moran's criticism.[27] It is reminiscent of Browning's suggestion that Erikson's seventh stage of generativity is more nearly normative for adulthood than is the final stage of integrity.[28]

SOCIAL INTERACTION

The cognitive and the emotive approaches to faith and morality are fundamentally contradictory, as they have been formulated. In the cognitive view persons progress through a limited number of stages; in the emotive views everyone passes through all stages.

Cognitive
    Cognitive judgment, perception,
    Invariant stages, limited progression through stages

Emotive
    Emotions and motives, ego structure
    Invariant stages, progression through all stages

Interactive
   Interaction and interpretation
   Stages qualified by narrative sequence

The cognitive approach assumes that both faith and morality are grounded in the perceptual process. The aim is a universalized morality and faith. The emotive approach is grounded in certain emotional responses to social relationships. The aim is a healthy personality and a productive contribution to the culture.

A social interactive approach focuses upon the interaction between people within committed communities. Individual believers are understood to be searching the tradition under the guidance and direction of the spirit that constitutes the faith community. That is to say, individual Christians are in dialog with one another, searching the Scriptures, seeking the mind of Christ, under the direction and guidance of the Holy Spirit. In their relationships with one another, believers come to the living center of their way of life. In the grace and power of God they come to love and care for one another.

The community and the individual re-create one another. The search of individuals for new relationships is the way that the community is re-created. At the same time, the faith community re-creates the individuals who make it up. In the interaction with a community of faith persons are formed and transformed. In this interaction persons discover their talents.

The individual and the community mutually transcend one another. The integrity, commitment, belief, and freedom of each person is beyond the community. At the same time, community processes are beyond each individual. In the dialectic between community and individual the community changes and the individuals grow.

As the critics of cognitivism point out, morality is an expression of the individual's interactional stance, the person's way of being in relationship to others. The life narrative and the individual's way of life come closer to the root of morality than do formal arguments for a particular moral decision. In the same way, faith and belief are closer to a person's and community's way of being and relating than to formal cognitive judgments. Faith is a basic attitude of trust in and gratitude to the living center, in whom faith, doubt, and guilt are overcome. The way of being and relating, the interactional process, includes both perception and motives. Concern about stages gives way to concern about narrative and moments of transition.

The narrative approach cannot properly be carried out without awareness of cognitive and emotive changes. A person's morality is not complete without knowing his or her "core beliefs."[29] A social interactive approach does not discard psychosocial attitudes and cognitive judgments, but sets them within the interactive process. The religious educator pays closer attention to both the interaction and the narrative and to cognitive judgments and motives.

STUDY SUGGESTIONS

Exercises

1. Describe the main values of your group (family or church). What activities does your group do together? What celebrations do you have? What activities are encouraged? What attitudes are encouraged? What activities and attitudes are discouraged? What values are represented by these activities, celebrations, and attitudes?

2. Tell Piaget's story about John and Henry to children of different ages from four to twelve. Compare the answers you get to Piaget's three

stages. Do the children you question give the kind of answers you would expect for their ages?

3. Tell children the story about Moses going to Mount Sinai to receive the Ten Commandments. Ask them the questions that Goldman asked. Do you get the same answers at the same age levels as those described by Goldman? What do you conclude about children's readiness for religious teaching?

4. Tell Kohlberg's story of Heinz and his wife to children from ages six to twenty. Ask the questions posed by Kohlberg. Do you get the same answers at the same age levels that Kohlberg did? What do you conclude about the development of the understanding of justice?

5. Use Fowler's questions to conduct an interview about faith development. On the basis of your interview attempt to characterize the stage of faith development of your interviewee. What confidence do you have of your stage assessment? Do you feel that you could get at the person's faith through Fowler's questions?

6. Write out your own life story according to the outline provided by Fowler's psychosocial attitudes. If several of you do this, share your stories with one another. Talk to an elderly person and try to reconstruct each of Erikson's stages. The person may have a sense of earlier stages even though he or she cannot remember detailed events. After you have done one or both of these exercises, discuss the extent to which the psychosocial attitudes illumine a person's life story.

7. Write out two or three of the most significant transforming moments in your own life. If several of you do this, share your accounts with one

another. Interview someone you know to find out her or his transforming moments. Compare notes with others in your group to consider how important transforming moments are in a person's life story. Should Christian education pay more attention to transforming moments?

8. Separate the men and women in your group. Let each group discuss Kohlberg's Heinz dilemma for a half hour and record what Heinz should do. Come together again to compare how men resolved this problem with how women did it. Is Gilligan right that women are less willing to choose either of the given options of stealing or letting the wife die? Is this because women consider relationships more important and men consider rights to be of more importance?

Questions for Discussion

1. Do public religious instruction and prayer strengthen the morality of children and youth?
2. Does morality develop from an attitude of unilateral respect to an attitude of mutual respect, as Piaget suggests?
3. When are children able to take the intentions of others into account in their moral judgments?
4. How does the teaching of religious ideas to children before they can understand them affect their faith later in life?
5. What are the primary dimensions of morality? Is justice the most basic dimension?
6. What is Gilligan's criticism of Kohlberg's male bias in describing justice? How do you evaluate this criticism?
7. How do you define faith? Is Fowler's definition of faith adequate?

8. Why are the final stages of both Kohlberg and Fowler difficult to describe? Are they invalid?
9. What is the contradiction between cognitive and emotive conceptions of stages?
10. Can a stage approach to moral development be reconciled with a narrative approach? What are the problems of a stage approach and of a narrative approach?

Suggestions for Further Reading

Craig R. Dykstra, *Vision and Character: A Christian Educator's Alternative to Kohlberg.*
This book had a major impact on religious educators' acceptance of Kohlberg's theory of moral development.

James W. Fowler, *Stages of Faith: The Psychology of Human Development and the Quest for Meaning.*
Fowler's account of the development of faith has been enormously influential.

Carol Gilligan, *In a Different Voice: Psychological Theory and Women's Development.*
A convincing feminist criticism of moral stage theory.

Mary Wilcox, *Developmental Journey: A Guide to the Development of Logical and Moral Reasoning and Social Perspective.*
Wilcox presents the cognitive stages of Piaget and the moral stages of Kohlberg in an interesting and readable style.

Chapter Eight:

THE FAITH JOURNEY

DESCRIBING THE JOURNEY

Everyone knows that she or he goes through life with an unfolding life story, but this statement is full of presumptions. The idea of an unfolding story held together by purpose and direction is peculiarly Western and is very much the reflection of the biblical tradition. This idea of person, character, and life story is so much a part of Western tradition that we easily forget it to be a faith assumption. Radical skepticism and certain Eastern traditions have questioned these ideas, but Christianity has regularly supported them.

To describe the course of life is an exercise in metaphor. Whether we speak of life journey, pilgrimage, life cycle, or "course of life," each reflects the perspective of the describer as much as what is being described. Christianity has often thought of life as a pilgrimage, a journey to a holy place. Believers move through life in anticipation of being with God at the end of life, thus it is a journey to a holy place.

In recent years social science has spoken of the life cycle, which in effect is to speak of a circle. The suggestion is that there is a circular path through which every life moves. The life cycle includes birth, infancy, childhood, youth, adulthood, later maturity, and death. There is some justification for a cyclical view of biological maturation; beyond that a cyclical view is questionable.

Developmental psychology has lately become a well-established discipline and has produced many descriptions of the life cycle. Even so, such descriptions are based on many presumptions about the nature of life, presumptions that go beyond the empirical data of modern science. The reason for making this point is that time and again a description of the life cycle is found to be wanting because the assumptions of the writer are too limited. We have already noted Carol Gilligan's observation that Lawrence Kohlberg's description of moral development is really a description of *male* moral development.[1]

In the following pages you will find a description of the life cycle that is dependent upon a number of recent research studies.[2] Like all such descriptions, it cannot escape the problem of circularity mentioned above. We simply acknowledge it and proceed. The description of each stage of faith below is accompanied by educational suggestions.

SEPARATION AND PARTICIPATION

The individual faith pilgrimage occurs within a network of relationships that make up the community context of life. In these relationships the primary meaning of life is carried. The original relationship is between the infant and the mother. Then father and siblings become part of the primary relationship. Later, teachers and playmates enlarge the circle. During adolescence, the peer group and the community become more important, then the spouse, adult friends, work associates, church members, and others.

Throughout life, individuals experience a series of separations and reunions. Every relationship moves toward a separation and every separation anticipates a reunion. At the time of birth the infant separates from the mother, but becomes related to her in a new way. Maturity leads to individuation and growing independence from the mother, balanced by a constantly developing new relationship to the mother.[3] The primary relationships to parents and siblings are strained with the beginning of school, where new relationships are established. Adolescence means a new independence from parents, and graduation from high school often means leaving the parental home.

The themes of separation and participation are present throughout adulthood. Marriage means a separation from older relationships to establish a new relationship. Marriage is a promise "until death do us part," so marriage anticipates the final separation in death. Should divorce intervene, then the separation comes earlier. Parents experience the pain of the separation of children. For all adults there is a sequence of separations and new acquaintances. There are the moves to new jobs, new neighborhood, new activities. When adults do not move, then others around them move. Finally, the separation of death comes to all.

If the theme of separation becomes dominant, then life is lived under the domination of judgment and death. One can view every relationship as separating and dying, full of transience and passing. Life becomes as grass thrown in the oven (Matthew 6:30), as vanishing smoke (Psalm 37:20). The power of not being seems to overwhelm being, and relationships lose their reality. Paul Tillich speaks of sin as separation. By this he means that sin is the threat that all things in life are being separated.[4]

When the theme of participation becomes dominant in life, then life is lived as blessing. Life is lived in the context of participation. No separation is stronger than the participation that underlies it. Each separation has its own potential blessing: acceptance, accountability, faith, dedication, love, maturity. Every separation pushes individuals to recognize the deeper levels of participation in life. Separation is ambiguous in that it may either become a curse or be the occasion of growing blessedness.

For the Christian, no separation is greater than the crucifixion and death of Christ, and that has been overcome in the resurrection. Therefore the apostle Paul is persuaded that nothing in creation, or beyond creation, can separate us from the love of God. All of the greatest powers of separation have been overcome in Christ: principalities, powers, heights, depths. In Christ every separation pushes the believer to greater participation (Romans 8).

This way of focusing the question of faith puts the emphasis on the living center of life rather than on the ultimate environment.[5] In fact, the living center and the ultimate environment must participate, otherwise separation reigns. However, the ultimate environment is more cognitive in nature and the living center is more participative and relational. Let us look at the faith journey from the vantage point of the living center.

Religious educators such as Mary Wilcox and James Fowler identify characteristic stages in the life cycle. Each stage can be identified by common characteristics, and each stage leads to a pre-established successive stage. However, stage theory presumes that there is a series of transitions from one stage to the next. Stage theory therefore adds weight to the arguments of those who consider the transitions of the life journey very important.

216

In what follows we will refer to the stages that Wilcox, Fowler, Kohlberg, Gilligan, and others have developed,[6] but we are most influenced by Erikson's psychosocial stages. They give a frame within which other stage theories can be assessed. They fit our focus on participation and separation, and give an account of transition.[7]

INFANCY AND EARLY CHILDHOOD

Our purpose is not to describe the behavior of young children in great detail, but to mention representative events and processes whereby the unique dispositions and character of persons are established. Efforts at Christian nurture and education presume such a description.

Birth is a paradigmatic transition of life—all other transitions pale in relation to it. Christianity has spoken of the most radical transition later in life as being "born again." At the time of birth an infant is thrust from total dependency on a very protected environment into a much more threatening one. The mother provides protection, nourishment, and care. (We speak of the primary caretaker as the mother, although it can also be the father.) The attitudes, dispositions, and character of the mother surround the infant; they are taken in with the milk.

During the first year of life an infant ordinarily learns coordination of hand, eye, and body movements. At about eight months the infant gains a sense of the permanency of objects and of the constancy and personhood of the mother. By the end of the first year the infant may be walking, and by sixteen months it may be solving basic problems. Language begins to develop in the second and third year. By age two many children are capable of bowel control and can follow basic parental expectations to hold and loosen, come and go. By three years of age the child has an identifiable concept of self.[8]

217

Erikson has suggested that the psychosocial attitude that children develop during the first year of life is basic trust and hope.[9] During the second and third years the attitudes of autonomy and purpose are established. Trust comes mixed with some degree of mistrust, and autonomy comes mixed with some degree of the shame of being exposed or soiled. Fowler describes these years as undifferentiated faith, which is to say that faith is not yet identifiable.

Cultures differ and expert advice constantly changes regarding the proper way to respond to the very young. First-century Hebrews apparently wrapped infants in swaddling clothes. One American Indian tribe apparently allowed children to nurse until they were six years old or more. A generation ago parents cared for children according to a strict schedule and believed that crying is good for the lungs. Another generation attempted to attend every whimper of the child and to give the child unlimited freedom. More recently expert opinion suggests always attending the infant's crying, but also putting limits on the child. Temper tantrums are felt to be the result of too few rather than too many limits.[10]

Much of the learning of infants comes from imitation of the parents and others. Many of the infant's basic attitudes come from immediate awareness of the basic attitudes of the parents. Therefore the infant's sense of basic trust will reflect that of the mother. Children differ in temperament and circumstances, of course. A child with chronic colic may simply develop less trust than another child. A mother's attitude may change from one child to another. Parents are normally more anxious to "do things right" with the first child, whereas they have more confidence with later children. First children are normally more anxious to be good children, thereby reflecting the attitude of the parents.

218

The religious nurture of infants comes indirectly from the faith of the parents. If faith in God gives the parents more confidence, courage, and trust, then the infant lives in the presence of those attitudes. If their faith in God is full of anxiety, vindictiveness, judgment, or despair, then the children will respond to those attitudes. Again let me say that the child's attitude is unique to the particular child. Children of the same parents may differ radically, and parents themselves may differ radically from one time to another. However, the immediate impact of parental attitudes seems well established and accepted. Children come to the living center of life through their parents' experience of the living center.

The church's primary ministry to very young children is to encourage the faith of the parents. Worship, friendship, loving care, and presence in times of trouble are given to the parents and indirectly to the children. The church can also have literature and discussions about parenting. Comfortable toddler rooms with good equipment and confident adults can also be a place to leave infants while parents are at church.

Years three, four, and five are a time when the child develops remarkably in the use of imagination and symbolic play. The use of imagination seems to come with an increasing vocabulary. Objects and symbols can be manipulated in a variety of ways; a stick, a stone, or a ball can be anything the child's imagination will allow. Play may wander fluidly from one construction to another, almost like daydreaming. Fantasy play may occur alone, with several children in parallel play, or with other children cooperatively. There may be imaginary playmates, such as Christopher Robin's playmates in *Winnie the Pooh*.

The preschool years are great story and dramatization times. Fowler notes the importance of imagination during the preschool years, and then he indicates the importance of imagination in the development of faith. Demanding and threatening parents and teachers apparently can foreclose a child's religious imagination by forcing on her or him on strong judgment images. More liberal parents can trivialize a child's religious imagination by purging stories of all references to judgment, pain, and death. Children need stories that have both the reality of pain and the depth of love.

The telling of stories is so important to preschool children because they are unable to hold the plot of a story in mind as they tell the episodes. Adults may be unaware that the child is dependent upon the adult for the story because the child will correct the adult if the story is told in a different way. The child remembers each episode as it comes along, but the child cannot hold all the episodes together within the plot. The preschool child's imagination is episodic.

The story gives words to what the child is otherwise unable to express. Great stories serve a similar function for all ages, but young children have no way to get at their emotions unless an adult helps them express themselves. Great stories therefore give voice to great experiences. *The Wizard of Oz* gets at the wonder and terror of everyday experience. *Winnie the Pooh* gives voice to conflict between strong personalities. Bible stories give voice to the holy.

The research of Ronald Goldman persuaded a generation of educators not to speak to children about God until they reach the age of eleven or twelve. Preschool children have a very garbled and anthropomorphic view of God according to a number of research reports. Goldman argued that "God" is an abstract concept that only adult intelligence can comprehend. Better, then, to avoid all reference to God until the young person is able to comprehend the idea rightly.

Goldman's research is sharply challenged by that of Rizutto.[11] In her studies of preschool children, she showed that they have a definite and vivid image and concept of God by the time they are three years old. This is the same time that a self-concept is strongly established. Apparently children in Western cultures have a vivid image of God by age three. Fundamental characteristics of God are there, even though expressed in anthropomorphic imagery.

Parents and teachers can tell stories from the Bible, stories of the church, and other religious stories to children because from at least age three most children can understand that God loves them. Children will not separate hearing and playing the stories. They will be able to relate to the drama of worship if it is not too dreary. Of course, children may mix up the stories according to their episodic imagination. Jesus may get mixed with Santa Claus and with a television superhero. The five-year-old may try to baptize the cat. However these are ways the child makes the stories her own. When the story is told again, the child knows anew that God really loves her. The ministering church tries therefore to provide the experience of care to which story, worship, and play can give voice.

MIDDLE CHILDHOOD

If infancy and early childhood is a time for the development of trust, purpose, and a sense of God's love, then middle and late childhood is a time to discover God's justice, creativity, and continuing love. Somewhere around age five, six, or seven a child gains a sense of the causality and coherence of the world. Objects farther away no longer seem smaller, and dead animals are no longer expected to come to life. The child of this age develops a permanent sense of conscience that will endure throughout the life journey. Whether it is called a new sense of reality or the establishment of conscience, a dramatic change has occurred.

Now children can be given directions and they will carry them out. They can be told why things happen, and will understand. They can also remember the plot of a story, and suddenly younger children's stories seem babyish because the adult is no longer needed to keep the story in mind. These changes in world perception and self-understanding are often accompanied by dramatic religious experience, but adults are often too busy teaching to listen to the experiences of children. Furthermore, children are seldom able to express themselves. Occasionally adults remember those early religious experiences of their own.

Questions of fairness now become primary. Brothers and sisters or classmates argue endlessly about whether each is getting a fair share. Gilligan suggests that boys generally are taught to demand an equal share. Girls are taught to give in for the sake of boys. Thus boys and girls are socialized in different directions, something that perceptive parents and teachers may decide whether to continue supporting.

Both girls and boys of school age are learning skills, rules, rituals, procedures, and values. They may have difficulty reading the motives of other people. Piaget found that children of this age have difficulty distinguishing between an intention to falsify and an exaggeration. They have trouble distinguishing between accidental damage and damage due to intention. It is an age of learning to read one's own motives and those of others.[12]

School age is a time of learning the various cultural skills basic to adulthood: reading, writing, getting along with others, doing chores around the house. While practicing such skills children are learning values and routines. Erikson suggests that during this time children develop a sense of competence mixed with some degree of inferiority.[13] Nearly all children choose to master skills for which they receive respect. Often they stay away from skills already mastered by an older brother or sister. Susan will not play a trumpet because her brother already does that well. In larger families, school age children learn to take care of younger children. Not to learn such skills, to remain in the imaginary world of the preschool child, brings a sense of inferiority.

Fowler's interviews suggest that school age children tend to understand Bible stories in a literal way, but they also carry along the imagined story of the preschool child. Both levels of the story are carried at once, and therefore he speaks of mythic/literal faith. In our view the child is close to the living center in the very concrete values that are embodied by the rules, rituals, procedures, and skills that are being learned.[14]

The routines of church can become much more significant for the child of this age. Receiving and reading the Scripture can be an event of great importance. Participation in worship can be meaningful when the child experiences assurance or wonder. Prayer can also become an important part of the child's life. Children can help with parts of the worship service, sing, and produce dramas for all. The sense of justice can make a child sensitive to world injustices: ecological disasters, militarism, colonialism, oppression. Music can become important. Above all the child needs stories, expressions, and opportunities to discuss the wonder, holiness, and love of the living center of life.

YOUTH

Just as for school age children, youth begins with a major transition in the perception of self and the world. The world changes from a place in which the values of one's own group are all-inclusive to a place in which the values of many groups are real. The self moves from inherited values to responsibility for choosing among the many values and beliefs available. It is, in the terminology of Erikson, a time of identity formation.[15]

Critical for youth is the task of forming friendships in which they can test the values and beliefs in which they have been formed. They need to decide which of the patterns of their lives they will accept as part of their own identity, and which they will reject. For early teens, a group outside the family may serve this function. For older youths, an opportunity to be away from home for an extended period—a moratorium—may be necessary to uncover those beliefs that are genuine and enduring.

Many observers point out that youth tend to form friendship groups around those values in which they have been reared and formed.[16] In this sense youth are usually very conservative. The youth culture develops its own symbols of identity, symbols which change frequently enough that the older community will not understand. Yet within the youth culture are the values of the family. Parents often expect youth to follow standards that they themselves do not, for example regarding alcohol consumption. Youth tend to practice what parents practice rather than what parents idealistically expect. Even the most rebellious youth often form friendships in which the friends put heavy expectations on one another. In all these ways youth tend to be conventional.

Fowler focuses upon the cognitive ability of youth, their newly developed capacity to think abstractly and to synthesize;[17] he speaks of youth as a synthetic/conventional period. Erikson stresses the search of youth for a basic attitude that has continuity with past values but that can also be genuinely at home in the broad range of adult

224

experience. Inability to find a fitting self-concept for the demands that all youth feel leads them to identity confusion. Youth search for a dependable identity in the midst of some degree of confusion.

Youth understand that people live within communities that are more than a set of friendships. Much of the experience of youth oscillates between the vagaries of friendship and the formation of larger groups. They also have mixed feelings about becoming independent, believing that they are capable of more independence than adults will allow. Adults in turn feel that youth are often more independent than they should be. Youth and adults therefore may find themselves in a double bind that is nearly impossible to break.

If one interprets youth in terms of the relational and interactional perspective rather than the cognitive, one moves from synthesis to belief. Youth is a time of investing in beliefs that give meaning to the habits, patterns, and routines that bind one together with others. Some youth will find themselves struggling with atheism. They may accept some of the treasured beliefs of their church, but cast out others. It is a time of developing a unique story of oneself that is more than what has been given in the past. Belief is as much uncovered as chosen and is often tested in youth. The experiences of adulthood lead to belief that is more deliberately chosen than the belief of youth. Youth may have dramatic religious experience, or perhaps very little religious experience, but youth seem destined to forge and adopt some kind of belief.

The church can minister to youth by providing a trustworthy congregational environment, and by supporting a youth group that is allowed to test the limits of belief. Testing the limits of belief can be taken in two directions. One direction is toward discovering levels of commitment that are absent in the church, while the other direction is to question cherished beliefs. Youth need adult sponsorship and guidance, not adult control or manipulation. Talented adults who understand this can help youth in the formation of belief. Youth are often capable of making a distinctive contribution to all phases of the life of the church, when they are interested and welcome. However, youth want, and should be allowed, the possibility of accepting or rejecting belief as they participate. The faith of the church in the face of the doubts and questions of youth can be a powerful ministry. Finally, belief is the power of trust over doubt about who one is and to whom one belongs. The holy, loving, living center of life gives such power of trust over doubt. Belief is evidence of the grace of God.

EARLY ADULTHOOD

Descriptions of the life journey of adults seem far less persuasive than those for children and youth. Adulthood does not offer the sharp physiological and psychological transitions that marked those earlier ages. Furthermore, adulthood encompasses so much of the unlimited wealth of human experience that most descriptive efforts seem to miss the reality of adult life. With these reservations we shall make some brief suggestions about the experience of adulthood.

In a limited sense adulthood refers to biological maturity of the body, and in a larger sense, to an ideal of moral and spiritual maturity. The mixture of these two meanings confuses any description of adulthood. Adulthood also refers to a status or position in a community. Adults are those who are committed to activities that sustain a culture and a way of life. Adolescence is a time for schooling, apprenticeship, and the testing of belief. Adulthood comes as belief and commitment become secure enough for people to begin following a way of life. In simpler societies children can move directly into adulthood without the extended period of apprenticeship and testing. The complexities of modern societies seem to create adolescence, an intermediate period between childhood and adulthood.

Engaging in the activities of a way of life is characteristic of adulthood in all societies. Young adults who leave home for college, military service, work, or travel may go through a period of radical relativism before coming to a more articulate belief. Western culture since Socrates and the Hebrew prophets has encouraged radical criticism of inherited cultural values.[18] Fowler describes young adults as becoming more articulate about their beliefs, and he finds this process is based on young adults' ability to dichotomize experience according to abstract categories. The problem is that Fowler's description misses many young adults.

Erikson seems closer to the point when he suggests that young adults develop a pattern of intimacy which is a mixture of love and isolation.[19] Whether or not young adults marry, they develop such a pattern of intimacy with friends. The pattern of intimacy is part of what I have called the way of life. Some young adults find their way of life easily and naturally. For others there is self-doubt, struggle, and changing activities. As youth test belief, so young adults test the way of life. Indeed the way of life is an embodiment of belief, so the testing of one tests the other. Young adults have come to accept certain beliefs which they then refine, articulate, and begin to act upon.

The problems with Fowler's individuative/reflective stage for young adults are several.[20] As we have said, it applies to only a limited number of young adults. Furthermore it is based on a cognitive judgment. By contrast, the concept of way of life is based on interactions, relationships, and institutional patterns within a narrated story. Every young adult is testing a way of life and in doing so is close to the living holy center of the life journey. Testing a way of life is the locus of faith for young adults.

Churches have been notoriously inept at working with young adults. This is true whether young adults go to college or not. The radical doubt of the college experience causes many young adults to question the church. But the problem is actually deeper. Most churches presume an established way of life; in fact, most churches function to legitimate an established way of life. Rare is the congregation that can actually encourage and support the testing of a way of life. Those young adults who participate in the church usually are established in a way of life. Church institutions that encourage the testing of a way of life have been able to address young adults; service programs, schools, experimental congregations, and travel programs are examples. Educators should reconsider the whole presumptive basis of the church's relationship to young adults.

MIDDLE ADULTHOOD

As with early adulthood, there is no sharp transition leading to middle adulthood. The difference between early and middle adulthood seems to be the difference between testing a way of life and contributing to one, which is more an attitude than anything else. When an adult has accepted a way of life, then the crisis revolves around whether it is a demanding fate or an opportunity for self-expression and response to the living center of life.

Fowler speaks of conjunctive faith and universalizing faith, but only a few adults reach those levels of cognitive maturity.[21] More to the point, Erikson speaks of the crisis of generativity among adults, when adults find that they either stagnate or are able to contribute to the culture of which they are a part. The prototypical generativity is the procreation and rearing of children, but all work oscillates between stagnation and generativity. Contributing to a way of life is a matter of generativity.

Gail Sheehy's book, *Passages,* has focused much attention on the mid-life crisis. The mid-life crisis seems to be whether one's life is being fulfilled by the way of life one has chosen. It is a return to the testing period of early adulthood. Sheehy has pointed out that the years thirty, forty, and fifty are particularly difficult because they represent the end of decades rather than simply the end of another year. The radical question of generativity and contribution to a way of life is raised, if it has been lurking unexpressed.[22]

The life story of adults is dramatically affected by health, friendships, occupational success, and historical epoch. A debilitating disease, an automobile accident, the death of a spouse or child, the loss of a job, or the outbreak of war can have a radical effect on one's life journey. Such events often precipitate a crisis of faith.

Neill Hamilton's study of ministers suggests that many begin their ministries with a strong sense of mission and prophetic concern.[23] Churches, however, are more interested in someone who will keep the institution functioning. The pastor's desire to be successful, to move to a larger church, or to become a church executive is nearly always disappointed. The person becomes aware that the dreams of youth and early adulthood can never be fulfilled as they were dreamed. At that point the pastor is thrown into a crisis of faith—a mid-life crisis, if you like.

As the result of such a crisis of faith a pastor either continues with an underlying despair or comes to terms with what is happening in her or his life. A pastor may be able to see and accept the pattern of what is being given by the power of the living center. Such a person has a new spirituality and a new sense of being caught up in God's mission. Though Hamilton's research was done with pastors, it is likely true for many people. The mid-life crisis is one of coming to terms with the disappointment of unfulfilled dreams of youth and young adulthood.

To be able to contribute to a way of life means accepting one's own limitations, acknowledging the shame of unfulfilled dreams and the guilt of injury to others, accepting the pain and loss that come in life, and finding the courage and confidence to express what is given one to express. To contribute to a way of life is to acknowledge one's sin and to place one's confidence in the love of God in Christ. The mid-life crisis is another form of the basic human urge to attempt the impossible task of creating one's own worth and prestige.

Fowler draws a contrast between vocation and destiny. Those who live by destiny either serve or are served by institutions for their own gain and self-enhancement. Those who live by vocation serve institutions or are served by institutions for the sake of what God is doing in their lives. Responsiveness to God's call and purpose is the character of vocation. Fowler suggests that vocation lifts the life journey above mere psychosocial development. In this sense vocation is characteristic of all periods of life.[24]

The concept of vocation is drawn from Martin Luther, who taught that everyone has both occupation and vocation. Occupation describes how people spend their time. Vocation is the challenge of God's call in life. The crisis of adulthood is the cry for vocation, for a pattern of activities that expresses rather than violates the living center of life.

Research in adult learning suggests that adults are often taught as though they were children. Children must be given particular values and directions for learning, but adults can discover truth for themselves. The skill of helping adults discover for themselves is the heart of teaching adults. Adults learn by genuine conversation in which the results are not predetermined.[25]

The church is often locked into teaching patterns for adults that are heavily dependent on lectures. Adults may find lecture satisfying if it serves to legitimate a way of life to which they are committed. However, more open, exploratory classes can get at issues that genuinely probe the way of life. Mission groups can give expression to God's call, and free discussion can banish despair over the absence of generativity. The particular experience will be heavily influenced by the Christian tradition to which it belongs.

OLDER ADULTHOOD

Like the other phases of adulthood, older adulthood has no transition that definitively marks it off. Social, psychological, cultural, and physiological factors converge to determine older adulthood for any given person. Physiologically, older adulthood is marked by a decline in the vitality of the body. An accident, a disease, or a chronic malady can require a person to withdraw from habitual adult activities. Since persons differ so radically in their health and vitality, the time of the transition to older adulthood can vary just as radically. A forty-year-old person with diabetes may be more of an older adult than a seventy-year-old person in excellent health.

Socially, older adulthood tends to come with retirement, which is established by law and social practice. Many businesses have a mandatory retirement policy for persons of a certain age, regardless of their health or productivity. After that age, they are treated as older adults. They then usually have lower income, loss of prestige, and often face the necessity of changing residence. Aging is also affected by the illness and death of lifetime friends, particularly a spouse. Older persons in Western culture do not have the status of carrying the cultural technology, as is the case in many simpler societies.

Psychologically, older adults tend to continue the life patterns established in early and middle adulthood. Studies of life satisfaction show that older adults are much more likely to continue earlier attitudes than to change according to circumstances, fortunate or unfortunate. Furthermore, older adults must finally adopt a withdrawal pattern. The declining energies of the body finally demand a change from the earlier adult way of life.

Fowler suggests that some adults achieve a universalistic faith wherein they are able to synthesize the various dimensions of life, beyond the many paradoxes. However, only a few persons, such as Gandhi, Martin Luther King, and other saints are able to do this. The rest live on a lower plane of faith. As in earlier stages, Fowler's concept of faith is governed by cognitive judgment, namely the synthetic judgment.[26]

Erikson speaks of later adulthood as a time when a person achieves some balance between integrity and despair and disgust. Integrity is the acceptance of one's own life story as worthy and significant. Despair is "an unconscious fear of death," a sense that there is not sufficient time to live out an alternate approach to integrity. The integrity that is able to separate the significant from the insignificant in life is summed up in the virtue of wisdom.[27]

Erikson's concepts of integrity and wisdom are enormously helpful. Integrity points to a unity of what now is, what has been, and what is to come. Wisdom is the ability of older adults to sense what is significant, but wisdom is not a gift of the many, and wisdom is often not highly regarded by younger adults. It has some of the limitation of Fowler's concept of universalizing faith.

The inevitable withdrawal of later adulthood requires a simplifying of life. The loss of friends, spouse, status, and physical energy requires focusing upon what is genuine. Otherwise, despair sets in. Kierkegaard spoke of purity of heart as willing one thing.[28] In terms of social interaction the theme of withdrawal and willing one thing is the simplification of life. Genuine simplicity is to love God beyond all things; everything else will find its place. Such simplicity of living is an ideal throughout adulthood, but it becomes critical in later years. To live simply is to be in the living center of life. For those who are able, simplicity is wisdom and universalizing faith. For everyone, it is a challenge to find a more fundamental truth when one's way of life can no longer be lived according to long established lifetime patterns.

What is clear from our discussion is that adulthood cannot be described with the same clarity and detail as childhood. In part, this is because adulthood cannot be described outside the life story that each person lives, and life stories cannot quickly be reduced to a few themes. However, every life story is an ongoing exercise in faith, hope, and love. It is a call to love and be loved, a restlessness to be near the living center of life.

The church's ministry to older adults must therefore take into account the unique life story of each. Ministry can encourage and support awareness at a time when there are many new opportunities for this. Older persons can be supported in their intentions and decisions. Ministry can encourage relationships between persons of various ages. Respect for older adults is as significant as respect for children in terms of the integrity of the whole community.[29]

THE FAITH JOURNEY

The view of the faith journey given above is a social interactional view that is centered on the love of God in Jesus Christ. The presumption is that everyone reaches for the living center of life, and that we do this as individuals interacting within communities. The living center is none other than the power of the love of God. Our account is in dialog with a number of views that have been very influential among religious educators. Its themes can be stated in summary and tabular form:

The Faith Journey

Early Child-hood	Child-hood	Adoles-cent	Young Adult	Middle Adult	Older Adult
Playing a story, drama					
	Discovering routine and value				
		Searching for belief			
			Finding a way of life		
				Contributing to a way of life	
					Simplifying a way of life

The diagram has the value of showing that each stage is closely related to the others. The focus is not on the social attitude, as is Erikson's account, nor is it on cognitive judgment, as is Fowler's account. Rather, it uses story, value, belief, and way of life as an unfolding narrative that holds individual and community life together. The different stages are related as parts of a narrative, and they are therefore open to the multiple meanings and interpretations to which all narrative is open. The link between the community's story and the individual's story is intended to become clearer in this account.[30]

The concepts above stand in immediate relation to interactional patterns. The story takes its significance within the community in which it is told and in the social patterns that it legitimates.

Symbol

Individual   Community

Interaction

So the faith journey is not to be seen as isolated and independent, but as social and interactional.

STUDY SUGGESTIONS

Exercises

1. In a group of several people, take turns telling your life story. This can be done in a brief or a more extensive way. Each of you may take an hour or two to tell your story. Going around the group may take several weeks or months. The story can be enhanced if participants bring in articles or possessions that are precious to them.

2. During medieval times, individuals and families sometimes had coats of arms which consisted of a striking symbol. Let each person in the group develop a coat of arms for herself or himself. Divide a large piece of cardboard or paper into four equal rectangles. Within each rectangle let each draw a symbol of one chapter of their lives, for a total of four symbols. When the coat of arms is complete, each person explains the meaning of the symbols to everyone else.

3. Let students list the seven greatest losses of their lives. Then let them list the seven greatest achievements of their lives. Share and discuss these losses and achievements with others in the group.

4. Write your life story in the form of a traditional fairy tale. When these fairy tales are complete, they can be shared with one another.

5. Recall the time when you first remember feeling like an adult. Recount the experience and the feelings to others in the group.

6. Recall the ceremonies that have been most meaningful in your life. Were they ceremonies that occurred only one time, or were they a part of a sequence of repeated ceremonies? Recall the most meaningful ceremonies of the church. What has each of those ceremonies meant to you?

7. Spend some time observing the play of small children. After making your observations, write down an exact account of an episode you observed, including the child's conversation, if any. On the basis of your observations discuss with one another the place of story and imagination in the lives of preschool children.

8. Talk to a school age child about when something happened that was unfair. Let several children talk about something unfair at home or in the school. What do they understand fairness to be? Is this the same way you would understand fairness?

9. Interview a group of youth about where they consider their parents views to be out of date. What do these youth consider to be a more up to date point of view? In what way do you see the views of youth being formed? Do you find them to be conservative (i.e., like their parents) or not?

10. Talk to a group of young adults about their problems choosing a vocation, a marriage partner, or a style of life. What considerations go into such a choice? What makes the choice difficult?

11. Interview a person in her or his forties or fifties who acknowledges having experienced a mid-life crisis. Have the person describe the crisis. What brought it on? If resolved, what helped resolve it? Has the person's faith been tested by the crisis, or helped to overcome the crisis?

12. Interview a retired person who has clearly changed her or his way of life. What led to that change? In what way does the person find life satisfying now? Has the person's Christian faith been tested by the change, or has faith sustained the change?

13. Take any one of the interviews above and compare the experiences of girls and boys, men and women. For example, what is the difference in choosing beliefs for a young man and a young woman? In a similar way conduct these interviews with different ethnic or minority groups and compare their experiences with those of the majority group.

14. Interview persons of different ages, asking them to recount their most significant religious experience at that age or at an earlier age. What observations do you have about religious experiences at different ages?

Questions for Discussion

1. Can one have a description of faith that does not assume what it hopes to describe?
2. Are separation and participation applicable to all of life?
3. Compare faith as the relationship with the living center to faith as an attitude toward the ultimate environment.
4. How is faith relevant to one- and two-year-olds?
5. To what extent do preschool children understand or misunderstand teaching about the love of God?
6. What is the special character of the faith of school age children?
7. How do the beliefs of youth compare with the beliefs of children and of adults?
8. Compare Erikson's concept of psychosocial attitudes to the concept of a way of life developed in this chapter.
9. How is mid-life crisis related to the faith journey?
10. Compare "simplifying a way of life" with "wisdom and integrity."

Suggestions for Further Reading

William M. Clements, ed., *Ministry with the Aging.* Clements has collected a number of commentaries on the church's ministry to the aging.

Neill Q. Hamilton, *Maturing in the Christian Life: A Pastor's Guide.*

Hamilton challenges developmental theory from a New Testament point of view.

Maria Harris, ed., *Portrait of Youth Ministry.*

A creative and imaginative portrayal of youth ministry.

Donald E. Miller, *The Wingfooted Wanderer: Conscience and Transcendence.*

Some of the ideas of the present chapter were first formulated in this book.

Kenneth Stokes, ed., *Faith Development in the Adult Life Cycle.*

A collection of the responses of various specialists to hypotheses about faith development.

Chapter Nine:

WORSHIP AND EDUCATION

In their life journeys, faithful individuals participate in communities of faith whose patterns of worship and practice interact with their journeys. Worship, learning, and living are thereby intimately related to the roots of faith. The interrelationship of worship, learning, and living is assumed throughout the Hebrew Bible and the New Testament, but recently a new and vital understanding of this interrelationship has come about. Religious educators are attempting to recover the educational functions that belong to the worship and practice of communities of faith.

EDUCATION AS ENCULTURATION

The most forceful advocate of the interrelationship of worship, learning, and living is John Westerhoff.[1] In Westerhoff's view, the heart of education is enculturation: the process of persons being shaped by basic cultural symbols. He calls for congregations to look to their worship patterns as the primary source of religious enculturation, for the symbols of worship are assuredly more powerful than teaching within formal classes. Westerhoff calls attention to the fact that festivals and celebrations have always served to incorporate members of all ages and renew the sense of belonging by festivals and celebrations.

In celebration, a community's story is acted out in ways that allow everyone to participate. Worship is always a drama, a community event. The pattern of worship becomes the common pattern of behavior for all participants, a norm of behavior. At the same time, worship unfolds a narrative or dramatic event. Even in non-liturgical communions where prayer, hymns, and preaching constitute the worship, the ritual is in the form of a simple drama. The dramatic elements of liturgical communions are more evident, but even the quiet worship of the silent Quakers has its own drama.

In the drama of worship, roles and relationships are developed and coordinated. The worship leader directs the movement. Choir and congregation become singers or listeners at different moments. One attitude is assumed in prayer and another in hearing the sermon. So the various roles of a worship event are orchestrated. In most congregations, the festival dimension of the worship drama is evident during holy days such as Christmas and Easter.

Worship has a language of its own, deeply informed by biblical tradition, and norms of behavior which may be violated only to one's embarrassment. It encourages certain appropriate emotions, such as reverence, penitence, gratitude, joy, and generosity. The worship narrative becomes a part of each person's own narrative. Worship rehearses and recalls an originating event, the event of God's grace in Jesus Christ. Worship is the acceptance of a common commitment, a covenantal

242

renewal, a community's search for the mind of Christ. Since worship is deeply formative for persons, it is educative in the profoundest sense.

THE CRITIQUE OF ENCULTURATION

Westerhoff's account of enculturation has given rise to a debate about whether this concept is adequate to describe religious education. One objection is that worship cannot replace the small study group as a center of learning and understanding. Worship remains mute until the worshiper enters into dialog with others. Children remain uninformed until worship is explained to them.

Study groups and classes within congregations offer primary relationships without which a congregation cannot survive. Researchers have often documented the fact that congregations of all sizes need primary groups in which individuals can participate. Sociologists use the term "primary relationships" to describe close, intimate, caring, supportive, committed relationships.[2] Secondary relationships are defined by formal functions, work, or usefulness to one another. Secondary relationships may vary from cordial and friendly to simply carrying out the expected function. Church school classes have been a fundamental locus of primary relationships in the congregation; worship alone cannot carry this function. Without primary groups, attendance dwindles. Indeed, attendance at church school classes is a good indicator of future church attendance.

Another critique of enculturation is that the socializing process can get caught in the prejudices of local traditions. Peter Berger describes how church schools tend to reflect the dominant culture, including its prejudices toward minorities.[3] Oppression of women, native Americans, blacks, and immigrants comes along with the dominant cultural symbols.

A number of recent studies of American churches document the fact that religious education tends to inculcate the dominant cultural values without bringing a concern for justice.[4] Belonging to church seems to make little impact upon people's basic American values; people seem not to understand how their religious faith might affect their secular life and public commitments. People give verbal allegiance to their faith, but primarily because it supports, or at least does not conflict with, dominant cultural values such as individual initiative and national pride.

If enculturation is simply the adoption of the dominant cultural values, with their oppressive and self-serving tendencies, then enculturation can hardly be an adequate theory of religious education. One must, however, acknowledge that the teaching of liberation, concern for minorities, and the love of neighbor creates its own kind of culture. The Hebrew prophets had followers who created a culture of protest, as did the reformers of the sixteenth century. Hence the name "Protestant." One cannot deny the fact of enculturation, but one can question the type of enculturation. If religious education is enculturation, then the question of what kind of enculturation it is must be addressed.

Another attack on the idea of enculturation comes from those who find the enculturation process too peripheral to human experience to touch faith directly. Faith has to do with one's ultimate commitment, one's relationship to God, one's sense of the grace of God in Christ. Enculturation deals with cultural symbols and social process. It is important, but has nothing directly to do with faith. For education to focus on enculturation means to leave the realm of faith.[5]

AN INTERACTIONAL VIEW

An interactional view focuses upon an ongoing response to God, the living center of life. Persons interact with the environment, with other persons, with community norms and symbols. Communities interact with the environment, persons, meanings, and with the wider public ethos. There is a constant and continuing process of interaction, which taken as a whole is a response to the living center.

Westerhoff is correct to say that the worship and practice of the community is formative for all people who participate in the community. Cultural norms and symbols can be and often are an expression of deep experience and commitment. Cultural norms and symbols are the form of religious commitment, and religious commitment is the substance of cultural norm and symbol. All profound religious movements produce a distinct culture, and to participate in any religious movement is to be enculturated. Even the Quaker move to silence, away from ministers, church buildings, and all symbols, in itself led to a new culture.

When the focus of commitment shifts from the living center to the cultural expression, then cultural symbols no longer serve to point to their source. When the names and practices related to God become more important than the relationship to God, then the problem of idolatry arises. An interactional view accepts the significance of culture, but always points to the more fundamental interaction with the divine center of power and value.

An interactional view calls educators to reach beyond the dominant cultural values to the values of prophetic faith. Evangelistic concern for those who do not know God's grace can be joined to social concern for the oppressed peoples of the world. Community worship and practice need not simply reflect the dominant cultural values. The problem with studies linking religious education and popular values is that researchers have chosen to study congregations known to reflect those values. They could instead have chosen to study religious groups known to be critical of dominant values. In spite of the fact that some congregations simply adjust to the culture, the power of prophetic religion can be present in the worship and practice of a faith community. Those who participate will feel its power.

Finally, an interactional view acknowledges that worship cannot carry all primary group functions. While a worshiping group often becomes a primary group, informal discussion and dialog after worship or around a meal table are also important. The interactional view points to the total interaction of group participants as formative. True enough, worship plays a decisive role in group formation because it is an expression of the centermost values of the group. But worship is part of the wider practice of a faith community and the latter is the larger context for any formal education. It is important therefore to follow Westerhoff in examining worship and celebration more closely, but always within the context of congregational practice.

TRANSITIONS

The life journey is characterized by a series of transitions, to some extent controlled by the separations of life. The young person leaving home is involved in a separation that is also a transition. Separation literally means to set apart or divide, while transition means to relocate. The relocation may not be a physical one; it may simply be a different social position. In any case, separations often involve transitions in a person's life.

A well-known anthropologist, Arnold van Gennep, studied the ceremonies of simple societies in relation to transitions in life. He found that critical and important ceremonies often accompany the customary transitions in a given society. A rite of passage is a ceremony that prescribes how a person moves from one social position to another. In some tribes adolescent boys must go outside the village, live alone for some days, and be scarred according to ritual procedure before returning to the village as a man.[6] A parallel ceremony prescribes how a girl becomes a woman.

In van Gennep's view, marriage is a rite of passage by which two persons who are located singly in the society take on the social location of a couple. The marriage ceremony serves to mark the transition. So also the funeral ceremony designates a transition from the status of a living person to the status of one who has died. Rites of passage are not limited to simpler societies; in Western societies ceremonies have also grown up around transitions. Unfortunately, however, the complexities of modern society offer multiple transitions and few ceremonies.

Van Gennep distinguished between repeated and unrepeated ceremonies. Daily, weekly, monthly, or annual rituals seem to help maintain a sense of continuity and regularity. One-time rituals mark the disjunctures in life, the transition from one time of life to another. Such rituals mark the movement of life. Both repeated and the one-time rituals celebrate separation and participation.

The concern for transitions has been strengthened by James Loder's study of transformation.[7] A previous chapter discusses how both the cognitive and emotive approaches to faith development can be grouped into certain stages. Loder is critical of stages because they seem to refer more to social process than to faith itself. Faith has to do with the deepest level of a person's commitment and orientation. At the time of the transformation of such deep commitments and orientation a person's faith becomes quite evident.

Loder is interested in what leads us to negate our assumptions about reality, and then what leads us to go beyond that negation. He calls transformation a process of the negation of negation. At such moments a person searches for a new orientation, and when the new orientation comes, life takes on a different character. Loder suggests that religious educators ought to be concerned about moments of transition.

In the interactional view, transitions can occur throughout life, and there are many such times within the life story. They include birth, beginning school, initiation into adolescence, coming of age, marriage, parenting, employment, recognition, illness, divorce, death of a loved one, retirement, and certainly others. Institutions also have times of transition, as can be seen in a narrative of the congregation's story. A congregation's story might include the beginning of the congregation, growth, pastors, other leadership (teachers), purposes and mission, a new building, covenantal renewal, the saints of the congregation, and important celebrations. Beyond its particular circumstances, the congregation interacts with denominational events, ecumenical events, the church year, and public events.

The faith community's worship and life take place within the context of a series of transitions, occurring between individual life journeys, the congregational story, the denominational story, the larger Christian story, and other public events. Worship can be a decisive expression of these transitions. Worship brings both a sense of continuity through repeated festivals and a sense of movement in one-time festivals. It supports the worthiness of life and of the need to work for mission. Throughout all it points to God's power, grace, love, and justice, the living center within the transitions of life.

WORSHIP AND EDUCATION

Traditionally, worship was understood to be educative. One need only look at the medieval cathedrals to see the way in which stained glass, stone relief, and carved wood all served to tell the story of the church. To be in a cathedral was to be surrounded by the church's story in visual imagery. Similarly, the ancient synagogue with its scrolls and readings from the Scripture surrounded people with the story of the faithful community.

The sixteenth-century Reformation recovered the didactic element in worship. Luther intended preaching to be not only the proclamation of God's grace but also the Word rightly interpreted. Hymns should carry the message of the gospel. The people must be rightly instructed if they are not to fall into idolatry. So also Calvin understood the minister to be a teaching elder. The minister should be trained in right doctrine (teaching) so that the people may be properly taught. The sharp line between preaching and teaching was not a Reformation view.[8]

The Anabaptists also saw worship as an encouragement in the way of discipleship. Those who spoke from the Scripture were to edify and encourage. Those who listened were to consider, question, and strengthen their resolve to live in the Christian way. Pietism and the Sunday school movement tended to separate worship and teaching in the modern Protestant church. Pietism led to conventicles for the study of Scripture at times other than the worship service, although the conventicles were also times of worship. John Wesley encouraged lay study groups, in keeping with the Pietist influence upon him. The Sunday school movement led to a group of lay teachers who took teaching as their special divine vocation, with worship left to the minister. So worship and education tended to divide.

Much of the twentieth century has seen an effort to reintegrate worship and education. The Sunday school has been renamed the church school; classes study stories and hymns that are a part of the worship. Church school study is now planned to undergird worship.

Westerhoff's suggestion, considerably more radical than the effort to integrate the Sunday school into the church, calls for recovering the educative function of worship. Worship itself should be the primary form of education; any other education is secondary. What is studied in a formal class should be taken directly into worship. The one who plans and conducts worship should consider what is being taught as a part of worship.

RELIGIOUS EXPERIENCE

The religious education movement of the twentieth century was based on the idea of enhancing religious experience. The moments of wonder, dread, care, and reverence belong at the center of teaching. Education is for the sake of evoking such moments.

The neo-orthodox critism of liberalism objected that education can never bring the moment of revelation. God's revelation comes in its own way in spite of human efforts, certainly in spite of our educational efforts. Neo-orthodoxy has brought more concern for indirect methods of education. Drama, story, and narrative can be the occasion in which God confronts us. Education becomes a kind of prayer for God's revelation. The next step is for formal worship to understand itself as educative.

Religious experience always comes as from another realm. It is not under the control of the receiver. In fact, the worshiper is convicted by her or his unworthiness. The person is "taken" or "led" into a new experience of wonder and awe. The person is "sent forth" with a message or a task. The being "taken" and "sent" shows the way in which the believer feels beyond herself or himself.

Whitehead spoke about the utter privacy of religious experience.[9] Religious experience is private, but surrounded by the communal. Isaiah's vision in the temple of seeing the foundations shake and seeing the seraph bring a live coal was formed around communal images of worship within the temple (Isaiah 6). The experience was utterly private, but the symbolic expression of the experience was utterly communal.

If the symbols of religious experience come from the tradition, i.e., from the community's holy stories and narratives, then private experience is also to be tested by the community. Isaiah was sent out to proclaim the message, thereby allowing his experience to be tested in the community life. So the privacy of religious experience is community oriented in its ground and in its effects. In religious experience we see how both the individual and the community transcend each other. Whitehead's assertion that religious experience is utterly private and Durkheim's assertion that religious experience is utterly communal need one another.[10] In John Wesley's view, private religious experience was to be tested by the Scripture and the community of faith. Otherwise private religious experience may move to the fantastic and the immoral.

The close relationship of worship and education is leading some educators to reconsider disciplines of prayer and meditation. An example is the use of guided meditation. The worship leader makes a series of suggestions for the meditation of the listener, who responds in her or his imagination. A study of Luke 24, where a stranger joins Cleopas and another disciple as they return to Emmaus, might include the following guided meditation:

> You are walking along a hot, dusty path. You have been walking for some time and you are quite tired by now. You are also discouraged. You had thought that you understood where your faith was taking you and what it all means.

251

Then something had happened. Your belief suddenly seemed unrealistic, childish, out of touch with reality. You were disoriented, shaken, afraid, afraid to admit that you were afraid. Suddenly, everything seemed oppressive and uncertain. You are no longer sure where things are going in your life.

Walking beside you is a friend you have known for several years. In fact your friend was the one who first spoke to you about Jesus. You have often talked together about your faith since then, and your friend's faith has always lifted you up. Now as you talk, you realize that your friend is as confused and uncertain as you are. The words of disappointment and discouragement rush forth from both of you.

Suddenly you are aware of someone else's presence. You were so engaged you did not notice him approach. He asks if he might join you. Simply agreeing relieves your mood a bit. He wonders what you are speaking about, and you surprise yourself by being very forthright about feelings that have hurt so much. What does one do when disappointment comes? Where does one turn when one's faith is shaken? The stranger's words are gripping. He knows the Bible well and is able to refer to many passages where despair is the beginning of faith. You become aware that you no longer feel trapped by your despair.

As you come to your own place, you invite the stranger to join the two of you for a meal. At first he insists upon going on, but then he agrees to accept your invitation. The meal is soon prepared. You ask him to pray. Something is happening to you. As he finishes the prayer, he takes the bread, breaks off a piece, and gives it to you. Your eyes meet his directly for the first time, and suddenly you know. You know the presence of Jesus. Joy rushes over you and you hear in his words the promise you have been waiting for so long.

As you meditate you begin to realize that the one who broke bread with you is gone. Reluctantly you shake yourself away from your meditation. Should you tell others what you have just experienced? You are returning to the others; what should you say? The meditation is over and now you are ready to speak to those around you.

252

Such a meditation can make the Lukan passage immediately present for the class. The leader must be sensitive both in leading the meditation and in encouraging people to speak about it afterward. A sharp and definable experience may come to some, a more amorphous and undefined one to others. The meditations may be quite different and are to be received in their differences.

Worship is not only private meditation, and meditation should be tested by Scripture, reason, and the experience of others. The discussion of meditation is important to test its authenticity and to enliven community life. Worship is also prayer, proclamation, singing of hymns, and communion. Community traditions provide a variety of ways of calling for and responding to God's presence. The intermingling of worship and education needs much more exploration.

WORSHIP AND PUBLIC EDUCATION

The American constitutional tradition guarantees the separation of church and state. The guarantee came in part from political necessities of the time. The colonies adhered to different religious traditions, from Roman Catholic to Anglican to Reformed to Separatist. The only possibility of joining them together was to allow religious diversity. But more than this, the writers of the Constitution apparently wanted to guarantee that the state would not dictate religious belief to any group.

In the twentieth century, many Americans believe that public prayer in the school could strengthen the moral conviction of the students. The Supreme Court has not allowed prescribed prayer in the public school. Our discussion in the previous section shows that private religious experience can go in many ways unless it is tested by Scripture, reason, and the experience of others.

Prayer in the public schools cannot be tested by Scripture, for that would be a further violation of the separation of church and state. It should be tested by reason and by others' experience. But that also would get deeply into the mingling of church and state. Silent prayer, done alone, may have many effects; there is certainly no guarantee that it will deepen morality.

Prayer depends upon deepening the intuitive side of understanding. Public school teaching can deepen the intuitive dimension of thought in many ways, and students can also be encouraged to state publicly understandings that come from their own religious convictions. Such encouragement trains young citizens to see the implications of their religious convictions for public policy. These suggestions fit the Supreme Court's interpretation that religious practice may not be prescribed by the schools, but that religious practice may be studied in the school.

EDUCATIVE WORSHIP SERVICES

The relationship of education and worship can be seen by looking at particular worship services. Consider the service of baptism. The Christian tradition splits in its interpretation of baptism. The more sacramental view focuses on the sign of God's gracious forgiveness of original sin. Less sacramental views, especially those of adult baptists, focus on the participatory response of the believer to God's gracious love and forgiveness in Jesus Christ.

Those who espouse adult baptism nevertheless offer a service of dedication for infants. This is not only a dedication of the infant to God's gracious love, but also of the parents and the congregation to seek to nurture and surround the child in the ways of faith. Infant baptism implies the same promise to nurture of the child in the

Christian faith, usually symbolized by the appointment of godparents.

A service that includes a baby dedication or a baptism offers a perfect occasion for a sermon on the character of God's grace and on the congregation's power to nurture one another. A Sunday school class might study the way in which the congregation nurtures their faith. The class could then prepare a litany or a drama to be used in the worship service.

A group of adults might discuss over a period of weeks how the congregations of which they have been a part have nurtured their faith. One or several of the adults might give brief statements about the nurturing power of the congregation in their own lives. One or more families might discuss at home the significance of the church in their lives, presenting the results of their discussion to the whole congregation at the time of dedication or baptism. Those who have special relationships to children in the congregation, e.g., godparents, might comment upon that relationship as a part of the worship.

Still another approach would be to have a younger class study their own babyhood. Then they might prepare gifts for the new baby. A children's choir might sing something for the baby being dedicated or baptized. All of these suggestions are ways of including formal or informal study within the worship service itself. Families with preschool children might all come forward during the dedication or baptism, and then all these families could rededicate themselves to the nurture of their children. Worship, then, may combine what was prepared by various groups, shaping it into a dramatic, unified event.

The giving of Bibles can be another opportunity for educative worship. Many church schools and congregations give Bibles to children who have learned to read, usually around the third grade. Often the Bibles are given and worship quickly proceeds to something else. But this can be a great and significant worship event. Six-, seven-, and eight-year-old children have dramatic religious experiences, but seldom is anything done publicly to recognize them. The giving of Bibles to children can be an opportunity to celebrate their growing faith.

Until the invention of the printing press, only a handful of educated people could read the Bible. The printing press brought the Bible to the common people, and many were astounded at what they read. The availability of Bibles was certainly an important factor in the coming of the Reformation. In the twentieth century, reading is taken for granted, even though there is much illiteracy around the world. The receiving of Bibles symbolizes the receiving of the Word of God, and to receive the Word of God is to be permitted to come into God's presence, which is the saving power in all human life. Without God's presence human life is lost and, finally, doomed. A child's receiving the Bible is an enactment of the possibility of everyone receiving the Word of God. It is a fine occasion for a sermon about the impact of the Word of God on human life.

Study groups can make special preparations for the giving of Bibles. Each of those receiving Bibles can read a selection for the congregation. They might very well read the Scripture passages for the worship service. They might spend several weeks or months preparing a summary about what they know about the Bible, presenting this at the worship service. Perhaps the teacher can give a brief description to the congregation about what is happening in the life of each child who receives a Bible.

Other classes may also be involved. A junior high class might study the various translations and versions of the Bible and give a summary about what they have learned. Perhaps a local librarian could bring examples of different versions of the Bible. A class might present a drama about the translation of the Bible. Another class might work out a litany telling what the Bible means to them.

In preparation for the giving of Bibles the congregation might be schooled in the memory of several passages, such as the Twenty-third Psalm or Romans 8. Such a passage could be recited as a part of the worship for several weeks in preparation. Then the children and the congregation could recite the passage together when the children receive their Bibles.

The relationship between worship and education should be transparent in the above suggestions. Various groups help prepare for the worship service. Their preparation is itself the content of their study. The worship focuses on the growing faith of a group of third graders, and is done in a way that symbolizes how all receive God's word. The dramatic account of the church's story intersects with the spiritual journey of a group of eight-year-olds and becomes an occasion for genuine worship.

IN THE TEMPLE

We have examined dedication/baptism and the giving of Bibles as examples of how worship and education can intersect. Still another example related to the spiritual journey concerns the spiritual recognition of eleven- and twelve-year-olds as they approach adolescence. This age is almost universally recognized as a time of transition from childhood into youth or early adulthood. Almost all religious communities have ceremonies for children of this age, from the Hebrew bar mitzvah to the Christian confirmation service. The following service is designed for most early adolescents, whether or not they choose adult baptism or confirmation.

The story we have of Jesus' life at age twelve occurs when his parents take him to Jerusalem for Passover (Luke 2:41–51). As they are ready to leave Jerusalem to return home, they cannot find him. Finally they find Jesus in the temple asking questions of the religious teachers. The story of the twelve-year-old Jesus can be used to form a worship service for children of the same age. The heart of the worship service is a dramatization of Jesus in the temple, with the twelve-year-olds asking questions of people in the congregation, and the congregation giving their answers.

The youth and their teachers are responsible for planning their part of the worship service. They begin by formulating questions about the Christian faith during six weekly sessions, as spelled out below. The youth are told that the beginning of genuine faith is to ask honest questions, and that during the next six weeks they will be searching out their heartfelt questions.

Preparation for an "In the Temple" Service

Session	*Title*	*Scripture*
Session One	Your Questions	Joshua 4; Matthew 7; John 14, 16; Isaiah 7, 45
Session Two	Jesus in the Temple	Luke 2
Session Three	Questions the Disciples Asked	Matthew 18, 19; Mark 10, 13; Luke 12
Session Four	The Questions of Parents	
Session Five	Preparing Your Questions	
Session Six	Planning to Lead Worship	

Session One: The youth look up the following passages: Joshua 4:6-7, 21 ff.; Matthew 7:7-12; John 14:12-14, John 16:23b-24; Isaiah 7:10-16; and Isaiah 45:9. They then discuss the contrast between "Ask and it shall be given," and "Don't question God." The students go off privately and write several questions about right and wrong, faith, the church, or whatever else they choose to ask about.

Session Two: The youth study and discuss Luke 2:41-51. They consider what Jesus' questions might have been. Together the students write a play about Jesus in the temple. They identify the characters, the plot, and the dialog.

Session Three: The disciples asked questions to which Jesus gave simple and direct answers: Matthew 18:1 and 18:21. The disciples asked other questions to which Jesus gave complex and difficult answers: Matthew 19:27; Mark 13:3-10; and Luke 12:41-42. Finally, the disciples asked questions which were answered by Jesus with other questions: Mark 10:35-38. The youth study and discuss these questions and Jesus' answers. They then further develop the play about Jesus in the temple and practice it. During the week they discuss with their parents the kinds of questions they were asking at the age of eleven or twelve.

Session Four: The youth share with one another and discuss the questions of their parents. They practice the play and put it on for another class. During the week the students are to think more about their own questions and write them down.

Session Five: The students discuss the different parts of the worship service in which they will participate. They discuss such items as the play, Scripture, reading and comments, children's story, and questions for the elders. Someone from the congregation comes to listen to the questions of the youth. They talk together and allow the youth to reformulate their questions. They work out the way in which "the elders" will be questioned during the worship service.

Session Six: The pastor is invited to join the class session. Together they decide the parts of the service for which the youth will be responsible. They rehearse the parts of the worship that they have planned, and the pastor makes suggestions to them. Each student chooses someone from the congregation to respond to her or his question. Each youth has the responsibility of contacting the chosen adult and giving her or him the written question. Final details of the worship are worked out.

The following week the worship service takes place. If there are a number of questions from the youth, the "questioning of the elders" may well take the place of the sermon. The pastor performs the opening of worship and announces the worship plan for the morning. The youth read Luke 2:41–51 and comment on it, then act out the play they have written. Next, persons are called up from the congregation and each youth asks a question. Each adult responds briefly, and gives the youth an opportunity to ask further questions of clarification. Each person will have been coached about how much time she or he has. Finally, the youth group thanks the adults and asks the congregation to continue to be willing to respond honestly to their questions. The pastor answers the requests the youth have brought the congregation. The youth are blessed in their ongoing questioning with a prayer by the pastor, and then are challenged by the pastor to continue questioning. Those who are baptized and/or confirmed are encouraged to grow in their faith in their Lord. All are reminded that sincere desire is the beginning of faith. The pastor then concludes the worship appropriately.

Here we have an extended example of a strengthened relationship of study and worship. Similar services could be worked out for high school graduation, commitments to adult vocation, weddings, and stewardship commitments, to mention only a few. In these services adults, youth, and children can all contribute. The consideration of the educative dimension of worship opens the question of the place of children and youth. The examples given above show they can have a significant place not only as participants, but in guiding worship.

STUDY SUGGESTIONS

Exercises

1. Recall the church's celebration for last Christmas. List all the church events that are part of the Christmas season. Consider how people of different ages are related to Christmas celebration. What captures the attention of both young and old? How is Christmas worship different from worship at other times of the year? How is education related to Christmas celebration? How are family events, worship, and teaching interrelated? Set down your conclusions about the relationship of education and worship.

2. Consider how the form of your church's worship reflects the life of your congregation. How does the order of service relate to the congregation's life? Is the worship dramatic or undramatic? Is the pace frenetic or relaxed? Is the worship structure coherent or incoherent? Are certain routines unchanged no matter who leads worship? Which age group is most engaged by the worship service? What are your conclusions about the relationship of worship and community norms?

3. Study the number of primary groups in your congregation. Are any or all of the classes primary groups? You might do this by asking persons which group they feel closest to at church. You might ask who are their five closest friends, and how many of these are at church? In which groups are your respondents together with one or more church friends? How many have no primary relations at church? What are your conclusions about the relationship between primary groups and church attendance?

4. Find a number of church members who grew up in the church and another several who came to the church as adults. Interview each of these two groups regarding their view of the church. What are your conclusions regarding those who were enculturated in the church and those who were not? Are the enculturated persons less likely to be concerned about questions of justice? Is there a difference between the two groups regarding the depth of their faith?

5. Read anthropological studies of rites of passage. Then consider one of the services of the church as a rite of passage, e.g., baptism, marriage, or funeral. What do you learn about these different services?

6. Interview one or more persons to discover the greatest moments of transition in their lives. To what extent were these moments also religious experiences? To what extent was the church related to these persons in their moments of transition? What are your conclusions about the church's capacity to minister to persons at their times of great transition?

7. Discuss with one or more people their most moving religious experiences. Did these experiences come when they were alone or when they were with other believers? Do they consider these experiences to be utterly private or shared? When worshiping, do they feel the presence of others, or do they feel ultimate solitude? What do you conclude about the relation of the communal and the private in religious experience?

8. The present chapter develops a guided meditation based upon Luke 24. Choose other passages and develop guided meditations based on them. Offer to use these meditations in various church school classes.

9. Hold a debate about prayer in the public school. As an alternative, set up a panel discussion on the topic. Invite a public school teacher or official, a minister, and a lawyer to speak on the panel. Allow opportunity for general discussion.

10. On the basis of the discussion in this chapter draw up lesson plans for the baby dedication/baptism, the giving of Bibles, or the "In the Temple" service. Ask the pastor and the worship committee to carry out one or more of these services. Develop lesson plans for graduation, adult commitment, or stewardship in such a way as to integrate worship and education.

Questions for Discussion

1. What are the arguments for and against viewing religious education as enculturation?

2. To what extent can worship fulfill the educational mission of the church, and to what extent must worship be supplemented with other educational activities?

3. Is faith located primarily in the cultural process, or beyond?

4. What are the major life transitions in the modern Western world? How is worship related to them?

5. Does worship function differently in different religious traditions?

6. Is there a separation of education and worship in your church? If there is such separation, is it of significance?

7. To what extent is religious experience utterly private and to what extent communal?

8. What are the limits of the constitutional doctrine of the separation of church and state?

9. Do the suggestions in this chapter about coordinating education and worship diminish or enhance the worship experience? The educational experience?

10. Is the integration of education and worship equally possible within both the free church and the liturgical traditions?

Suggestions for Further Reading

Robert L. Browning and Roy A. Reed, *The Sacraments in Religious Education and Liturgy.*
The authors explore the relationship between education and liturgy in this extensive study.

Ruth C. Duck, ed., *Bread for the Journey.*
Presents a variety of worship resources based upon the church year.

John H. Westerhoff and William H. Willimon, *Liturgy and Learning Through the Life Cycle.*
The authors explore the way that liturgy and learning can be joined together.

John H. Westerhoff and Gwen Kennedy Neville, *Generation to Generation: Conversations on Religious Education and Culture.*
Draws upon anthropology to show how the values of one generation are transmitted to the next.

IV
TEACHING

Chapter Ten:

TEACHING AND LEARNING

Learning is the process by which story and community practice interact with an individual's changing awareness of self and others. Learning is constantly occurring at both conscious and unconscious levels. Teaching is the process of purposefully enhancing learning by means of attitude, activity, and discourse. Teaching is therefore intentional, although it may be more or less informal. A person who is not conscious of being a model for someone else is hardly teaching, whereas a teacher is usually aware that he or she is a model for students. When so defined, teaching is a function that can be shared to various degrees by all members of a group.

In what follows we will look at several theories of learning, and then at theories of teaching and instruction. We shall continue to view learning and teaching as part of a larger community process, but we shall also account for the relationship of the individual to the community. Learning occurs not simply in the community or in the individual, but in the relationship between the individual, the community, and the ongoing story of both. Therefore we shall look both at formal study and at what is called contextual learning.

THE STORY OF LEARNING

Learning theory in its modern use is an attempt to put the philosophy of human understanding into more empirical and scientific terms. So the philosophy of human understanding and learning theory are very close. In Western thought the debate about learning has centered on several key issues. One is the relationship between concept and experience.

The Platonic tradition taught that learning begins with experience but moves by means of disciplined study and dialog to the fundamental concepts or structures at the base of all experience. The Aristotelians took the opposite point of view, arguing that the fundamental reality is individual experience. Concepts can enrich experience, but they are never more real than the experience itself. Twentieth-century religious education has seen a constant debate about the place of experience. By and large, the modern religious education movement has insisted that all genuine education must begin with experience, but the common practice is often more Platonic, teaching ideas with little reference to experience.

The ancient world also split over the question of whether understanding is primarily an activity of the intellect (Plato) or an activity of the will (Augustine). Plato taught that the intellect alone can comprehend something in its true nature. Augustine held that genuine understanding is a matter of the will. One cannot understand what one is unwilling to understand, therefore repentance and confession are the beginning of understanding.

The relationship of action and reflection has also been greatly contested. Plato stood in the Socratic tradition, holding that to know something is to do it. Knowledge that does not include action is less than knowledge. Aristotle understood concepts to be enriching to action. He presumed that thought gives direction and vision to the active life. Thought is therefore simply an extension of the normal process of living.

In the modern world the priority in action is assumed by both Marxism and pragmatism. Marx's famous dictum was that the task of philosophy is not to analyze the world but to change it. Every reflection is therefore based upon action and directed toward action. Pragmatism holds to a similar belief: Thought is a kind of activity, posing alternative actions and anticipating their consequences. Carrying out the activity is the only way that thought can become useful.

Knowing in the biblical sense is relational. It is a relationship between God and the community, God and a person, or one person and another. At the same time, knowing is active. The Word of God is creative. To know the Word of God is to participate in God's life-giving activity. There is no separation of being and doing or knowing and doing. Knowing is close to the covenant, which is a relationship within the community.[1]

Even such a brief discussion of the ancient issues related to learning indicates how contemporary they still are. Discussions about concept and experience, intellect and will, action and reflection, individuality and relationship are all very much alive. The experimental science of learning theory may be largely a twentieth-century development, but the fundamental issues are part of an age-old debate.

LEARNING IN COMMUNITY

A basic issue in contemporary discussions of learning concerns individual experience and community process.

271

C. Ellis Nelson has drawn on the social sciences to show that learning about religion takes place as a part of customary and common social practices.[2] Learning is therefore more than a private experience—it is a change in social perception and interaction. Participating in the life of cultural groups like church or family is a process of adjusting to their patterns of behavior. To some extent groups must also adjust to the behavior of those who come to them. Such a process of learning social patterns is normally called socialization.[3]

In a community, learning is closely related to customs, traditions, habits, courtesies, procedures, worship, and other patterns of communal life. One learns such patterns more by participation than by discussion. To participate means to be able to understand the rules being followed, to see the activity of others in relation to each other and to oneself. Many four- and five-year-olds exasperate their older playmates by wanting to play a game when they do not yet understand the rules. They imitate older children by moving a token on a board, but they do not move it in the proper direction. They do not yet fully grasp the rules or interactions, even though they have an external sense of the game.[4] To learn to play the game means to learn the rules, i.e., the common practice, and to see one's action in relation to others.

From a community perspective, learning to take the role of a student in a classroom or the role of a teacher is at least as important as learning guided by the stated objectives of a session. Quickly, we must acknowledge that following stated objectives helps to define the role of both teacher and students. Taking part in worship and social activities in a congregation are also a part of the learning process. To participate is to be touched by the values implied by shared practices. To be able to take part with discernment is itself to learn. Learning is to accept a role, to receive a social position, to act from an implied value.

We have been discussing learning as socialization. As was mentioned earlier, John Westerhoff prefers to speak of enculturation, by which term he stresses the learning of cultural meaning. Westerhoff has pointed to the work of social anthropologists who show that persons learn the meanings and mythology of a group by taking part in the celebrations. The community rites are the acting out of the religious beliefs. In celebration the most basic story of the community becomes a living reality. In the rites of passage persons not only assume a new position in the community, they also participate in the re-creation of the community's story.

Celebration, pageant, community activity, story, and drama are the ways in which religious learning occurs. In such activity the unity of story and life occurs. Each person embodies the story from a particular role and each relates to the other as part of the story. Westerhoff is persuaded that enculturation occurs not only in pre-literate tribes, but also in contemporary communities. The most powerful Christian education comes from celebration and liturgy that embody the Christian story. The ancient traditions and liturgies give a living tie to the community of the past.

SHARED PRAXIS

The praxis view of learning has been powerfully set forth in the theologies of liberation.[5] Praxis is the Greek word referring to the unity of theory and practice. Liberation educators are reluctant to use the word "practice" because it seems to stand in opposition to theory. Practice is commonly understood to be the application of theory. The concept of praxis refers to a dialectical relationship between theory and practice such that theory springs from practice and constantly returns to it.

A praxis understanding of learning always begins with present plans and activities. Discussion rooted in present practice is never to be merely theoretical. As practice is revised, the discussion evaluates it. Praxis implies a constant dialectic between action and reflection. Since action is always intended by those who act, praxis is a thoughtful consideration of intended activity. Theoretical discussion can be merely hypothetical; action can be uninformed. Praxis is neither blind activity nor purposeless discussion but purpose in search of understanding.

Paulo Freire's account of praxis begins not simply with present practice and reflection, but with community patterns that he calls life themes. There are many life themes, but oppression is the most pervasive and basic. The disclosure of oppression leads to fundamental learning, a new level of critical self-consciousness. Only as persons examine their cultural practices critically can they become aware of themselves as oppressed or oppressors.[6]

The praxis theory of learning has been articulately restated by Thomas Groome. Lamenting the theoretical approach to learning of much religious education, Groome calls for a critical dialectic between the Christian tradition and living praxis. Learning occurs when one identifies present praxis and sets it beside the tradition. This critical dialog affirms the present praxis and the tradition, and finds limitations in each of them as well as contradictions between them. From such dialog a new praxis arises. Groome calls this approach shared praxis because the critical element of dialog occurs within a community. Unlike Freire, Groome does not insist that the theme of oppression always be present.

Groome has shown how the praxis approach to learning can be widely used. The call to begin teaching with what students are experiencing is commonplace among educators.[7] However the focus on praxis goes beyond perceptions, emotions, or "lived moments" (Ross Snyder) to the activities and intentions of those who discuss. While experience may include all of this, it may also be limited to feelings and present events that illustrate a biblical or theological concept. Praxis is experiential in the sense of experience related to ongoing activity and is reflective in the sense of critical discussion of living traditions. Praxis is therefore an identifiably distinct and influential learning theory.

INDIRECT LEARNING

Some religious educators insist that learning is more indirect than the above theories propose.[8] In their view, learning occurs when dependable perceptions or concepts are brought into question. Doubts may be evoked by the questions of other persons, the contradictions within experience, or the threat of pain and failure. When one's understanding of what is genuine or true does not account for new experiences, conflicts arise.

When severe conflicts with familiar ideas occur, then established understandings fail. To some extent a person is brought into the limits of morality, the sense that life is passing and will soon be finished. At that point a person scans her or his experience for a new image that will hold experience together. In an unexpected moment some event or image gleaned from the search takes on symbolic meaning and gives continuity and coherence to a whole range of other experiences, far beyond the original one. That transforming experience or image becomes an analogy for other parts of life, through which many other life-events can be reinterpreted.

Transforming moments sometimes occur when a person has a brush with death. Previous life projects and plans lose their importance. Conflict between awareness of the brevity of human existence and the futility of past commitments throws a person into doubt about what is true. A period of scanning may then occur in which the person reviews her or his life to find its meaning. The person may decide that the accident was God's way of awakening her or him to genuine faith. Perhaps a resolution to begin Christian service becomes the point from which the person's whole life is reinterpreted.

The Christ-event can be understood as the central transforming moment for humanity. The conflict between the predictions of the prophets and the oppression of Israel led to anticipation of the Messiah. When Jesus was executed by the Romans, his followers were thrown into a state of hopelessness. They scanned their experience with Jesus and the Hebrew tradition to make sense of it all. The gospel testifies to the dawning awareness that Jesus is the Christ. From that point on his followers were in a process of reinterpreting their lives.

Indirect learning theory does not attempt to predict what will be learned. Rather, it deals with the conflicts, the breakdown of meaning, the scan for new coherence, and the reorganization that it proposes are essential to learning. This ongoing process of reinterpreting life is how story develops. Story, drama, and art encourage indirect learning because they do not try to control the outcome. Indirect learning is not solving a problem or developing a habit, which are both examples of direct learning. Rather, indirect learning continues one's story or drama so as to preserve continuity with who one has been while discovering who one is coming to be. The learning of a person's story or character is fundamentally indirect.

The indirect view of learning is in contrast to the structuralism of some educators.[9] Structuralists see new perceptions arising out of conflict, but the new perceptions follow predetermined patterns. Preschool children experience things in a way that confuses interior imagination and external reality. School age children perceive immediate conditions, but they cannot imagine hypothetical conditions. Teenagers can think abstractly because they are not bound by immediate perceptions.[10] According to structuralism every person's perceptions will change, but they will follow the preschool, school age, and teenage patterns just enumerated.

Indirect learning theorists believe that learning does not occur according to universal patterns or structures, but rather according to an ever-changing and unique story for every individual and every group. While universal structures may be present in a limited way, they do not define the individuality of persons and groups. Loder argues that Fowler's stages do not touch the center of personhood; rather, it is the transforming moment that penetrates to the deeper dimensions.

Indirect learning puts more emphasis on dialog and less on problem-solving. Not that problem-solving is unimportant, but the more important learning regards the ongoing story within which problems are set. Religious educators may or may not be concerned about particular problems, but they certainly should be concerned about dialog between persons about their life stories.

We have not exhausted the various theories of learning. We might also consider behaviorism, pragmatism, and psychoanalysis. However, the learning theories given above are the ones most discussed by religious educators. In addition to theories of learning, teachers also rely on models of teaching, and to these we will now turn.

MODELS OF TEACHING

Learning is a process that is constantly occurring whether or not teaching is attempted. The opposite is not true; teaching cannot be done without learning. Of course, teaching can be attempted without learning, but it is not proper teaching unless some of the intended learning occurs. Genuine teaching therefore requires careful attention to what is being learned. Teaching is not the same thing as telling, listening, or encouraging, although it may include all of them. Teaching is a relationship that purposefully influences learning.

Teaching is not primarily controlling, for genuine learning is voluntary discovery. Teaching does indeed involve the management of the politics and power of a group, but power must be subsidiary to voluntary discovery by group members. Teaching is always a relationship whose purpose is to influence learning. The teacher's responses must therefore be adjusted to the learning that takes place.

Teachers normally do four types of activities: planning, managing, evaluating, and counseling. Planning is preparation for group activity. Managing occurs during the designated teaching time; the teacher has priority in deciding procedures. Evaluation occurs as the teacher considers what learning is taking place. Many individual counseling conversations may occur before and after teaching events.

In her book, *To Set One's Heart*, Sara Little offers a classification of models of teaching. She suggests that there are five different models: information processing, group interaction, personal development, indirect communication, and action/reflection.[11] Each of the models has a different focus, each favors different procedures, and each contributes something different to belief.

278

Information Processing

Information processing models of teaching focus on building concepts related to experience. Almost all learning involves the ability to use concepts in relation to experience. Religious education requires concepts to interpret spiritual experience. To the extent that teaching aims at thinking and understanding, it will attempt to communicate concepts.

The focus of information processing can be more the process of disciplined thinking than the concepts themselves. It can be inductive, as when many examples are given and the students are encouraged to find the common concept. It can also be deductive, with concepts described and then applied to different situations. Programmed learning can be used either inductively or deductively, but it is nearly always information processing.

A variety of assignments feature information processing. Research projects or reports get students into the background of a topic. Debate allows persons to explore different points of view. Guided classroom discussion is a way of letting students analyze and evaluate different points of view. A group interview permits a class to interact with an expert. Questioning is a basic way to get at issues, lecture a way of presenting concepts. In a symposium various students present different points of view. The use of team teachers (more than one teacher) allows different points of view to be represented.[12]

Group Interaction

Group interaction models recognize the social character of learning. The focus is not only on concepts, but on relationships, roles, and interactions within the group. The content is therefore both conceptual and relational, and the teacher must be adept at group process. Students are encouraged to suggest ideas, make group decisions, evaluate what occurs, and generally share responsibility.

In group interactional teaching much time may be spent in group planning, formulating a procedure, carrying out a task, and evaluating the process. Role-play situations encourage students to interact emotionally as well as verbally. Simulations provide opportunities for acting out more complex situations. Case study methods enhance intense group interaction. Choric reading is a way of reading together according to the directions of the director. Jury trial is an interactive simulation.

Planning and carrying out a field trip is very engaging. Work camps, service projects, and visits to other communities are more than field trips—they are participative learning experiences. They require group planning and cooperation. Worship is another group interaction; either as a small group or as a part of a congregation, it is clearly group oriented. The teacher may ask several students to be on a panel. A group of students or the whole class may attack a problem together or work on a project together. The class can be divided by age, sex, interest, skill, culture, personality, etc. Intergenerational events are designed for interaction between persons of different ages.

Interest grouping is done by setting up several interest centers. Students can then choose the center they like. One interest center approach for school age children had the following activities: woodwork, computers, creative writing, choir, drama, clowning, puppets, sewing, signing for the deaf, and painting. A teacher with the appropriate skill was at each center. There were an equal number of tags for each center; a child could go to a center as long as a tag was available. She could go to a different center at any time by exchanging her tag for that from another center whenever one was available. The degree of group interaction depends on the activities at the different interest centers.

Personal Development

The focus of personal development is the enhancement of the powers of selfhood, self-awareness and self-expression. Teaching is carried on through the acceptance of feelings and the encouragement of self-expression. The uniqueness of each individual is recognized and celebrated. The teacher is sensitive to the growth of individuals and to the spiritual awareness of each person.

Activities for the personal development model are those that allow individual expression, such as writing a faith statement, poetry, a play, or other kinds of creative writing. A group of teens may write a litany on baptism for the ceremony of one of their number.

Another kind of expressive writing is keeping a journal. A person writes not principally about what is happening, but about what he is feeling, his shifting moods, his day-by-day sense of reality and meaning. Such writing can move in the direction of stream of consciousness, simply following the sequence of thoughts. Plumbing the depths of feeling can lead to new insight and emotional depth. Journals should be kept daily, but they can be done effectively less often. Groups can share excerpts from journals for mutual enrichment.

The composition of a piece of music, creating a painting, or developing a wood carving are examples of individual expression. A group may plan a worship service for the congregation for which they have written the prayers, litanies, and hymns, and designed the worship center. For the Scripture reading they may prepare a paraphrase written by themselves.

The writing of children's stories can be a unique and interesting experience. Each student writes his or her own life in the form of a children's story. These stories are used during the regular worship service, or children are invited in to hear the stories. Another approach is to write the story of the congregation or the denomination as a children's story.

Another form of creative expression is to produce a slide show by either taking the pictures or creating the slides. A more ambitious but exciting project is to produce a movie. The students may write the play, work out the sets, act out and film the sequences, and, finally, edit the film. Such a film could be produced for a special event in the church.

Awareness training is still another form of personal development. The plight of the hungry can be experienced by having a foodless banquet. To get the sense of being handicapped, let some wear blindfolds and others be confined to wheelchairs. Let adults get down to the height of children and imagine how the world looks from that perspective.

Assertiveness training is a variation of awareness training; it is particularly useful for women. Let persons in a group practice behaviors that they need in order to be more effective or fulfilled persons. The encouragement of one another to be assertive, in such disciplines as dieting or exercising, or in greater stewardship of resources, can be a very powerful incentive.

It is only a small step to spiritual training. A group can take on a discipline of prayer, Bible study, and service, which can be done in private as well as together. The private and the group spiritual disciplines supplement and strengthen one another.

An important way for a teacher to encourage the personal development of students is for the teacher to practice the art of active listening. The teacher listens intently to each student, often attempting to rephrase what has been said in a manner that captures the person's emotional as well as conceptual meaning. To move beyond rephrasing, the teacher can try to intuit the feeling being expressed by a student and then respond to that

282

feeling. If the student in turn reveals more of the feeling, then the teacher has been successful in active listening. If the student stops responding or changes the subject, then the teacher has misread the student's feeling-tone.

A teacher concerned about students' personal development will encourage them to learn in their own way. They may write contracts for what they will do. They may work at their own pace, submitting what they have done when they are ready. The evaluation process is not simply lodged with the teacher; they evaluate their own or one another's work. The whole community shares teaching and evaluation.

An appropriate approach to encourage the self-expression of children is the "magic circle."[13] The children are brought together in a circle, and then are told the two rules of magic circles: (1) only one person may talk at a time, and (2) everyone has an opportunity to speak (although no one is required to). A theme is suggested around which each child can speak; for example, "Has anyone here ever been lost? How did it feel?" The teacher encourages the expression of feeling. For almost every biblical passage a magic circle can be held. For Joseph and his brothers the question could be, "Is anyone the favorite in your family, or in your class at school?"

The method of synetics developed by William Gordon is one of finding similarities between disparate things, situations, and persons.[14] For example, how is a Bible like a mule? Various answers may be given: They both carry your load for you; they will take you where you want to go if you don't try to force them; Jesus comes to us both on a mule and in the Bible. Exploring strange contrasts can expand self-awareness.

Indirect Communication

This teaching model focuses on the examination of conflict and the anxiety of freedom. Out of such anxiety come new analogies, new imagination, and a new understanding, which we spoke of under theories of learning. The truth is dramatic, revelational, beyond the cognitive. The teacher's role is one of sensitivity, timing, and awareness of genuine freedom and truth. The student's role is to risk and discover.

Storytelling is a powerful mode of indirect communication, but of this we have already written at length. Such forms of artistic expression as stories, parables, music, film, and other media are often indirect; they raise questions beyond the cognitive and leave persons with a restlessness to be answered.

Clowning is a form of indirect communication. In clowning, a person takes on a costume and a special face that is unique to him or her. The clown may not speak, but must communicate by mime and suggestion. Developing a clown routine can be an interesting learning experience, and most biblical passages can be interpreted by a clown or a group of clowns. Using clowns as a worship aid to the reading of Scripture or a litany can make for powerful drama.[15]

A third form of indirect communication is Socratic dialog. The point of the dialog is not to reach a predetermined conclusion, but to explore a topic in terms of the personal reflection of all participants. The teacher encourages all to challenge and question one another. The mutual stimulation may raise anxious questions, but that is the risk of freedom. Not the final answer, but the genuineness of the search is the critical objective. Therein persons understand themselves better. Like a story, the dialog is unpredictable because it is genuinely free.

Again, worship must be mentioned. As people express themselves individually or together, they develop a sense of new truth beyond the surface meaning of worship symbols. But of this we have already written.

Models of Teaching

Information Processing

Induction
Deduction
Research
Reports
Debate
Discussion
Group interview
Questioning
Lecture
Symposium
Teaching team

Indirect Communication

Story telling
Artistic expression
Clowning
Socratic dialog
Worship

Personal Development

Creative writing
Keeping a journal
Artistic composition
Children's story
Slide show
Awareness training
Assertiveness training
Spiritual direction
Active listening
Contract learning
Community evaluation
Magic circle
Synetics

Group Interaction

Group planning
Role play
Simulation
Case study
Choric reading
Jury trial
Field trip
Work camp
Service project
Cross cultural visit
Worship
Panel
Project team
Intergenerational events
Interest groups

Action/Reflection

Covenantal renewal
Naming present praxis
Representations of life
Life story
Life planning
Value clarification
Service projects
Worship
Participation in movements
Discussion
Analysis
Planning

Action/Reflection

This is the fifth and last of Sara Little's teaching models; it is based on the praxis learning theory discussed earlier in this chapter. The focus is on relating any discussion to actual practice, with the intent to keep reflection from being merely theoretical. In this method, discussion is based on what individuals and groups are actually committed to. Little acknowledges that the process may involve more than action and reflection. A fuller paradigm might include awareness, analysis, action, and reflection.[16]

Action/reflection has been heavily influenced by the Latin American experience. The Basic Ecclesial Communities in Roman Catholic parishes have been formed to become aware of the situations of all participants, to pray together, to study the Scripture, and to attend to problems of their neighborhoods.[17] Such an approach involves a renewal of community covenant, an active caring for one another. Our own discussion has very much emphasized covenantal renewal.

Identifying present praxis is important, and can be done by describing experience related to life themes. For example the theme of fear can be considered by discussing fearful experiences in the lives of those present. Paulo Freire insists that life themes must come out of the actual experience of people and not be introduced as hypothetical situations. The use of photographs or other representations of daily existence can provoke analysis of present praxis.

The life story is a way of allowing others to get close to a person's praxis. Life planning can also be used. A closely related approach is that of value clarification. A value is an ethical commitment implicit in one's present praxis.

Reviewing how a person spends time can become the basis for discussing the person's values.

Action/reflection calls for participation in life issues. Groups do not take "field trips," which implies that the purpose is the discussion at home base. Instead, groups engage in service projects because the service is needed; groups protest armaments because the threat of armaments is real; groups worship because worship is basic to abundant living.

Action/reflection brings people to issues and movements; praxis gives birth to study, not the other way around. A group may join those acting to protect the environment. A group may begin asking others to join with them in dedication to Christ. Action usually involves conferring and discussing with those who are already engaged and experienced with a concern, and requires discussion, planning, and study.

These models of teaching show the variety of approaches to teaching. Certainly teaching is as much an art as a technique or a science. It is very personal, powerfully expressing the uniqueness of each person. Teaching is also a function of a group. Though one may be designated as teacher, teaching becomes more powerful when the teaching function is shared in the group and when the designated teacher becomes a model learner.

STORY AND CONTEXT

We have reviewed several learning theories that are influential in Christian education. Socialization theory describes how learning occurs as persons participate in a community. Shared praxis assumes that learning occurs as actual praxis is identified. Indirect learning focuses on the transformations that occur beyond the immediate intentions of teacher and student. There are many other learning theories, but these three are of special importance.

We have identified and illustrated five models of teaching. Information processing rests on the classical concern about ideas. Personal development addresses the creative possibilities of the individual. Group interaction uses group process to teach. Indirect communication concentrates on the revelatory moments of life. Action/reflection is rooted in present praxis. Again, there are many other models of teaching, but such a typology may be useful to identify the range of possibilities.

Teaching is deeply affected by perceptions, styles, training, and community context. The community will act as teacher no matter how much formal teaching is done. Individuals are formed by such teaching, but they also transcend it. In the interplay between individual and community is born the possibility of an increase of global awareness.

STUDY SUGGESTIONS

Exercises

1. Hold a series of debates on topics critical to the ancient world: the relationships between experience and concept, intellect and will, action and reflection. Study the sources referred to in this chapter in preparation for the debates. You may also want to discuss how biblical knowing is related to each of the three issues just named.

2. Observe four-, five-, and six-year-old children, or attempt to play some simple games with them. When do children begin to understand the purposes and rules of games?

3. Attend a film or read a book about one of the community rites of a pre-literate tribe or group. How does the rite relate to the religious belief of that group?

4. Let the members of your group share transforming moments with one another. Did each person experience a period of conflict and of scanning? How did resolution come about? In what way did each person sense God's presence or absence?

5. Interview several teachers and attempt to discover their unique approach to teaching. What are their primary considerations in planning and class management? What unique styles do they bring to the art of teaching? Do their approaches fit the types described in this chapter?

6. Hold a group interview with an expert teacher. Let a panel of persons prepare questions to be asked. Then let the whole group enter the discussion. What does the teacher consider to be the most important elements of teaching? What learning theory does the teacher follow?

7. Plan a series of interest centers for the children of your church. Consider the skills of church members that are of interest to children of different ages. Can you include the following: woodwork, computers, creative writing, choir, drama, clowning, puppets, sewing, and painting? You may think of many more. Perhaps the planning can be a part of Christmas, Easter, or summer celebrations.

8. Keep a spiritual journal or diary for several weeks. Look in the library for suggestions about keeping a journal. You may want to share your entries with someone else. Perhaps several of you can do this and share your discoveries weekly.

9. Work with a group of children or youth to produce a movie. The movie might be based on a contemporary interpretation of one of the Bible stories—perhaps a parable. Invite others in to see the movie after it is produced.

10. Practice the art of active listening. Active listening can be practiced with one other person while being recorded. Then the recording can be played to the larger group. Together they can discuss whether the listener was acute in intuiting the meaning and feelings of the other person.

11. Interpret a Bible story by clowning. Decide upon the number of participants needed, and let each develop a clown face and dress. Decide how the action of the story can be mimed without words. Then present the story to a group of children.

12. Interpret some particular theme of your community's life by taking photographs. The theme may be a source of either concern or joy. Present the photographs to your group and discuss the community praxis related to them.

Questions for Discussion

1. What is the relationship between experience and concept in learning?
2. What is the relationship between what we want (will) and what we learn?
3. How are action and reflection related to one another?
4. How are socialization, shared praxis, and indirect learning theories complementary and/or contradictory?
5. How is teaching related to learning?

6. How are the science and art of teaching interrelated?
7. What are the limitations of inductive and deductive approaches to teaching?
8. How is the model of teaching related to the message being taught?
9. What theological differences underly the models of teaching discussed in this chapter?
10. Will action/reflection lead to the abandonment of classroom teaching?

Suggestions for Further Reading

Paulo Freire, *Pedagogy of the Oppressed.*
Freire's book is not easily read, but it has been enormously influential in promoting a praxis theory of learning.

Thomas H. Groome, *Christian Religious Education: Sharing Our Story and Vision.*
Groome's is a groundbreaking book calling for a praxis theory of learning in religious education.

Sara Little, *To Set One's Heart: Belief and Teaching in the Church.*
The author develops a typology of different approaches to teaching and shows how each is related to belief.

James Loder, *The Transforming Moment.*
Loder's is the best contemporary statement of indirect learning theory and is inspired largely by the work of Kierkegaard.

Chapter Eleven:

CURRICULUM

The kingdom of God is the curriculum of the community of faith. The kingdom of God is the power of Christ's forgiveness, an ecumenical vision transforming present traditions, a mission of love concerned with inclusiveness and social justice, a search for global consciousness amidst local circumstances, a sense of individual and communal vocation, an action toward liberation and hope. A community that experiences and awaits the kingdom of God will find the power and love of the heavenly kingdom present and expected in all that it does. The relationships, life, and practice of a congregation, which interact with and influence every individual participant, constitute its hidden curriculum.

The root definition of curriculum is the Latin word meaning "a circular race track." By analogy, a curriculum is the overall design, round of activities, planned experiences, and subject matter to be followed in a course of study, or collectively in all of them. The curriculum is the means by which a chosen focus of experience, knowledge, or belief is made available for students' participation and response. Through curriculum the traditions, convictions, and practices of a faith community become matters of consideration, commitment, and response by participants.

It is customary to distinguish, between narrow and broad meanings of the term "curriculum," and then to dismiss the broadest. The narrowest for religious education is, (1) the biblical passage to be studied. Larger is (2) the printed material being used as a guide and aid to study. A still larger view includes (3) all the lesson resources, materials, student experiences, and the total teaching plan. Broadest of all is the view that (4) curriculum is the total set of activities, relationships, and resources that give shape to a community's educative structure. Normally the last concept is dismissed as impractical, resulting in an unfortunately narrow perspective in the creation and use of curriculum. To recover its relationship to social process and personal experience, curriculum must be reconceptualized in this broadest sense. Nothing is more practical.

The conception of curriculum must be reformulated so that the symbolic content interacts with social process, individual commitment, and particular circumstances. Not simply reinterpretation of the community's story is called for, but transformation of the community itself is needed to enable its members to see their own story within the larger Christian one. Curricular change begins not with more expensive printed materials for children, but with community recommitment. We turn on its head the statement of George Betts: "What you would have in the life of a people you must first put into its schools"; the truth is more nearly that what you would teach the new generation in the classroom you must first find in the aspiration and commitment of a people.[1]

COMPONENTS OF CURRICULUM

D. Campbell Wyckoff distinguished between five components of curricular design: objective, scope, context, learning tasks, and organizing principle. *Objective* is the overall aim or purpose of the curriculum. *Scope* is the arena of knowledge and experience to be explored. *Context* is the whole set of relationships within which learning tasks and procedures are set. *Learning tasks* are the activities and procedures for teaching and learning. The *organizing principle* is the design by which objective, scope, context, and learning tasks are held together.

Wyckoff relates his formal categories to the congregation by suggesting what ought to go into each of the categories of curriculum design.

> The context of Christian education is seen as the worshiping, witnessing, working community of persons in Christ. The scope of Christian education is the whole field of relationships in the light of the gospel. The purpose of Christian education is awareness of revelation and the gospel, and response in faith and love. The process of Christian education is participation in the life and work of the community of persons in Christ. The design of Christian education consists of sequences of activities and experiences by which the learning tasks may be effectively undertaken by individuals and groups.[2]

By featuring context as "the worshiping, witnessing, working community of persons in Christ," Wyckoff is very close to the emphasis of this book. His view, like the interactional one, balances the relationship between symbol and circumstance, individual and community, memory and anticipation. However, his purpose is more nearly awareness and response than participation in the transformation of persons and communities. The sense of vocation and justice is notably absent.

The term *design* does not exhaust the meaning of curriculum. Wyckoff also speaks of *theory*—the rationale by which curriculum is planned, produced, and evaluated. *Content* refers to stories, activities, and procedures that go into a curriculum. The curriculum *materials* are the resources that are used. These categories have decisively influenced the discussion of curriculum in religious education for at least two decades.

THE CURRICULUM STORY

The development of coordinated printed curriculum came with the schooling movement. In the sixteenth century the Bible became the new curriculum for the people. What the printing press did for availability of the Bible, Pietism did for motivation to Bible study. The Pietist movement of the seventeenth century led to conventicles of believers studying the Bible and praying regularly. Pietism is sometimes credited with giving impetus to the movement for public education.[3] Other than the Bible, the curriculum for children in churches was the formal series of questions and answers in the catechism.

The New England Primer was an attempt to provide Bible-based curricular material for children learning to read. The Sunday school, which began in England in the late eighteenth century, created a demand for new and more curricular materials. The American Sunday School Union in the early nineteenth century offered a set of books for teachers and their classes in newly founded Sunday schools. By 1825 a five-year study cycle of the Scriptures was available.[4]

The mid-nineteenth century saw a wealth of printed materials become available for the religious instruction of children and adults. Winona Walworth considers this a time of curricular confusion and refers to it as the "Babel" period of 1840–1872.[5] One must remember that the American Sunday School Union nearly collapsed in 1837, that denominations took over the Sunday school, and that public controversy over slavery issues was increasingly acrimonious.

Following the Civil War, Sunday schools were reorganized under the International Sunday School Convention. At its convention of 1872 a committee was appointed to develop the first International Uniform Lessons. At the beginning of the twentieth century, in 1903, the Religious Education Association was founded, partly to promote the principle of graded lessons, and soon the International Graded Series became an alternative to the Uniform Series. By 1918 the International Uniform Lessons were revised to allow for age differences. Many denominational materials followed the outlines produced by the International Uniform Lesson Committee. The expense of producing materials along with a growing concern for ecumenism eventually moved denominations to cooperate in producing materials.

By 1933 the All Bible Graded Series was developed to give more Bible content, more recognition to the child's perspective, and more concern about evangelical principles. It later became Scripture Press. The same year Henrietta Mears' concern for closely graded evangelical materials led to the founding of Gospel Light Publications. In 1944 the National Association of Evangelicals authorized the production of uniform lesson outlines separate from those of the National Council of Churches.

Under the challenge of neo-orthodoxy, religious educators began to question whether educational methods can bring people to faith. Curriculum was redesigned to put revelation and theology at its center. Christian Faith and Life (Presbyterian Church, U.S.A.) and Covenant Life (Reformed) as well as the United Church Curriculum

(United Church of Christ) were developed under the influence of the new theological orientation. While the importance of theology was generally accepted, most Protestant denominations were not about to dismiss educational theory. In the 1950s and 1960s sixteen Protestant denominations joined in the Cooperative Curriculum Project to produce a curriculum that was both educationally and theologically informed.

In the 1970s more than a dozen Protestant denominations joined to form Joint Educational Development. They decided that no one curriculum could be acceptable to the diversity of religious convictions within their communions, so they decided to develop four separate but interrelated curriculum series. Knowing the Word was to be strongly biblical, simply structured, and similar to the Uniform Series. Interpreting the Word was to be organized around scholarly interpretation of the Bible. Living the Word was to feature creative teaching and learning activities within congregational life. Finally, Doing the Word was to explore issues of social engagement and justice.

Other noteworthy curricula include that of the Lutheran Church in America, which has done extensive research on religious development and on the relationship between various church agencies. Fortress Press has developed a program for the urban experience called *Hey, God!* Roman Catholic curricula are usually related to official statements of bishops and councils. Various publishing houses develop curricula on the basis of official doctrine. For example, Paulist Press has produced *Growing in Faith Together*, organized around adult needs, as well as a multimedia curriculum for families. The United Methodist Church produces its own curriculum which stays close to the outlines of the Cooperative Project mentioned above.

THE CURRICULUM DEBATE

The above account shows that curriculum has moved from the simple study of catechism or Scripture to more and more complex, specialized plans which take into account the diversity of users.

The curricular vision of the twentieth century has been an ecumenical approach to Christian education that would include all Christians. The movement toward a unified approach seemed stronger at the beginning of the twentieth century than it does now. Not only is there a split between those who call themselves "evangelical" and "mainline" churches, but cooperation among the latter has run into many difficulties. The Cooperative Curriculum Project was replaced by the Joint Education Development project, but the latter produced four curricula instead of a unified perspective. The denominations find themselves caught between the economic necessity of cooperating and the economic reality that many of their congregations choose to purchase materials from independent publishers.

The present situation is one of conflicting directions. The century-long effort for a unified curriculum continues, but is hindered by lagging loyalty among denominational users, a variety of approaches, and the split between evangelical and mainline efforts. It is, in the phrase of Mary Jo Osterman, "Babel II," a situation like the nineteenth-century "Babel" period mentioned above.[6]

Some critics of unified curriculum resources suggest that such resources are hopelessly separated and disconnected from the people who use them.[7] Most prepared curriculum materials represent a compromise between subject matter, method, and persons. Curricular themes are often unrelated to one another. Curricular materials often seem irrelevant to those who use them. The use of a curriculum seems to be separated from other processes in the life of the church.

A number of commentators believe that a curriculum should help persons find meaning, make connections, and explore their own experience of life, instead of giving them additional information that only serves to alienate them from their world and from the curriculum.[8] Dwight Huebner believes that teachers should encourage students to explore their own experience and invent new meaning. The old catechetical method of question and answer can be very educative if the questions are genuine and the questioner works at trying to understand the response. The responses may change the questioner and ultimately the catechism.

Some critics believe that curriculum can be reconceptualized to allow for the faith journeys of persons and communities, and to enhance their own process of finding meaning along the way. Others argue that the curricular system should be abandoned. The latter say that large curricular enterprises are produced by an educational technology that merely reflects a highly technological society. Curricular materials are developed around specialized goals, methods, and procedures that dominate people rather than help them find meaning and purposeful activity. The materials are inevitable compromises reflecting more middle-class values than committed Christianity.[9]

The criticism can be carried further. The schooling model of education in the church is based on managerial and industrial concepts. The objectives and procedures, the management and promotion reflect the social structure of a factory or a business. The materials, buildings, and equipment require a heavy financial investment. Improvement is measured by more elaborate facilities, more sophisticated equipment, more material resources.

All is controlled by particular objectives against which progress is measured. Schooling, with its curriculum, therefore reflects the structure and process of industrialized society. The large, expensive, and highly organized procedures for producing cooperative curriculum reflect the same technocratic structure.

Radical critics therefore call for a total restructuring. Such a restructuring should move to inexpensive curricular materials, locally developed. Such critics call for communities to become actors in their own environment rather than consumers of the products of a large bureaucratic structure. They call for attention to life-style, commitment, and praxis in the local congregation as the place where genuine reflection can occur.[10]

So the curriculum discussion stands between continuation of present methods of developing and using curriculum, revision, reconceptualization, and total restructuring. Curriculum theory is in a considerable state of indecision and confusion.

CURRICULUM PREPARATION

Curriculum preparation may be illustrated by telling the story of one small curriculum project. The Foundation Youth Curriculum is produced cooperatively by the Mennonite Brethren Church, the General Conference Mennonites, the Mennonite Church, the Brethren in Christ, and the Church of the Brethren. After a conference of Mennonite educators concluded that a new youth curriculum was needed, a publishing council was established to develop one, and an editorial council was appointed to be responsible to the publishing council.

The editorial council was to design the new curriculum and the publishing council was to test the feasibility of publishing the new design. Therefore the editorial council kept the publishing council informed of its developing

301

plans in order not to have its work vetoed. The publishing council soon employed a college teacher of theology to act as editor of the new materials until they could be handled by the regular professional editors of the various participating denominations.

The editorial council began by reviewing the reasons for a new curriculum. The older youth curriculum was being discontinued. The churches were asking for effective materials for their youth, in view of the threat that youth were becoming disaffected with the churches. Other available curricula did not present the Believers' Church perspective forcefully enough. The first decision was the matter of the *curriculum objective* or goal. For whom was the curriculum to be designed? What was it to communicate? The editorial committee took stock of the fact that many of the congregations were small and rural. Some were inner city, and some were predominantly Latin or black. The majority were in the United States, but many were Canadian. The message to be communicated was that of the Believers' Church, featuring the lordship of Christ, adult commitment of faith, and a life of discipleship.[11]

The editorial committee decided that the curriculum must be centered in the Believers' Church understanding of the Bible, interesting to youth, simply written, relatively unsophisticated, and easily taught. Black and Latin representatives were asked to sit on the editorial council to promote their points of view. The committee was regularly reminded of what the teacher of a class in one rural church said: "Don't tell me to break the class into buzz groups, set up a learning center, or use a film strip. We have only two young people, and we don't have a film projector. Just give us some good questions to discuss."

The comprehensive objective of the Foundation Curriculum had already been established: "to encourage persons to live in response to the creating God, the redeeming Christ, and the sustaining Spirit, so that they and others may participate in the mission of God in the world as the particular people they have been and are."[12] The purpose of the youth curriculum was formulated as follows: "to provide educational materials containing information, methods and resources which will facilitate a continuing exploration of the teachings of Scripture and an examination of the beliefs of the Christian faith and the particular emphasis of the Anabaptist tradition. The curriculum will promote a supportive context in the midst of the congregation within which youth can discuss opportunities and problems facing them at their stage of growth and place in life, so that youth may commit their way to Jesus Christ as Saviour and Lord and to the church as the people of God."[13]

The second decision was that of *curriculum concept*, or what Wyckoff called scope.[14] A number of considerations influenced the committee: continuity with themes in the children's curriculum, the study of Scripture, basic theological beliefs, and issues facing youth. Admittedly, these latter three concerns are interdependent.

The committee spent much time outlining possible units. Here is a partial list of their topics:

I. Biblical Studies
A. The making of the Bible
B. Survey of the Bible's literature
C. Twelve book studies

II. Examining Our Beliefs
A. Basic beliefs
B. Peacemaking
C. Becoming a Christian
D. Believers' baptism

III. Living in Today's World
A. Christian life-style
B. Sharing the good news
C. Making choices
D. Vocational decision making

The third decision was that of *learning tasks.* To choose appropriate learning strategies, a group of representative youth and teachers from the cooperating denominations were called together in a conference. They considered together the theology of the Believers' Church, differences of belief among the cooperating denominations, the developmental and spiritual interests of youth, models of learning amenable to the Believers' Church, the variety of local contexts within which youth live, and interesting and appropriate activities and media. The conference developed a list of possible teaching strategies, including bibliodrama, brainstorming, and case method. They listed dozens of learning activities and media. These lists were then made available to curriculum writers.

By the end of the conference of youth and teachers, the editorial committee arrived at a fourth decision. The *organizing principle* established was to develop learning activities and relationships that would draw youth into the life and practice of the local congregation, encouraging them to a commitment to Christ as Lord and to the way of discipleship. Current learning theory and developmental descriptions of youth were accepted. The relationship between particular doctrines like discipleship or peace and learning activities within congregational life was also accepted.[15]

A fifth decision concerned the *format* of curricular materials. A set of topics was outlined for a four-year cycle. The decision was made to have printed materials with much artwork and with supplementary songs, folders, posters, buttons, pennants, etc. Furthermore, it was decided to let the printed material for each quarter be a different format. One might be a pocket-sized book; another, a newspaper format; still another, a magazine, etc. The intention was to have enough variety and additional resource materials to keep youth interested. By way of contrast, the teacher's guide for every unit was to be of uniform size and format.

The decision to adopt a four-year cycle was a difficult one. Developmental studies suggest a great difference between thirteen-year-olds and seventeen-year-olds. If the material is written for the younger group, it may be uninteresting to older youth, and vice versa. The publishing council made it clear that a two-year cycle would be too expensive. The editorial council therefore instructed writers to include suggestions and adaptations for both younger and older youth.

The sixth set of decisions regarded *content and style.* The lesson format was assumed to be for a forty to fifty minute session. The lesson writer was to introduce the topic, give background information, suggest resources for further study, and set forth the objectives for the lesson. Next, the writer was to give specific steps for each lesson, indicating their relationship to the objectives. Alternate suggestions were to be offered for different ages or different contexts, perhaps even an alternate lesson plan might be offered. Suggestions for evaluating the lesson and for preparing for the next lesson were to be given.

Writers were to remain aware of denominational and racial differences. Materials were to have an international character, not assuming that America means United States when Canada and Latin America are also a part of America. Writers were to keep rural-urban differences in mind and to remember that readers are both male and female. Judaism was never to be depreciated. Writers were to be sensitive about the overuse of male language in reference to God. References to family were to keep the variety of households in mind, especially singles and single parent families.

The biggest task of the editorial council regarding content was to produce writer outlines. One was produced for each unit, which included a synopsis of the total unit's content, content suggestions for each session, statements about the significance of the unit for young people, a list of intended learner outcomes, and recommendations for learning experiences. The book of writer outlines set the stage for finding writers.

A seventh decision regarded the *production of materials*. Writers were chosen who could communicate with youth and who represented the various points of view of the denominations. Each writer was to have three consultants: a high school youth, a teacher or leader of youth, and a person from a denomination other than that of the writer. The mechanics of setting deadlines and finding substitute writers for those who could not complete assignments took time. The writers were to write students' and teachers' materials as well as suggesting other media for their units. The completed manuscripts were then edited by the professional editors of each denomination and reviewed by at least one editorial council member from a denomination other than that of the writer and the editor.

An eighth and final decision involved *marketing the materials* and supporting their use. Fliers were developed with colorful diagrams and vivid prose to introduce the curricular materials to the churches. A set of lessons was written as a teacher instruction manual. A series of workshops were set up to explain the curriculum in various districts of the churches, and plans were made to translate the materials into Spanish for Latin churches.

This case study is intended to show the complexity of producing curricular materials. Normal lead time for producing a new curriculum can be as much as ten years. The lead time breaks down as follows:

2 years to assess need and plan the curriculum concept

2 years to produce writer outlines and select writers
2 years to write
2 years for revision and editing
1 year to begin publishing
1 year to promote and allow users to order materials

Production of curricular materials requires great expense and effort, and the writing usually lags several years behind current issues and events. Nevertheless some similar process is used to produce most curricular materials for religious education.

LOCAL CURRICULUM PLANNING AND EVALUATION

Any group attempting to choose a set of curricular resources will have some set of selection criteria. If these criteria are not made explicit, they will operate implicitly. Any list of criteria will reflect the chooser's point of view, for there can be no wholly objective choice of curriculum. Many congregations choose their own curricula, and many use a "mix and match" approach.

One helpful curriculum evaluation guide is published by the Evangelical Covenant Church.[16] The guide suggests many evaluation categories: What are the basic costs and will they fit your budget? Do the materials cover Christmas, Easter, the Old Testament, the New Testament, church history, and the church today? Are the lessons grouped around a common theme? In addition, the user should consider the method of biblical interpretation, the way mission is treated, the educational philosophy, teaching methods, ease of use, the degree of family involvement, aesthetics, and level of social concern. Individual churches may have other questions they want to ask.

A set of questions derived from considerations in this book might include the following:

1. What is the theological perspective? Is the theology more oriented to propositions, stories, or relationships?
2. How does the biblical interpretation handle the analogy between the biblical community of then and now?
3. Are the beliefs and traditions of Christians and others considered within their historical context?
4. How are worship, the life of the faith community, and education related?
5. Is personal growth considered to occur in stages, as part of a life journey, or otherwise?
6. What is the relationship between the gospel, evangelism, and contemporary injustice? Is public expression of faith encouraged?
7. Are the stories of minority cultural groups included? Is language inclusive of male and female?
8. Is conflict creatively addressed?
9. What learning theory is assumed? Does the learning theory spring from active social interaction and praxis or is it primarily cognitive?
10. Are persons encouraged to converse, dialog, and discover their own meaning, or are they given the answers?

This list of questions could be expanded a great deal. It reflects considerations discussed in previous chapters, which may not be present in other lists of evaluative criteria.

The Joint Educational Development approach encourages local congregations to be involved in curriculum planning and evaluation. Iris Cully believes that the initiative of local congregations is a major trend in curriculum development.[17] Local planning allows for the life of a congregation to be taken into account in a way that cannot be done by nationally produced curricular resources.

According to the Joint Educational Development approach, a local congregation should have a curriculum planning and evaluation committee. The committee should attempt to keep the demands of the gospel in touch with the people's needs and their social situations, both locally and worldwide. The committee develops educational goals according to the local congregation's theological and educational assumptions. A variety of educational settings are identified and educational objectives are written for each. For example, one setting is the membership class. The objective there might be to understand and appreciate the beliefs of the church, and to be willing to confess one's faith publicly. The committee considers its assumptions about leadership, and then enlists, trains, and supports leaders as needed. Finally, the committee chooses material resources for teaching fitted to identified needs.

Congregations that take the Joint Educational Development suggestions for local planning seriously may select from a whole variety of available curriculum resources according to their own interests. They are no longer bound to the single set of materials recommended by their denomination. Congregations may also create their own curriculum; for instance, a local committee may use sermon topics to create experiences for a Wednesday evening group. Such serious planning is being done by many congregations.[18]

Local planning allows for a wide variety of resources, with the major resource being the life and worship of the community of faith. Local planning can feature different members and activities of the congregation. The prayer book, hymnals, and other worship resources can be a part of the curriculum. A wide variety of media are available for those who look.[19] Decentralization of curriculum, local initiative, and planning give new power to curriculum in the faith community.

CURRICULUM EXPERIMENTS

Some years ago, Paul Freire conducted an influential curriculum experiment in Brazil. His account of this experiment is a major source of the praxis theory of learning discussed in earlier chapters. Working to teach illiterate peasants to read and write, Freire began by bringing a team of educators and social scientists to live in a local community. After studying the lives of the illiterate peasants over a period of years, they noted common themes, which they called "generative themes." Freire observed that all the generative themes were related in one way or another to the oppression of the poor. Their small huts, lack of education, long hours of work, drunkenness, poor clothing, lack of plumbing, low social status, and general poverty were all related to their being oppressed.[20]

The next step was to find symbols encoding these generative themes. A symbol code would allow them to see their situation objectively, thereby raising their consciousness about their condition. Photographs of people were chosen to illustrate generative themes. Symbols showing the contrast of rich and poor were used. For example, a picture of a hut was set beside that of a mansion. Students were then given the word for their own huts and the word for the landowner's mansion. So the awareness of oppression came at the same time the students learned the language.

310

The teaching procedure was to let the coded symbols be the occasion for discussion among the people. Rather than being told what proper reading is, the people were to discover how to read by seeing the words for hut and mansion and discussing together the meaning of both these words and their situation. Learning became a matter of decoding the symbols in order to discover the underlying generative themes. The learners formed a community of concern around their plight. Far from being competitive, learning was cooperative; instead of being graded, they encouraged one another. The competitive status orientation of most of Western society was not assumed by Freire. The relation of politics and reading became clear as the people began to inquire into the political conditions of their poverty.[21]

Freire's method caused great controversy because it was seen as political agitation. He was jailed and finally banished. He has, however, continued to use his methods in other parts of the world. Efforts to import Freire's methods to the United States have largely failed.[22] American churches quickly try to turn liberation into a program or curriculum, rather than actually changing their way of life.

The challenge to curriculum is to recover the authenticity of local worship and practice for learning the Christian story. Let dialog be in relation to what is actually done and in relation to the poverty of the world. The challenge is to let decisions about lifestyle be the setting of learning. Local groups can find or create materials that symbolize their own oppression or that of many people around the world. The challenge is to live in the power of the coming of God's kingdom.

HERMENEUTICAL INTERACTION

The thrust of this chapter is to recover the broadest meaning of curriculum as the total set of community relationships and interactions within which learning takes place. The worshiping community in its life and practice *is* the teacher and the curriculum. The idea of curriculum presumes direct planning and action. One may speak of the hidden curriculum as unplanned experiences that teach. Religious educators have long known how powerful the community is as teacher. Because the community seems too unwieldy, they have taken up the more practical task of creating centralized printed curriculum.

In this decade, congregations are turning to their own resources. Centralized curriculum has in its very structure reflected the high level of organization of modern Western society. Local congregations can regain their sense of decision, commitment, and vocation, but they must begin in their own life commitments. Then, worship and common practices become the occasion to consider mission, outreach, and justice, and their questions of mission come to grips with what can actually be done. Study groups begin to contribute to the worship, life, and mission of the church, rather than simply discussing them. Curriculum becomes an interaction of story, community practice, commitment, environing events, and circumstances.

What is needed is a curriculum theory that is ecumenical, global, public, praxis oriented, shalom directed, and vocation related. We need a curriculum theory that allows for local creation, but transcends local bias and oppression. It should be ecumenical without being coercive. It should use appropriate technology without wasting resources. It would allow local theologies to be expressed without losing the story of God's redemption in Jesus Christ.

We live in a day when there is loss of community, confusion of identity, lack of vocation, anticipation of imminent destruction, worldwide poverty, squandering of resources, mass manipulation, worship of consumption, despair, and alienation from God. In such a day congregations may carry a sense of God's power and Christ's presence, an ecumenical vision in touch with local tradition, a conviction about public issues, a dialog with actual praxis, a global consciousness, a search for an attitude of peace, a sense of vocation, and an effort to rid the world of injustice. Perhaps the term curriculum is too slender to carry such a vision.

CURRICULUM RESOURCES

A wide variety of curriculum resource materials are currently available for churches. The four perspectives of Joint Educational Development were mentioned above. The following list of some other available resources is based upon Carol Wehrheim, ed., *Guide to Curriculum Choice* (Elgin, Ill.: Brethren Press, 1981). For a more complete list, consult the Cully volume mentioned below.

The Bible-In-Life Curriculum (Elgin, Ill.: D. C. Cook).
Materials are Bible-centered, life-related, and developmentally based. Study for nursery through adulthood is unified around the same themes.

The Bible Way Curriculum (Grand Rapids, Mich.: Christian Reformed Church).
Features Bible study from a reformed perspective for ages three through adult.

Centerquest Curriculum (St. Louis, Mo.: The Education Center).
Interweaves biblical and classical literary material to serve as a guide for a person's life journey toward meaning. Available for kindergarten through adulthood.

Gospel Light Living Word Curriculum (Ventura, Calif.: Gospel Light Publications).

Bible-centered, evangelistic, and church growth oriented. Undated materials are available from infancy through adulthood.

Great Commission Publications (Philadelphia, Pa.: Great Commission Publications).
Sponsored by the Orthodox Presbyterian Church and the Presbyterian Church in America, and based on the view that Christian education is for evangelism and personal commitment. Materials are available for preschoolers through adults.

Joy Series (Minneapolis, Minn.: Winston Press).
Presents religion "as a personal, joyful experience, a part of everyday life," without reference to denominational creed and tradition. Available for preschool through high school.

Lutheran Church in America Curriculum (Philadelphia, Pa.: The Lutheran Church in America).
Aims at helping persons respond to God's continuing activity as they cope with life involvements. Closely graded from age three through adults.

Scripture Press Curriculum (Wheaton, Ill.: Scripture Press).
Very Bible-centered, aimed at personal salvation, and organized around age-level needs. Departmentally graded, and includes resources for both children's church and weekday Christian schools in addition to Sunday church schools.

Southern Baptist Life and Work (Nashville, Tenn.: The Southern Baptist Convention).
Useful for studying and interpreting the Bible in relation to the life and work of Southern Baptist churches. Materials are available for youth and adults.

Standard Curriculum (Cincinnati, Ohio: Standard Publishing)
Aims at Bible knowledge and personal commitment to Christ. For toddlers through adults. Early grades are based on two-year cycles and later grades on three-year cycles.

United Methodist Curriculum (Nashville, Tenn.: The United Methodist Church).
Influenced by the Cooperative Curriculum Project design; features the relationship of Bible and life, paying careful attention to human development.

Paulist Press, Ramsey, N.J.; William H. Sadlier, Inc., N.Y.; and Silver Burdette, Morristown, N.J., offer graded materials from a Roman Catholic theological perspective.

STUDY SUGGESTIONS

Exercises

1. Interview a number of church school teachers to find out what they understand "curriculum" to mean. Ask them about the strengths and limitations of the curriculum they use.
2. Take a curriculum you are familiar with and analyze it according to Wyckoff's categories: objective, scope, learning tasks, organizing principle, content, and materials. Summarize your discoveries.
3. In the library try to find religious education materials that were written prior to the Civil War. Compare those materials with materials used today. How would you characterize the differences?

4. Compare *The New England Primer* or the McGuffey readers with modern primers and readers. How are religious and moral teaching treated? What changes do you see?

5. Set up a debate between those who believe that the church school is a significant factor in changing the social values of participants and those who believe that the church school simply confirms the prevailing social values.

6. Use the story of the Foundation Youth Curriculum, to be found under the heading *Curriculum Preparation*, to do a simulation. Set yourselves up as the editorial council. Consider any one of the eight decisions listed in the case. Come to your own conclusion about what that decision ought to be. Discuss more than one decision if there is time.

7. Using one of the curricula listed in this chapter, evaluate it according to the questions listed on page 308. If there are several of you, divide the questions among yourselves. If there are many of you, compare different levels of the curriculum you are evaluating.

8. Using the suggestions of this chapter create a curriculum plan for your own local congregation. You may want to limit the task by planning one educational setting or one event.

9. Use Paulo Freire's method of codifying a generative theme of a group you are a part of or that you teach. You may want to take photographs that contrast their situations and the situation of others, develop drawings, or make tape recordings of actual situations. Use these to recover the generative themes during your discussion. What is your assessment of Freire's method?

Questions for Discussion

1. What gains and/or losses come from considering curricula to be the total set of relationships, life, and practice of a congregation?
2. Compare local and centralized curricula in terms of advantages and limitations.
3. Compare the assertion, "What you would have in the life of a people you must first put into its schools," with the statement, "What you would effectively train the new generation in you must first find in the aspiration and commitment of a people."
4. How does public instruction from *The New England Primer* compare with public primary instruction today?
5. What curricular trends from the nineteenth-century Sunday school movement have continued through the twentieth century?
6. What effect did the neo-orthodox movement have on church school curricula?
7. What are the moderate and radical criticisms of mid-twentieth-century church school curriculum trends?
8. What must a congregation consider in choosing a curricular approach?
9. To what extent can Paulo Freire's curricular approach be used in nations other than Brazil?
10. What curricular resources are available to churches?

Suggestions for Further Reading

Iris V. Cully, *Planning and Selecting Curriculum for Christian Education.*

317

Cully's is the most complete recent survey of curriculum planning.

Evangelical Covenant Church of America, *Curriculum Evaluation: Measuring the Material.*
This is an excellent tool to help congregations evaluate curricular materials.

Shirley J. Heckman and Iris L. Ferren, *Creating the Congregation's Educational Ministry.*
Heckman and Ferren have produced a brief manual to help local churches create their own curriculum.

Carol Wehrheim, ed., *Guide to Curriculum Choice.*
Wehrheim has edited a set of standardized evaluations of many different curricular materials available to churches.

D. Campbell Wyckoff, *Theory and Design of Christian Education Curriculum.*
This is an old reference, but still the standard work.

Chapter Twelve:

ORGANIZING FOR LEARNING

Just as the community is the context of teaching and of curriculum, so also is the community the context of organization and administration. The local faith community, its ongoing story interacting with that of the global community, is the locus of the coming of the kingdom of God. Here is the place where planning, purpose, strategy, leadership, and administration for learning occur. Some settings for teaching reach beyond a local community of faith, such as retreats, conferences, camping, and higher education. But such settings are still subject to dynamics similar to those of the local community of faith.

Local communities are affected by environmental circumstances, regional and national attitudes, patterns of customary practices, forms of organization, and modes of leadership. Such social and historical factors interact with local commitments in an ongoing story. To the extent that personal commitments are extended beyond self-centered interests, local community commitments reach toward the formation of a global community, and persons and communities are graced by the living center of life, to such an extent that they experience the power of the kingdom of God. The purpose of the present chapter is to examine the influence of the sociohistorical context on administration, organization, and the leading of religious education.

THE ORGANIZATIONAL STORY

The New Testament meaning of organization is the building up of the body of Christ. The apostle Paul says, "And his gifts were that some should be apostles, some prophets, some evangelists, some pastors and teachers, to equip the saints for the work of ministry, for building up the body of Christ" (Ephesians 4:11-12 RSV). For Paul, the body of Christ is an organization that has singleness of purpose and commitment, multiplicity of function, and freedom for maturation, which is also a powerful description of the characteristics of an organization. Teaching is one of the "works of ministry" that belongs in a properly functioning organization.

Questions of purpose, strategy, leadership, and administration are closely related to how learning occurs within a given community. Furthermore, the organizational dimension of a community is not alien to ministry functions like teaching. The popular view that spirit touches reality while form alienates tends to depreciate interest in questions of organization.[1] Karl Barth is critical of the docetic tendency to separate "the Holy Spirit and the upbuilding of the Christian community" into spirit and form in this way.[2] According to New Testament teaching, form and spirit belong to one another in the image of the body. So the "works of ministry" bind teaching to the organizational form and leadership of the community.

The Reformation had a dramatic effect upon the modern concept of organization. In the medieval world the "body of Christ" meant that secular organizations found their fulfillment and completion in the church. All of society was within the body of Christ *(Corpus Christianum)*. Martin Luther wounded the religious hierarchy of organization. For Luther all organizations including the church are at once sacred and secular. The church does not fulfill or complete a secular organization. The church is a witness to the power and grace of God in all life. The church is to fulfill its religious purposes and secular organizations are to fulfill their secular purposes. Thereby, Luther gave a kind of legitimation to secular organizations.

Calvinism added a new element to organization. Calvin saw the church as a gathered body of believers acting out God's predestined purpose of organizing all life for the kingdom. The idea of a group of people organized around a mission to transform the world in some particular respect gave birth to the modern concept of organization. A modern corporation is a group of persons functionally related in order to achieve a given mission or objective. Where the medieval organization was governed by custom and tradition, the modern organization is rationally organized around specific purposes and objectives. Max Weber developed this thesis in his work.[3]

The colonies of pre-revolutionary America were organized in different ways reflecting religious traditions from Anglican to Separatist. The American Constitution attempted to allow these different organizations to live beside one another. Methodist revivalism had a dramatic effect upon the organization of the American frontier. Methodism combined elements of formal Episcopal church structure with charismatic power. Groups like the Anabaptists and the Friends influenced American concepts of radical equality. In these groups, all decisions require consensus and anyone can correct a sister or brother.

The Sunday school movement also affected the organization of churches. In their origin, Sunday schools were an independent, predominantly lay movement. Often Union Sunday schools were begun first, and worship services were added later. The Sunday school superintendent, teachers, and students formed their own organization, and the worshiping church had a parallel and largely independent organization. In spite of the fact that the Sunday school has become the church school, the pattern of separation continues in many congregations. In an effort to integrate the church school some churches give the leadership of nurture and worship to the same committee. Even so, the two activities tend to continue in parallel but separate directions. John Westerhoff's proposal to drop the church school may be seen as an effort to locate education centrally in the church.[4]

THE ORGANIZATIONAL DEBATE

Modern social science theories of organization and management have had a powerful effect on many churches. These theories propose that organizations are structured around goals and objectives. An organization gains power as it clarifies its objectives, structures itself to achieve those objectives, mobilizes resources, and constantly monitors results to see whether objectives are being accomplished.[5] Modern management theory speaks of management by objectives. Ironically, critics of management by objectives say that the church is being taken over by a secular business concept when historically the idea developed from the Reformed concept of mission.[6]

The Hawthorn experiments of the 1930s focused attention on group dynamics in organizations. The studies seemed to demonstrate that worker productivity is more influenced by the attitudes of fellow workers than by job incentives.[7] A person who lifts the job standard by working too hard will be criticized by fellow workers. That criticism adversely affects output much more than work incentives increase it. Churches have been influenced by these findings to employ group dynamics as a way of understanding apathy, lack of commitment, and poor teaching.

A strong advocate of the power of primary groups in the church is Carl Dudley.[8] He argues that small churches are single-celled groups of persons with primary relationships. The power of that relationship is greater than any formal structure. In their many associations people remember and extend the ongoing story; they "mend the nets." They want a lover rather than an organizer for a pastor. So Dudley argues for the power of relationship over structure; his argument applies equally well to education in the congregation.

More recently, structuralists have been critical of both goal theories and human relation theories of management.[9] Both try to eliminate conflict in an organization. Structuralists point out that human relations management can be as manipulative as goal-directed management. They believe that since conflict is inevitable, there will be no perfect fit between goals and relationship in an organization. Furthermore, individuals will interpret the situation from their own interests, and the organization will serve its own social interest. Because creativity comes from conflict, management should seek to let conflict be creative rather than eliminate it.

Churches have been much influenced by structuralists.[10] Many churches had sought to eliminate all conflict, but more recently conflict has been seen as a sign of vitality, so long as it does not become destructive. Educators are also emphasizing the significance of conflict.[11] Educational management in the church requires facing rather than running from conflict.

Most theories of educational management place high priority on goals and objectives, but many effective educational programs in congregations are just as concerned about friendship and conflict.[12] From a sociohistorical point of view, structure, goals, objectives, primary relationships, and conflict are all highly important, but they will vary according to social circumstances and the unfolding story. A congregation that wants to renew its educational program might well begin with goals and move to structure. Yet some problems will not be resolved by attending to goals unless basic conflicts within the congregation are also attended to, and only awareness of the actual situation can answer the question of which of these two is more significant. Goals or structures must be interpreted in the context of the ongoing story.

EDUCATIONAL PLANNING AND RESEARCH

All religious education involves some degree of planning; otherwise the learning process is without intention. Planning does not imply a total plan or detailed scheme. The book of Deuteronomy suggests that certain practices be followed so that when children ask about them, adults can relate the story (Deuteronomy 6:20 ff.). In Deuteronomy the teaching of the Lord's words to children means to "talk of them when you sit in your house, and when you walk by the way, and when you lie down, and when you rise" (Deuteronomy 6:7 RSV). This is hardly a total or formal plan, but it is certainly intentional. So education always involves some degree of wider vision, purpose, or procedure, i.e., some planning.

The rise of religious schooling and instructional materials has given teachers and students procedures to

follow. Graded, centralized curricula offer detailed instructional procedures. Pragmatic discovery learning
theory places more emphasis on creativity and spontane-
ity, usually within concern about precise objectives. With
centralized curricular materials, congregational planning
is primarily concerned about the question of which
materials to use. The planning may consist only of the
committee's decision to adopt one set of materials rather
than another.

However, many teachers prefer to choose their own
materials. The result is that curricular materials are being
mixed and matched, as was said in the last chapter.
Denominations sometimes offer guidance on how that
process of choosing can be done.[13] Many congregations
plan a series of elective courses to supplement the
centralized curriculum.

An alternative to adopting a standard curriculum or to
letting teachers choose their own materials is for the
congregation to create its own educational plan. One
approach is that suggested by Heckman and Ferren,[14] in
which the congregation establishes a planning and
evaluation process.

The planning and evaluating committee attempts to
keep in touch with the vision, commitment, and goals of
the people in the congregation. From their research they
establish a basic design for education in the congregation.
Then they decide on teaching/learning opportunities,
leader development/support, and material resources. The
committee continues to evaluate what happens. It may
decide that concern about world hunger means that an
intergenerational event on world hunger should be
developed for Thanksgiving. They create the event, find
leadership, and evaluate what happens. The planning and
evaluation committee works to maintain an ongoing and

individualized design for religious education uniquely suited to particular congregational needs.

John Westerhoff's suggestion about educational planning moves in the same direction of encouraging congregations to develop their own theology and program of education. However, Westerhoff recommends that planning be done around worship and celebrative events, where in his view the most powerful education takes place. Thereby the segmentation of the schooling model may be overcome. Westerhoff's suggestions are not intrinsically contradictory to schooling. A congregation might very well mix and match the recommendations of both Westerhoff and Heckman and Ferren.

Another approach to planning comes from the church growth movement and people like Carl Dudley, Robert Worley, and James Hopewell.[15] They advise carrying out a careful study of congregational life within the wider community. Look at the sociological data of the community, which can be found by asking for census data at the local library and by interviewing local leaders. Study the congregation's constitution and policies, comparing them with what actually happens. Why are procedures followed or not followed? Study the care people give one another and the mood or climate of the congregation. Look at the way the congregation is organized and trace the primary communication patterns. What is the leadership style and how is leadership supported? What does life in the congregation mean to individual members? Who participates and why? What is the role of the pastor? What are the pastor's primary experiences and skills? What is the story of this congregation?[16]

One can trace the story of a congregation by reading documents and talking to those who know it. The story may be reconstructed in relation to the primary events in the life of the congregation. When was, or is, or will be the golden period? James Hopewell has suggested that after the story has been described, it should be analyzed according to the classic literary categories of comedy, tragedy, romance, and irony.[17] A church in a changing community that knows it must close within a decade is living out a tragic narrative. A church that does not expect self-sacrifice because all persons act from self-interest lives in an ironic narrative. A church suffering great difficulties, but with admiration for the pastor, lives in a romance. A church constantly expecting difficulties to be soon overcome lives in a comedy. The narrative story of a church will have dramatic impact upon all of its ministry, including its educational ministry.

THEOLOGY AND PURPOSE

An institution is shaped around an ongoing narrative, and in the center of a narrative is a purpose or direction. Classical management theory requires a precise objective, but an objective is always embedded within a narrative. A narrative without a direction or purpose lacks coherence. A congregation's stated purpose and its actual function or task may be quite different. The actual task of a congregation may be studied by asking knowledgable persons inside and outside the congregation, and then comparing their answers to stated purposes.[18]

The purposes of an organization shift as time passes, and often other purposes take their place. A church may be established to minister to an ethnic group, such as Hungarians. When the Hungarians are replaced by another group, the church's purpose must shift. Goals also proliferate. The church may find that a Sunday school leads to a day care center. Every institution must struggle with a shift of purpose and with proliferation versus centeredness of purpose. The loss of purpose is a loss of power.[19]

Institutions are caught between effectiveness and efficiency. Effectiveness is a function of purpose because it can be judged only in view of purpose. Efficiency is a function of resources; use of fewer resources to achieve the same purpose is more efficient. An educational program may become more efficient by ordering less expensive curricular materials and by beginning fifteen minutes later. But, if there is also a loss of effectiveness, nothing may have been gained.

A primary struggle in Christian education has been between the purposes of nurture and evangelism. The goal of nurture is spiritual maturity. The goal of evangelism is church growth or personal salvation. Our contention is that church evangelism and nurture take place within a social process and an ongoing story of God's kingdom. In recovering its story the church must also clarify its educational purpose.

A Community Congregational Church clarified its purpose in these words: "We believe that Christian Education is the opportunity for opening life, where one would learn about God and about his church, would grow in faith, would learn to live with others, would experience Christian fellowship, and would, with self-awareness, become a responsible Christian who effectively responds to and participates in the world."[20] Each phrase was then expanded. "Learn about God" was expanded to becoming familiar (1) with the Bible, (2) with Jesus, (3) to experiencing a relationship with God, (4) to becoming acquainted with world religions, and (5) to participating in organized religion. Other phrases were expanded in a similar way. The statement reflected the beliefs of many persons in the congregation by the time it was adopted.

A goal or purpose is not something that is finished and complete. Rather, goals open the way for the next step.

328

Reviewing goals is a part of an ongoing narrative that opens as the journey continues. The purpose therefore needs reformulation. The larger story of God's purpose is to be found in the Bible and church history. The study of Scripture informs the discernment of purpose. Such a view recasts the strict view of management by objectives without casting out the whole concept.

STRUCTURE

Every group is structured by its relationships of power and influence. The formal structure consists of the roles of membership, the committees and offices, and the public whom the group addresses, along with the rules and responsibilities that shape those various relationships. The informal structure is the pattern of relationships of power and influence that are not part of official committees and positions. The informal structure has to do with the norms of common practice, the friendships and relationships by which information and influence are transferred.

Formal church structures are determined largely by historical church tradition. An episcopal pattern is hierarchical, with bishops, priests, deacons, and laity related to one another in descending order of power and influence. In a congregational pattern each person's voice is equal, so that everyone is related horizontally. In a presbyterian structure the presbytery governs the session and the session governs the laity. Each of these formal structures has a different pattern of power and influence.

The informal structure may be so powerful that it greatly modifies formal power. For example, a bishop in an episcopal system has authority to appoint or withdraw a priest from any parish. However, the bishop may consider that working through the consensus of the congregation is only good administrative practice. It is difficult to distinguish such an administrative style from a congregational pattern. On the other hand a given person of great influence and power in a congregational pattern may be able to dictate what will be decided. A congregational pattern with a person of great power may be difficult to distinguish from an episcopal pattern.

Educational patterns also differ from one church structure to another. An Episcopal or Catholic bishop has authority over what is taught. When the American Roman Catholic bishops issue a formal letter on peace and justice, it is authoritative and must be taught to the laity. Presbyterian and synodal (Lutheran) decisions also have great authority. Congregational polity allows congregations and groups much latitude in what is taught.

The relationship of structure and education helps one to understand why James Michael Lee is so insistent in showing the independence of educational method within religious education. Lee is Roman Catholic and he feels that episcopal authority tends to smother good teaching practice. In Protestantism's less centralized authority, many Protestant groups are more interested in a theological basis for educational practice.[21]

The separate structure of the church school and the worshiping congregation in many churches may dramatically affect education and nurture, even when the church school understands itself as evangelist and trainer for church membership.[22] One staff member may serve as pastor and the other as director of religious education. However the relationship can be structured otherwise. Some multiple staffs share both worship and educational responsibilities.

Robert Worley points out that communication patterns have a considerable effect upon organizational structure.[23]

If one person, e.g., the secretary, is the center of all information, then that person has great power. If all communication occurs within separate committees, the effect will be quite different than when there is open communication between all members of a group.

Administration requires careful consideration of the responsibilities of a working group. Teachers, students, and committees need to know their place within the overall structure. They need to share the purpose and vision of the larger group. Administration also requires consideration of communication patterns. Open communication should lead to greater creativity.

STRATEGY AND SETTINGS

The primary educational strategy of many Christian churches has been the church school. Catholics, Lutherans, and others have set up weekday parochial schools where religious influence can pervade the whole school life. Most Protestants have embraced the church school. Western Europe for the most part has religious instruction in the public school. Some religious groups have resisted schooling and depended upon the informal relationships of family and community ethos to enculturate people to the religious tradition.

Other educational strategies besides those just mentioned are movement education and contextual education. Both of these are much more active and engaging than is traditional schooling. Movement education seeks to engender commitment to a vision or program beyond traditional institutional loyalties.[24] For example the peace and justice movement and the right-to-life movement enlist the loyalty of people from many traditions. Movement education usually develops workshops, retreats, or rallies. At these events much time is given to studying and becoming familiar with particular issues.

Persons who have direct experience or who have been oppressed address everyone. The aim is to spread loyalty to the cause espoused by the movement. The liberation movement of the twentieth century parallels the emancipation movement of the nineteenth century.

Contextual education is also much more directly engaging than is traditional classroom teaching. Contextual learning takes place in the actual setting where an activity is done. Contextual education goes beyond field trips, which are on-site visits. Rather, contextual education puts persons into the activities themselves. Volunteers study about the conditions of poverty as they actually work with the poor. One learns about evangelism as one reaches out to evangelize other persons.

Receiving increasing attention is the strategy of *paideia*, a Greek word referring to the fundamental cultural values toward which all education aims. The aim of paideia is to influence the fundamental values of a culture. Such influence requires joining hands with those who share common values and compromising for the sake of wider influence. The strategy is to form alliances with other groups in the public debate by which common values are developed.[25]

Organizing for education involves a choice about settings, i.e., a choice about the particular time, place, persons, and occasion. Heckman and Ferren list the following educational settings for a congregation: church school, family cluster, vacation church school, education/action groups, membership classes, leadership development classes, and fellowship groups. Denominations and other publishers offer curricular materials for each of these settings.

Beyond those just listed might be added the following: contextual groups, evangelism groups, paideia groups, care groups, camping, conferences, and retreats. Contextual groups engage themselves directly in what they are studying. A study of the effects of warfare on the peasants of Central America means taking a trip to El Salvador and working with the people to harvest their crops. It means speaking to one's congressperson about armaments policies. It means volunteering to do literacy training in the inner city.

Evangelism groups are those dedicated to reaching out to other persons. The natural way of reaching out is through the network of friendships that each person has. A hospitality group in one church decided to invite all church visitors to lunch. From those invitations several new friendships developed.

Paideia groups are willing to join with other community groups for a common community cause and for the debate of public issues. Paideia groups are interested in meeting with other Christian groups to study common public issues. They are also interested in ecumenical events and other public events. They are willing to join statewide and national networks dedicated to public issues.

Care groups are found in many congregations. They may be formally constituted as the deacons or they may be informally constituted for brief periods of time. Care groups are willing to reach out to others in times of crisis or stress. Some hospitals encourage lay visitors to help visit the sick. Groups may be set up to encourage couples who are having marital difficulties. For care groups to be effective, they need to study and practice techniques of active listening. Many persons in a congregation can become skilled at caring if they are willing to commit themselves to the time and effort needed.

Camping is one of the most effective settings for Christian education. The essential character of camping is to leave the many cultural conveniences of affluence and to come more directly into contact with the outdoors,

normally under the leadership of a more experienced
guide. Camping therefore offers a natural setting for
concerns about the environment and ecology. Camping
also offers an occasion to develop a new set of relationships
beyond the normal routines of settled life. Camping also
offers a time to be away from mass media and to engage in
longer, unhurried conversations.

Camping is related to the biblical theme of wilderness.
Israel wandered in the wilderness before adopting a more
settled agricultural existence in the promised land. The
prophets constantly returned to the wilderness to hear the
voice of God again; so Elijah returned to Mount Horeb
when harassed by King Ahab, and John the Baptist
returned to the wilderness to call the people to repentance.
In the wilderness, away from settled routine, people come
again to their basic sense of identity.

Camping offers the occasion for people to confront what
is real and genuine in life. For that reason church camping
continues to be a powerful source of religious education.
Camping can be done with a routine of study, work, and
play, or camping can encompass a wider range of
possibilities, such as mountain climbing, hiking, bicycle
caravans, survival camping, small group camping, and
family camping.

One of the problems of camping is that it tends to pull
people away from the problems of injustice and public
issues. This can be partially overcome by having inner city
work camps, or by inviting minority persons to take part in
a camp. For camping to be effective the theology and
purposes guiding it must be as carefully considered as the
daily routine and activities.

Conferences are often intense educational experiences.
Participation in an annual denominational conference or
an ecumenical conference can revitalize personal commitment and motivation. Conferences have the power

to lift people's vision beyond local issues to more global ones. The administration of conferences also requires careful thought about the theology and purpose of the conference.

Retreats have many of the advantages of camping. They are by definition a withdrawal from normal routine to give time and consideration to a special subject or activity. Often retreats involve a special spiritual discipline. Church educators are becoming interested in spiritual discipline again.[26] The desire to recover spiritual discipline comes from the realization that virtue and character are shaped by worship as much as by action. Virtue and character may contribute more toward the global community than frenetic activity. Whether in retreats or other settings, the spiritual disciplines of meditation, prayer, and silence can be practiced.

Higher education offers a whole group of settings for Christian education, but they are beyond the scope of this discussion, even though story and context affect higher education as much as congregational education. The setting has a dramatic effect upon what is learned, simply because the setting reflects the interplay of purpose and environment. An interactional approach to setting features the relationships between persons in the interplay between purpose and environment. Just as global issues recast the meaning of camping, so they recast every setting. Settings are not simply chosen; they are a part of the spirit of the times. Settings are to be discerned, taken up, and given up according to the longer story of God's kingdom.

LEADERSHIP

Leadership is the capacity to move people together toward the accomplishment of commonly accepted purposes.[27] It is an exercise of authority, of which Max Weber has distinguished three classic types: traditional, bureaucratic, and charismatic.[28] To these may be added professional authority.

Traditional authority comes from established customs and patterns; the ministry has a long history of this type of authority. Bureaucratic authority comes from mutually accepted procedures to achieve common purposes. A group may vote to accept a constitution and by-laws that define the way people are to be appointed and what will be done. To receive such appointment is to gain bureaucratic authority. Charismatic authority comes from the personal power of an individual. That person may be able to perform and comprehend better than others, or may simply have the personal power to move others. In every group one or several such natural leaders will emerge. Professional authority comes from having achieved the understanding and level of performance required by a given discipline. Professional authority involves training, levels of performance, knowledge not generally known, and acceptance by others of the profession.

Some pastors operate principally from traditional respect given to them. Others act on the basis of a job description and ability to manage organizations. Some have great winsomeness or personal power to influence others. Some act out of the power of professional training. In fact, most pastors act out of some combination of all four. The same is true of teachers. Teachers have traditional authority, the authority of appointment, some degree of winsomeness, and some degree of professional training.

Leadership was spoken of above as the capacity to move people together toward the accomplishment of commonly accepted purposes. In this definition leadership can be considered the function of one person or of many. If ministry is a kind of leadership, then the apostle Paul speaks of the gifts of ministry being exercised by different persons within a community in order that the whole community might be built up (Ephesians 4:11-16). To the extent that teaching is leadership, it is also shared within a community.

Leaders have various styles, depending on disposition, training, and experience. Some leaders are primarily task oriented and others primarily relationship oriented. Task oriented leaders insist upon getting the task done even if personal feelings are injured in the process. Relationship oriented leaders prefer to keep a relationship and find a consensus even if the task must be delayed or changed. The same is true of teachers. Some are primarily task oriented, and some primarily relationship oriented.

Churches in North America are voluntary organizations. People of all ages must be invited and encouraged to participate. Leadership arises from the coincidence of people's personal goals and the congregational goals. When people move from simply taking part in the church to accepting responsibilities, then their "psychological contract" has deepened.[29] When persons move beyond accepting responsibility to becoming concerned about the mission and direction of the church, then they have formed a "covenant." When concern about mission is rooted in devotion to the grace of God in Christ, then the covenant has deepened.

Nourishing leadership in the church requires attending to the natural abilities of persons as well as their deepening motivation. Within a voluntary organization motivation is a function of intrinsic interest, feeling included, open communication, clarity of responsibility, and community support. Leadership in the church has these same qualities. Finding teachers for a church school, like finding leaders, means searching for those who have some interest, inviting them to teach, and helping them feel wanted. They are more likely to feel wanted if there is free and open communication, a clear assignment for a definite time, supportive training, supportive materials, supportive procedures, and recognition for service done.

The changing social structure of the twentieth century has resulted in more employed persons and more competing leisure-time activities. Consequently leadership in the church is more difficult to find. However, the basic principle of open communication and finding what people want and need, along with the other principles just named, are effective ways to motivate people.

ADMINISTRATION

Management is a primary function in every organization. Some kind of management will occur so long as an organization continues to function. The very word administration includes the word minister, to serve or care for. A minister is one who cares for the affairs of someone else. Administration is the management of the task of ministry. It is caring for the purposes and processes of the church. Educational administration is to care for the purposes and processes of teaching and learning.

The task of administration involves matching resources and purposes by means of structures of responsibility and leadership. Otherwise stated, administration is the management of the relationships between the various functions of an organization. Administration works at both forming a consensus and carrying out that consensus.

The forming of consensus and the management of tasks sometimes conflict within ministry, as within all leadership. Pastors who work at enabling their church members to share ministry functions are on the side of forming consensus. Pastors who take a stand and work to get a task done are on the task management side. Enablement has been popular with many pastors, but task management is often expected by laity. Laity continue to desire what H. Richard Niebuhr's study called "pastoral directors." Human relations and task management are held together with the priority on task management in the concept of pastoral director.[30] More recently the desire for a spiritual guide has come to the fore.[31] Consensus formation, task management, and spiritual direction are all involved in ministry and at times they will be in conflict.[32]

Theories of administration move between goal oriented and situation oriented approaches. Management by objectives is a process of setting specific objectives and organizing to achieve them. Situational management attempts to act out of a changing consensus and the movement of circumstances. Both have their difficulties. The most carefully considered objectives have to be changed according to circumstances. For example, the death of a church leader may dramatically affect stewardship planning, as may also a wave of unemployment.

On the other hand, situational management is even more subject to circumstances. Administration may become simply reactive. If planning time becomes quite short, then the church may be in a constant state of crisis. Situational management can become chaotic.

The alternative is management by goals within the narrative. Amitai Etzioni speaks of this as mixed scanning.[33] Long and short range goals are established, but they are constantly reviewed and adjusted according to changing consensus and circumstances. Etzioni's approach is close to a narrative approach. Goal and objectives are a part of the social setting and the ongoing story. Goals are established, but reviewed according to the changing story. Management can remain purposive without losing touch with circumstances. It should be said that more tradition oriented churches will give primacy to carrying the story and less time to clarifying objectives. Management oriented churches will give primacy to clarifying objectives.

A primary function of administration is to handle conflict. Some styles of administration take conflict immediately to the leading official. The more appropriate method is to have levels of appeal for conflict, always attempting to resolve conflict at the lowest level. The essence of Jethro's advice to Moses was to establish a procedure of appeal, rather than to carry all of the conflict resolution himself (Exodus 18). Jesus gives the same advice in Matthew's Gospel (Matthew 18). If a conflict between persons canot be resolved, let them bring witnesses. If that fails, then go to the higher authority, the church. In both instances the administrative principle is to handle conflict at the most immediate level possible.

Another central task of management is that of supervision. To the extent that persons have assignments to do, those who administer need to know whether the task is being completed. Management is therefore caught in the dilemma of giving people directions and questioning their activities versus letting them proceed on their own. The church is a voluntary association where openness of communication, acceptance of responsibility, clarity of task, supporting procedures, and community recognition are the modes of supervision. Voluntary church school teachers cannot be supervised in the same way as employed public school teachers.

Administration is a way of assisting an organization to find coherence and direction. Managers in the church therefore constantly balance consensus forming, working toward agreed upon goals, and giving spiritual guidance. The administrator is responsible not only to the congregation, but to the denomination and to the wider church. The administrator thinks organizationally and considers what an action means for the structure and purposes of the organization.[34] The realities of an organization within the larger community are set within the power and reality of God's kingdom. In so doing the administrator helps the congregation to give voice to its own commitments.

LEADERSHIP ROLES

Most religious education is carried out by lay people, often relatively untrained lay people. The role of the lay leader is not to be a religious specialist. The contribution of lay leaders is influenced by common goals, relationships between people, and their own spiritual commitment. Clarifying the common goals of a congregation is important, else each leader is likely to proceed according to her or his private goal. Participating in the life of the congregation helps to orient people to common goals, but discussion about educational mission can certainly clarify and sharpen goals.

In local congregations that do their own curriculum planning and evaluation, and in some cases create their own curriculum, lay people should articulate an educational vision and learn the processes of educational design. In the church, consensus and friendship are always a part of the educational process. Larry Richards emphasizes that nothing is more important to teaching the truth of Christ than a genuine friendship with those who learn.[35]

The role of the professional educator in religious education has been changing in response to new visions of the task and social circumstances.[36] Previously, directors of religious education were expected to coordinate and administer the educational program. This involved setting up classes, ordering curricular materials, finding teachers, and otherwise supporting the program.

While such a role continues for many, the director of religious education has increasingly been concerned with

341

the total educational vision of the congregation and all of the educative processes of the church. The educator considers all the age groups in the church, how they are receiving nurture or instruction, and how this relates to the gospel of Christ and to service in the wider community. The professional educator orchestrates the total educational process within and beyond the church.

This total approach has seemed overwhelming to some educators, and so they have begun to specialize in age groups or in educative procedures. Some have formed professional groups that offer specialized educational services to congregations. Some educators from various congregations have banded together so that each could become more specialized, thereby assisting the others. Some become specialized in worship, others in spiritual direction, and still others in age-level characteristics and programs. In criticism of both the total and specialized approaches, some are calling for a return to the ministry of religious catechesis, "which is intended to make men's faith become living, conscious, and active, through the light of instruction."[37]

What is clear from these trends is that unless a congregation clarifies just what it wants from a professional educator, the task is overwhelming. A congregation should be clear about what it wants done, assess resources, and decide whether to employ a professional educator. In negotiating responsibilities with a congregation an educator also should be clear about what she or he wants to do. Clarifying objectives, common practices, and available procedures within the context of the ongoing narrative are critically important.

In many instances the pastor must also serve as educator. Traditionally the pastor has allowed a split between the lay leadership in Christian education and other pastoral functions. This has been true even though the Sunday school was traditionally the evangelist and trainer of the congregation. Sometimes the pastor would give symbolic support to the school by being present. A closer relationship is that of participant, of attending committee meetings and attending teachers' meetings, perhaps teaching a course for teachers. A still closer relationship is that of coordinator, wherein the pastor coordinates and administers the education program, perhaps with the assistance of a lay leader. Closest is the pastor who becomes an educational specialist, perhaps in youth ministry or intergenerational education. The pastor may then take leadership in creating curriculum or encouraging laity to create curriculum.

The most recent challenge is for pastors to adopt the traditional role of catechist. In Lutheran, Reformed, Catholic, and other traditions the minister was responsible for the proper instruction of the people. This may be done with a total educational approach wherein the church's whole program is viewed in relationship to every age group with an eye to how everyone is being nurtured. It may be done by featuring the educative dimension of worship, even to the point of dropping the church school. The catechist has a primary responsibility for total education.

The educational role of the pastor must be determined by the pastor's experience and abilities, the common commitments and practices of the congregation, the ongoing congregational story, special purposes and objectives, resources, and the wider sense of responsibility to the global community. There is no question that the pastor has a primary responsibility for study and for training the people. Equally, the people have a primary responsibility to assist, even to correct the pastor. It is in the renewal of the covenant and in mutual correction that the pastor's role comes alive.

STORY AND CONTEXT

Organization and leadership in the religious community take place within the larger human community's need for God's love and justice. Education can be centralized, highly structured, total, and formal, or it can be decentralized, local, and praxis oriented. Administration is the task of keeping a larger vision without losing touch with a local praxis orientation. The local community can be a humanizing influence for the larger community, as a place where the public is being educated to God's purpose and direction for human life. From a sociohistorical approach to religious education, leadership stands critically within the community discerning and acting in the assurance of God's power to redeem all human life. The pastor has a primary responsibility to see that the teaching of the faith in the congregation is being cared for and administered well, although there are many ways that may be done. The particular educational program will fit the ongoing story of the local community of faith reaching to be responsible to God's global community.

STUDY SUGGESTIONS

Exercises

1. Read the official documents of a congregation to find its statement of purpose. Interview the pastor, leaders of the church, and other persons inside and outside the church to find out what they consider the special task of that congregation to be. How do the stated purposes fit together with the perceived task of the congregation? The same exercise may be carried out for the educational program of the church alone.

2. Interview a number of long-time members, recent members, and youth to determine the most significant customs and common practices within the congregation, beyond its formal program. How do people account for these common practices? What function do they serve in the life of the church? What would happen were these customs to disappear? How is the education program related to the common practices? Are the practices taught formally or informally?

3. Interview the leaders of a congregation to find an example of a time when the fixed goals of the congregation were interrupted by some accidental event, such as a resignation, a death, or a fire. How were the original goals affected by the interruption? How did the leadership of the church respond to the crisis? What have been the long range effects of their responses? What do you observe about the style of leadership?

4. Plan an educational event for the whole congregation. For instance, the event may celebrate something in the life of the congregation, or it may focus on awareness of the role of women in the world. Design the event to give a powerful presentation of the story.

5. Study the congregational rules and procedures as set forth in official documents. Interview people in the church and attend official meetings to discover the extent to which official rules and procedures are followed. Why are or aren't they followed? What effect do the rules and procedures have on communication with the congregation?[38]

6. Divide your group into smaller groups of five persons. Let each group be assigned one of the following communication patterns:

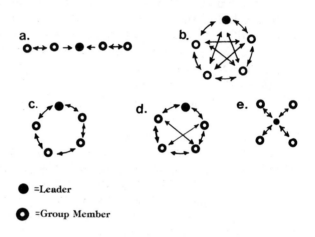

● =Leader

○ =Group Member

Persons may speak to each other only as indicated by the arrows. Designate the top or central person in each group as leader. For forty minutes discuss this question: What is the most significant problem facing this congregation and what is a strategy to meet it? Then bring everyone together to discuss the following questions: Was your group able to come to an agreement? Why or why not? How do you feel about other persons in your group? How did the communication pattern affect the task? How did it affect the leader? Which pattern is most effective?[39]

7. Interview persons in the congregation, including long-time members, to discover the significant events in the life of the congregation. On the basis of the interview formulate the congregational story. Has there been a golden period, or is it still expected? Is the story a comedy, tragedy, romance, or irony, as described in the present chapter?

8. Interview congregational leaders and pastors to formulate a list of the congregation's primary goals. Which are being fulfilled and which are not? What goals have been rejected? How do church leaders handle the tendency of goals to proliferate?

9. The struggle between effectiveness and efficiency often produces a lack of resources for the church educational program. Interview teachers in a religious education program to find out what missing resources are most needed. Then interview the administrator and treasurer to discover why these resources have not been purchased. What do you observe about the way the congregation handles the conflict between effectiveness and efficiency?

10. Interview the nurture commission to discover the official relationship between nurture and evangelism in the congregation. Then interview teachers to discover how they practice nurture and evangelism. What is the relation between the stated policy and the actual practice?

11. Work out what you consider to be a coherent and appropriate statement of educational purpose for your congregation. Let it be only one sentence long. Compare it to the statement worked out by

the Congregational Church cited in the present chapter.

12. Diagram the formal structure of organization in the church. Now diagram the informal channel of influence in a different color on the same diagram. Which is more powerful? How do the two work together? This exercise can also be done with the educational structure of the church.

13. Decide to study an issue where you can actually take part in the event. For example, study the reasons for becoming urban street people, then volunteer time at an inner city mission to street people. Discuss the merits of contextual versus classroom education.

14. Arrange to meet with a group from another denomination or with a secular group to discuss a contemporary issue such as disarmament or human rights. Ask a representative of a state-wide group concerned about public issues to be present.

15. Volunteer to the deacons or other official church body to visit hospitalized members of the congregation. Ask the pastor or deacons for training before you go.

16. Organize a weekend camping event. Decide the purpose and the kind of camping. (This might be combined with the next suggestion.)

17. Invite a spiritual leader to lead your group in a spiritual retreat. Ask the leader for study and discipline suggestions before you go.

18. Prioritize the kind of authority your pastor has according to the following types: traditional, bureaucratic, charismatic, and professional. If you are a pastor, rate yourself. Now consider

what kind of educational leadership the pastor takes. Is the pastor closely related to the educational program or not? Is the pastor primarily responsible for Christian education? Which is most important: task management, consensus building, or spiritual direction?

19. How does the nurture committee find and support teachers for the religious education program? What difficulties do they now encounter and how are they responding to them? Interview present and past teachers to find out why they teach or why they resigned. How does the nurture committee supervise teaching?

Questions for Discussion

1. What biblical concepts and passages are especially relevant to administering a church's educational program?
2. How did the sixteenth-century Reformation affect the concept of church organization?
3. Contrast management by objectives, by group dynamics, and by creative conflict.
4. What are the functions and responsibilities of a local educational planning and evaluation committee?
5. How are shifts and proliferation of purposes best handled in educational administration?
6. What is the relationship between formal and informal church structures?
7. Contrast and evaluate church educational strategies of the nineteenth and twentieth centuries.
8. Contrast and evaluate church educational settings of the twentieth century.
9. Compare the types of leadership authority.

10. What are the alternatives to goal oriented and situation oriented management?
11. What alternative roles are available to the professional religious educator in a local church?
12. Name and evaluate the alternative educational roles available to the pastor.

Suggestions for Further Reading

James D. Anderson and Ezra Earl Jones, *The Management of Ministry.*
Two church consultants offer a theory and suggestions about the management of ministry.

Carl S. Dudley, ed., *Building Effective Ministry: Theory and Practice in the Local Church.*
A number of theoreticians and practitioners reflect on the story of one local congregation.

Maria Harris, ed., *The DRE Reader: A Source Book in Education and Ministry.*
The discussion of the role of the director of religious education is helpful to both Catholic and Protestant.

Robert C. Worley, *A Gathering of Strangers: Understanding the Life of Your Church.*
A popular statement by a religious educator who considers administration to be key to the church's educational ministry.

NOTES

Notes

1. THE FAITH COMMUNITY AS TEACHER

1. Horace Bushnell, *Christian Nurture* (New Haven, Conn.: Yale University Press, 1953).

2. The most recent study is Thomas Groome, *Christian Religious Education: Sharing Our Story and Vision* (San Francisco: Harper, 1980). See also Larry O. Richards, *A Theology of Christian Education* (Grand Rapids, Mich.: Zondervan, 1975); any of the works of John H. Westerhoff III, e.g., *Liturgy and Learning Through the Life Cycle,* with William H. Willimon (New York: Seabury Press, 1980); Charles R. Foster, *Teaching in the Community of Faith* (Nashville: Abingdon Press, 1982); and C. Ellis Nelson, *Where Faith Begins* (Richmond, Va.: John Knox Press, 1967).

3. Alternative approaches are listed in Jack L. Seymour and Donald E. Miller, *Contemporary Approaches to Christian Education* (Nashville: Abingdon Press, 1982).

4. This analysis is influenced by the work of Talcott

Parsons et al., eds., *Toward a General Theory of Action* (New York: Harper, 1962), and Talcott Parsons et al., eds., *Theories of Society: Foundations of Modern Sociological Theory* (New York: Free Press of Glencoe, 1961).

5. The interplay of group culture and individual is analyzed by Peter L. Berger and Thomas Luckmann, *The Social Construction of Reality: A Treatise in the Sociology of Knowledge* (Garden City, N.Y.: Doubleday, 1967).

6. The horizon of meaning is a concept of James Fowler, *Stages of Faith: The Psychology of Human Development and the Quest for Meaning* (San Francisco: Harper, 1981). The center of value is a concept used by H. Richard Niebuhr, *Radical Monotheism and Western Culture* (New York: Harper, 1960). See also the commentary on Niebuhr's theology edited by Paul Ramsey, *Faith and Ethics* (New York: Harper, 1957). Ultimate concern is a concept used by Paul Tillich, *Systematic Theology*, 3 vols. (Chicago: University of Chicago Press, 1950-63). The sense of absolute dependence was used by Friedrich Schleiermacher, *The Christian Faith* (Edinburgh: T. & T. Clark, 1928).

7. This conception of idolatry is close to that of Tillich, Barth, Schleiermacher, Luther, Calvin, and Augustine.

8. This discussion on the meaning of education is influenced by the work of R. S. Peters, ed., *The Concept of Education* (New York: Humanities Press, 1967).

9. James Loder, *The Transforming Moment: Understanding Convictional Experiences* (San Francisco: Harper, 1981).

10. Bushnell, *Christian Nurture*.

11. Ibid., p. 4.

12. On pluralism and the church see Don S. Browning, *The Moral Context of Pastoral Care* (Philadelphia: Westminster Press, 1976).

13. The influence of social class is widely documented. See the works of Max Weber and Karl Marx. See also Ernst Troeltsch, *The Social Teaching of the Christian Churches*, 2 vols. (New York: Macmillan, 1956). See H. Richard Niebuhr, *The Social Sources of Denominationalism* (New York: Henry Holt, 1954).

14. The same point is made by Troeltsch, Weber, and Niebuhr in the works already cited. The church growth movement has used similar data to argue for "homogenous groups." By this they mean that churches grow when they are sociologically homogenous. See C. Peter Wagner, *Church Growth and the Whole Gospel: A Biblical Mandate* (San Francisco: Harper, 1981).

15. Jack L. Seymour, Robert T. O'Gorman, and Charles Foster, *The Church in the Education of the Public: Refocusing the Task of Religious Education* (Nashville: Abingdon Press, 1984).

16. Stanley Hauerwas, "The Family as a School for Character," *Religious Education* 80, no. 2 (1985).

17. Robert N. Bellah and Phillip E. Hammond, *Varieties of Civil Religion* (Garden City, N.Y.: Doubleday, 1961).

18. The typology of church and sect was introduced by Ernst Troeltsch, in *Social Teaching of the Christian Churches*. The denominational type was added to Troeltsch's typology by H. Richard Niebuhr.

19. Some may object that the theology of a sect group must include a partial view of society, so that early Christians or early Lutherans could not be called sectarian. However, no sect group is opposed in principle to the universalization of its views, even

though it anticipates that only a few will actually accept them. We understand the sect to be in sharp normative tension with the remainder of society.

20. In Nigeria much of Christianity has taken on' a denominational character, although some groups are sectarian. Islam generally aspires to be church-like, but it contains its own sectarian groups, e.g., the Maitazini.

21. The Roman Catholic strategy of private schools has become less urgent as Roman Catholicism in America has become more acceptable as a denomination.

22. Groome, *Christian Religious Education.*

2. THE FAITH COMMUNITY IN HISTORY

1. Walter Brueggemann, *The Creative Word: Canon as a Model of Biblical Education* (Philadelphia: Fortress Press, 1982).

2. Norman K. Gottwald, *The Tribes of Yahweh: A Sociology of the Religion of Liberated Israel, 1250– 1050 B.C.E.* (Maryknoll, N.Y.: Orbis Books, 1979).

3. Gilbert Highet, *The Art of Teaching* (New York: Alfred A. Knopf, 1952), pp. 190 ff. Highet revises his earlier view in *The Immortal Profession* (New York: Weybright and Talley, 1976).

4. Robert W. Lynn and Elliott Wright, *The Big Little School* (New York: Harper, 1971).

5. Gibson Winter, *The Suburban Captivity of the Churches* (Garden City, N.Y.: Doubleday, 1961).

6. *The New England Primer*, ed. Paul Leicester Ford (New York: Dodd, Mead, 1962).

7. Lynn and Elliott, *Big Little School.*

8. John H. Westerhoff III, *McGuffey and His Readers: Piety, Morality, and Education in Nineteenth-century America* (Nashville: Abingdon Press, 1978).

9. An example of the NCC material for public schools on peace is Shirley J. Heckman, *Peace is Possible: A Study-Action Process Guide on Peacemaking* (New York: United Church Press, 1982).

10. Robert W. Green, ed., *Protestantism, Capitalism and Social Science: The Weber Thesis Controversy* (Lexington, Mass.: D. C. Heath, 1973).

11. Lamin Sanneh, *West African Christianity: The Religious Impact* (Maryknoll, N.Y.: Orbis Books, 1983), chap. 6; Elechi Amadi, *Ethics in Nigerian Culture* (Ibadan, Nigeria: Heinemann Educational Books, 1982); Ogbu Kalu, ed., *Christianity in West Africa: The Nigerian Story* (Ibadan: Daystar Press, 1978).

3. THE GLOBAL COMMUNITY

1. Friedrich Schleiermacher, *The Christian Faith.*

2. Seymour, O'Gorman, and Foster, *Education of the Public*, chap. 2.

3. Ibid.

4. Refer to George Albert Coe, *A Social Theory of Religious Education* (New York: Scribner's, 1917).

5. Seymour, O'Gorman, and Foster, *Education of the Public*, chap. 4.

6. Eleanor A. Daniel, John W. Wade, and Charles Gresham, *Introduction to Christian Education* (Cincinnati, Ohio: Standard Publishing, 1980), pp. 64-65. For Paul Vieth's earlier statement see his *Objectives in Religious Education* (New York: Red Label Reprints, 1930), pp. 79-88.

7. Søren Kierkegaard, *Training in Christianity*, trans. Walter Lowrie (Princeton, N.J.: Princeton University Press, 1944), p. 134.

8. Lawrence Little et al., "The Objectives of Christian Education" as quoted in Daniel, Wade, and Gresham, *Introduction*, pp. 65-66. See also Lawrence Little et al., *The Objectives of Christian Education* (New York: National Council of Churches, 1958).

9. H. Richard Niebuhr, *The Purpose of the Church and Its Ministry: Reflections on the Aims of Theological Education* (New York: Harper and Brothers, 1956), chap. 1, pp. 27-39.

10. Seymour and Miller, *Contemporary Approaches to Christian Education.* The typology was first published by Seymour and then elaborated by Seymour and Miller with the help of Sara Little, Charles R. Foster, Allen Moore, and Carol A. Wehrheim.

11. Ibid., pp. 35 ff.

12. Ibid., p. 32.

13. Mary Elizabeth Moore, *Education for Continuity and Change: A New Model for Christian Religious Education* (Nashville: Abingdon Press, 1983), p. 132.

14. David W. Augsberger, *Caring Enough to Confront* (Glendale, Calif.: Regal, 1980).

15. Helmut Harder, *Guidebook for Writers: Youth Curriculum*, The Foundation series (Elgin, Ill.: Brethren Press, 1979), p. 5.

16. Seymour, O'Gorman, and Foster, *Education of the Public.*

17. Ibid., p. 152.

18. Wagner, *Church Growth*, p. 57.

19. Jack L. Seymour, *From Sunday School to Church School: Continuities in Protestant Church Education in the United States, 1860–1929* (Washington, D.C.: University Press of America, 1982), chap. 11.

20. Loder, *The Transforming Moment.*

21. Iris V. Cully, *Education for Spiritual Growth* (San Francisco: Harper, 1984).

22. Ibid., pp. 16-17.

23. Parker J. Palmer, *To Know as We Are Known: A Spirituality of Education* (San Francisco: Harper, 1983).

24. Browning, *Moral Context of Pastoral Care.*

25. Harvey Cox, *The Secular City: Secularization and Urbanization in Theological Perspective* (New York: Macmillan, 1965).

26. Harvey Cox, *Religion in the Secular City: Toward a Post-Modern Theology* (New York: Simon & Schuster, 1984).

27. Margaret Mead, *Coming of Age in Samoa* (New York: Morrow, 1971).

28. John H. Yoder, *The Politics of Jesus: Vicit Agnus Noster* (Grand Rapids, Mich.: Eerdmans, 1972), chap. 8.

29. John Naisbitt, *Megatrends: Ten New Directions Transforming Our Lives* (New York: Warner Books, 1983).

4. SHARING THE STORY

1. James D. Smart, *The Strange Silence of the Bible in the Church: A Study in Hermeneutics* (Philadelphia: Westminster Press, 1970), p. 27.

2. Harrison Elliott, *Can Religious Education Be Christian?* (New York: Macmillan, 1940).

3. Peter Berger, *The Noise of Solemn Assemblies: Christian Commitment and the Religious Establishment in America* (Garden City, N.Y.: Doubleday, 1961).

4. The ideas in this paragraph have been succinctly stated by Sara Little, "Revelation, the Bible, and

Christian Education," in Marvin J. Taylor, ed., *An Introduction to Christian Education* (Nashville: Abingdon Press, 1966), pp. 42-49.

5. Ibid., p. 46.

6. Iris V. Cully, *Imparting the Word: The Bible in Christian Education* (Philadelphia: Westminster Press, 1962); Dorothy Jean Furnish, *Exploring the Bible with Children* (Nashville: Abingdon Press, 1975) and *Living the Bible with Children* (Nashville: Abingdon Press, 1979); Brueggemann, *The Creative Word;* and Jack L. Seymour and Carol A. Wehrheim, "Faith Seeking Understanding: Interpretation as a Task of Christian Education," in Seymour and Miller, *Contemporary Approaches to Christian Education,* are four examples.

7. Sara Little, "Revelation, the Bible, and Christian Education," in Taylor, *Introduction to Christian Education,* p. 48, suggested that "perhaps . . . hermeneutic will replace revelation." Edward Everding, Jr., "A Hermeneutical Approach to Educational Theory," in Marvin J. Taylor, ed., *Foundations for Christian Education in an Era of Change* (Nashville: Abingdon Press, 1976), p. 41: "Infrequently has hermeneutics informed the theory [of education], even though teaching is interpretation." Brueggemann, *The Creative Word,* pp. 2-3, states that new developments allow biblical scholarship to take education more seriously, and so biblical scholars ought to enter into dialog with educators.

8. Julius Wellhausen, *Prolegomena to the History of Ancient Israel,* trans. J. S. Smith and C. A. Menzies, 1885, reproduction (Magnolia, Ma.: Peter Smith, 1973).

9. Paul Ricoeur, *Interpretation Theory: Discourse and the Surplus of Meaning* (Fort Worth, Tex.: Christian University Press, 1976), argues for the validity of the structuralist position without denying the limited validity of the historical approach. He believes that the two approaches supplement one another and stand in dialectical tension.

10. Brevard Childs, *Introduction to the Old Testament as Scripture* (Philadelphia: Fortress Press, 1979), pp. 71 ff. Brueggemann, *The Creative Word*, p. 3: "Thus the broad link I suggest is that *canon is a clue to education, both as substance and as process.*"

11. Brueggemann, *The Creative Word*, p. 21.

12. Everding, *"A Hermeneutical Approach,"* in Taylor, *Introduction to Christian Education*, p. 44, speaks about a "coincidence of the horizon of meaning" between a present and past interpreter. James D. Smart, *The Past, Present and Future of Biblical Theology* (Philadelphia: Westminster Press, 1979), p. 145, speaks of a "resonance" between biblical drama and our own.

13. Brueggemann, *The Creative Word*, p. 12.

14. Ibid.

15. Ibid., pp. 17-27.

16. Ibid., pp. 23 ff.

17. F. W. Beare, "Canon of the New Testament," in George A. Buttrick et al., eds., *Interpreter's Dictionary of the Bible*, vol. 1 (Nashville: Abingdon Press, 1962), pp. 520-32.

18. Groome, *Christian Religious Education*.

19. Paulo Freire, *Pedagogy of the Oppressed* (New York: Herder and Herder, 1970).

20. See Ross Snyder, *Contemporary Celebration* (Nashville: Abingdon Press, 1971) and *Young People and Their Culture* (Nashville: Abingdon Press, 1969).

21. See Warren F. Groff, *Christ the Hope of the Future* (Grand Rapids, Mich.: Eerdmans, 1971). Bultmann emphasized the future character of faith; Moltmann has developed this theme. Groome speaks of both story and vision.

22. Nancy Fuchs-Kreimer, "The Authority of the Bible in Modern Jewish Thought," *Religious Education* 77, no. 5 (1982): 485, makes the same point: "The telling and retelling of the story . . . was itself an essential part of the meeting between the Jewish people and that which is eternal. We cannot simply read and follow their results. We must *do* what they *did*."

23. See Warren F. Groff, *Storytime: God's Story and Ours* (Elgin, Ill.: Brethren Press, 1974).

24. See Patricia Griggs, *Using Storytelling in Christian Education* (Nashville: Abingdon Press, 1981); May Hill Arbuthnot, *The Arbuthnot Anthology of Children's Literature* (Glenview, Ill.: Scott, Foresman & Co., 1976); Groff, *Storytime.*

25. Smart, *Strange Silence of the Bible*, p. 170. Ronald Goldman, *Religious Thinking from Childhood to Adolescence* (New York: Seabury Press, 1968), is full of research findings documenting this view.

26. Goldman, *Religious Thinking.*

27. Fowler, *Stages of Faith*; Ana-Maria Rizzuto, *The Birth of the Living God* (Chicago: University of Chicago Press, 1979).

28. Mary Wilcox, *Developmental Journey: A Guide to Development of Logical and Moral Reasoning and*

Social Perspective (Nashville: Abingdon Press, 1979), pp. 234 ff.

29. Childs, *Old Testament as Scripture,* p. 72, states: "Canonical criticism is largely descriptive and doesn't assume a particular stance of faith or commitment on the part of the readers."

30. Harrison Elliott, *Can Religious Education be Christian?* (New York: Macmillan, 1940).

31. H. Shelton Smith, *Faith and Nurture* (New York: Scribner's, 1941).

5. EXPRESSING THE STORY

1. Brueggemann, *The Creative Word.*

2. C. H. Dodd, *The Apostolic Preaching and Its Development* (New York: Harper, 1944). My view differs from Dodd's in that I see both preaching and teaching arising from living the story. Dodd sees teaching as an application of preaching.

3. Paul Tillich, *A History of Christian Thought* (New York: Harper, 1968), p. 20.

4. David Tracy, *The Analogical Imagination: Christian Theology and the Culture of Pluralism* (New York: Crossroad, 1981).

5. Several educators calling for imagination are Maria Harris, Sharon Parks, and James Fowler.

6. James Michael Lee, *The Shape of Religious Instruction: A Social Science Approach* (Dayton, Ohio: Pflaum, 1971).

7. Charles Melchert, "Theories as Practiced," *Religious Education* 78, no. 3 (1984): 307-22.

8. Don S. Browning, "Pastoral Theology in a Pluralistic Age," pp. 187-202, and David Tracy, "The Foundations of Practical Theology," pp. 61-82, in Don S.

Browning, ed., *Practical Theology: The Emerging Field in Theology, Church, and World* (San Francisco: Harper, 1983).

9. Westerhoff and Willimon, *Liturgy and Learning.*

10. Larry O. Richards, *Theology of Christian Education.*

11. Thomas Groome, who is Roman Catholic (as is James Michael Lee), sets forth a concept of "shared praxis" that allows the interaction of functional and authoritative theology.

12. Two representative works are John B. Cobb, Jr., and David Ray Griffin, *Process Theology: An Introductory Exposition* (Philadelphia: Westminster Press, 1976), and Bernard Eugene Meland, *The Realities of Faith: The Revolution in Cultural Forms* (New York: Oxford, 1962).

13. Rosemary Radford Ruether, *Sexism and God-Talk: Toward a Feminist Theology* (Boston: Beacon Press, 1983).

14. Jürgen Moltmann, *The Theology of Hope* (New York: Harper, 1976).

15. World Council of Churches, *Baptism, Eucharist and Ministry*, Commission on Faith and Order, Faith and Order Paper No. 111 (Geneva: World Council of Churches, 1982).

16. Edward Farley, *Theologia: The Fragmentation and Unity of Theological Education* (Philadelphia: Fortress Press, 1983), pp. 190-95.

17. John Dewey, *Experience and Education* (New York: Macmillan, 1952).

18. Steven Toulmin, *Human Understanding* (Princeton, N.J.: Princeton University Press, 1972).

19. James N. Poling and Donald E. Miller, *Foundations for a Practical Theology of Ministry* (Nashville: Abingdon Press, 1985), pp. 62-99.

20. Here we are following James Gustafson's suggestion in *Ethics From a Theocentric Perspective*, 2 vols. (Chicago: University of Chicago Press, 1981–84).

21. Paul Ricoeur speaks of a "hermeneutic of suspicion" in terms of neurosis, power, and oppression. To these we add faithfulness. See Charles E. Reagan and David Stewart, eds., *The Philosophy of Paul Ricoeur* (Boston: Beacon Press, 1978), pp. 213-19.

22. Here we agree with Don S. Browning's criticism of Groome. Don S. Browning, *Religious Ethics and Pastoral Care* (Philadelphia: Fortress Press, 1983).

6. LIVING THE STORY

1. Kant's maxim is: Percept without concept is blind, and concept without percept is empty.

2. Max Weber, *The Protestant Ethic and the Spirit of Capitalism*, trans. Talcott Parsons, (New York: Scribners, 1958); Richard H. Tawney, *Religion and the Rise of Capitalism* (New York: Harcourt Brace, 1926).

3. T. W. Adorno et al., *The Authoritarian Personality* (New York: Harper, 1950).

4. Gordon W. Allport, *The Individual and His Religion: A Psychological Interpretation* (New York: Macmillan, 1950); Sara Little, *To Set One's Heart: Belief and Teaching in the Church* (Atlanta: John Knox Press, 1983).

5. Niebuhr, *Radical Monotheism*.

6. See Dietrich Bonhoeffer, *The Communion of Saints: A Dogmatic Inquiry into the Sociology of the Church* (New York: Harper, 1963).

7. Max Stackhouse defines the creed of a community in similar terms. For a description of Stackhouse's view, see Edward Le Roy Long, *A Survey of Recent Christian*

Ethics (New York: Oxford University Press, 1982), pp. 54-55.

8. John Rawls, *A Theory of Justice* (Cambridge, Mass.: Harvard University Press, 1971).

9. John Stuart Mill, *Utilitarianism* (New York: Macmillan, 1971).

10. William K. Frankena, *Ethics* (Englewood Cliffs, N.J.: Prentice-Hall, 1973), questions a third approach. Gustafson, in *Ethics From a Theocentric Perspective*, defends it.

11. Paul Lehmann, *Ethics in a Christian Context* (New York: Harper, 1963).

12. See James M. Gustafson, *The Church as Moral Decision Maker* (Philadelphia: Pilgrim Press, 1970).

13. See Plato, *The Republic of Plato*, trans. Francis M. Cornford (London: Oxford University Press, 1961). A recent book is by Brian Wren, *Education for Justice: Pedagogical Principles* (Maryknoll, N.Y.: Orbis Books, 1977).

14. Rawls, *Theory of Justice.*

15. Stanley Hauerwas, *A Community of Character: Toward a Constructive Christian Social Ethic* (Notre Dame: University of Notre Dame Press, 1981).

7. FAITH AND MORAL DEVELOPMENT

1. Paul J. Philibert and James P. O'Connor, "Adolescent Religious Socialization: A Study of Goal Priorities According to Parents and Religious Educators," *Review of Religious Research* 23, no. 3 (March, 1982): 225-316.

2. Lawrence Kohlberg, *Collected Papers on Moral Development and Moral Education* (Cambridge, Mass.: Moral Education Research Fund, 1973), p. 7; Ralph B.

Potter, "Justice and Beyond in Moral Education," *Andover Newton Quarterly* 19, no. 3 (January 1979):145-55; Carol Gilligan, *In a Different Voice: Psychological Theory and Woman's Development* (Cambridge, Mass.: Harvard University Press, 1982), p. 5.

3. Fowler, *Stages of Faith*, p. 33.

4. James W. Fowler, *Becoming Adult, Becoming Christian: Adult Development and Christian Faith* (San Francisco: Harper, 1984).

5. See works by Nelson, Little, Groome, Dykstra, Hauerwas, and Westerhoff in the bibliography.

6. Jean Piaget, *The Moral Judgment of the Child*, trans. Majorie Gaban (Glencoe, Ill.: Free Press, 1948), p. 118.

7. Ronald Goldman, *Religious Thinking from Childhood to Adolescence* (New York: Seabury Press, 1968), p. 117.

8. Ibid., pp. 118-19.

9. Ibid., p. 120.

10. See Ronald Goldman, *Readiness for Religion: A Basis for Developmental Religious Education* (London: Routledge & Kegan Paul, 1965), p. 196, for a more extensive chart.

11. Susan Pagliuso, *Understanding Stages of Moral Development: A Programmed Learning Workbook* (Ramsey, N.J.: Paulist Press, 1976), pp. 125-27; adapted to eliminate sexist language.

12. Ibid., p. 125.

13. Ibid.

14. Ibid.

15. Seymour and Miller, *Contemporary Approaches to Christian Education*, pp. 81-82.

16. Wilcox, *Developmental Journey*.

17. See Fowler, *Stages of Faith*, pp. 307, 310-12 for the full interview guide.
18. Seymour and Miller, *Contemporary Approaches to Christian Education*, pp. 86-88.
19. Erik H. Erikson, *Childhood and Society* (New York: W. W. Norton, 1950), and *Insight and Responsibility: Lectures on the Ethical Implications of Psychoanalytic Insight* (New York: W. W. Norton, 1964).
20. See Don S. Browning, *Generative Man: Psychoanalytic Perspectives* (Philadelphia: Westminster Press, 1973).
21. Craig R. Dykstra, *Vision and Character: A Christian Educator's Alternative to Kohlberg* (New York: Paulist Press, 1981).
22. Loder, *The Transforming Moment*.
23. Hauerwas, *Community of Character*.
24. Immanuel Kant, *Critique of Practical Reason and Other Writings in Moral Philosophy*, trans. and ed. L. W. Beck (Chicago: University of Chicago, 1949); Frankena, *Ethics;* Richard M. Hare, *The Language of Morals* (New York: Oxford University Press, 1968).
25. Hauerwas, *Community of Character*.
26. Gilligan, *In a Different Voice*.
27. Fowler, *Becoming Adult, Becoming Christian*, pp. 72-73.
28. Gabriel Moran, *Religious Education Development* (Minneapolis, Minn.: Winston Press, 1983).
29. Little, *To Set One's Heart*.

8. THE FAITH JOURNEY

1. Gilligan, *In a Different Voice*.
2. Principal sources are Piaget, Erikson, Kohlberg, and Fowler. See bibliography.

3. Margaret S. Mahler, Fred Pine, and Anni Bergman, *The Psychological Birth of the Human Infant: Symbiosis and Individuation* (New York: Basic Books, 1975).

4. Tillich, *Systematic Theology*, vol. 2, pp. 59 ff.

5. Fowler, *Stages of Faith*, speaks of faith as one's relation to one's conception of the ultimate environment.

6. See works by Wilcox, Fowler, Kohlberg, Gilligan, in the bibliography.

7. These views are given a more elaborate statement in my book, *The Wing-Footed Wanderer: Conscience and Transcendence* (Nashville: Abingdon Press, 1977).

8. See Mahler et al., *Psychological Birth*.

9. Erikson, *Insight and Responsibility*, pp. 111 ff.

10. Burton L. White, *The First Three Years of Life: A Guide to Physical, Emotional, and Intellectual Growth of Your Baby* (New York: Avon, 1978).

11. Rizzuto, *Birth of the Living God*.

12. Piaget, *Moral Judgment of the Child*, chaps. 2 and 3.

13. Erikson, *Insight and Responsibility*, pp. 122 ff.

14. Fowler, *Stages of Faith*, pp. 135 ff.

15. Erik H. Erikson, *Identity and the Life Cycle: Selected Papers* (New York: International Universities Press, 1959).

16. See Kohlberg, *Collected Papers*.

17. Fowler, *Stages of Faith*, pp. 151 ff.

18. Kohlberg calls this stage of relativity 4b.

19. Erikson, *Identity and the Life Cycle*, pp. 95 ff.

20. Fowler, *Stages of Faith*, pp. 174 ff.

21. Ibid., pp. 184 ff.

22. Gail Sheehy, *Passages: Predictable Crises of Adult Life* (New York: E. P. Dutton, 1976).

23. Neill Q. Hamilton, *Maturing in the Christian Life: A Pastor's Guide* (Philadelphia: Geneva Press, 1984).

24. Fowler, *Becoming Adult, Becoming Christian*, chap. 4.

25. Malcolm Knowles, *The Modern Practice of Adult Education: Andragogy versus Pedagogy* (New York: Association Press, 1970).

26. Fowler, *Stages of Faith*, pp. 211 ff.

27. Erikson, *Identity and the Life Cycle*, p. 98.

28. Søren Kierkegaard, *Purity of Heart Is to Will One Thing*, trans. Douglas V. Steere (New York: Harper, 1948).

29. William M. Clements, ed., *Ministry with the Aging* (San Francisco: Harper, 1981).

30. Donald E. Miller, "Conscience and History," (Ph.D. diss., Harvard University Press, 1962).

9. WORSHIP AND EDUCATION

1. John H. Westerhoff III and Gwen Kennedy Neville, *Generation to Generation: Conversations on Religious Education and Culture* (Philadelphia: United Church Press, 1974), and Westerhoff and Willimon, *Liturgy and Learning*.

2. Charles H. Cooley, *Social Organization* (Glencoe, Ill.: Free Press, 1956).

3. Berger, *Noise of Solemn Assemblies*; Berger and Luckmann, *Social Construction of Reality*.

4. Herve Varenne, *Americans Together: Structured Diversity in a Midwestern Town* (New York: Teachers College Press, 1977); Theodore Caplow et al., *All Faithful People: Chance and Continuity in Middle-*

town's Religion (Minneapolis, Minn.: University of Minnesota Press, 1983); Joan D. Chittister and Martin E. Marty, *Faith and Ferment: An Interdisciplinary Study of Christian Beliefs and Practices* (Minneapolis, Minn.: Augsburg Publishing House, 1983).

5. James Loder brings this criticism against the various stage theories, cognitive and emotive, and against Westerhoff's concept of enculturation. Craig Dykstra makes a similar criticism.

6. Victor Turner, *The Ritual Process: Structure and Anti-Structure* (Ithaca, N.Y.: Cornell University Press, 1977).

7. Loder, *The Transforming Moment.*

8. C. H. Dodd popularized the distinction between apostolic preaching and teaching (kerygma and didache); see *Apostolic Preaching.*

9. Alfred North Whitehead, *Adventures of Ideas* (New York: Macmillan, 1933).

10. Whitehead, *Adventures of Ideas;* Emile Durkheim, *The Elementary Forms of the Religious Life* (New York: Collier, 1954).

10. TEACHING AND LEARNING

1. Groome, *Christian Religious Education,* pp. 141-42.

2. Nelson, *Where Faith Begins.*

3. See Berger and Luckmann, *Social Construction of Reality.*

4. Piaget, *Moral Judgment of the Child.*

5. Gustavo Gutierrez, *A Theology of Liberation* (Maryknoll, N.Y.: Orbis Books, 1973); Jose Miguez Bonino, *Doing Theology in a Revolutionary Situation* (Philadelphia: Fortress Press, 1975); Freire, *Pedagogy of the Oppressed.*

6. Wren, *Education for Justice*, gives a straightforward interpretation of Freire's view of learning. Learning is a voluntary act in which the learner becomes more aware of the conditions of justice. The awakened person must then enter into the cultural and political conflict for justice.

7. Randolph C. Miller, James Michael Lee, and Iris V. Cully, to mention a few.

8. Loder, *The Transforming Moment*; Dykstra, *Vision and Character*.

9. Fowler, *Stages of Faith*; Wilcox, *Developmental Journey*.

10. These sentences refer to Piaget's egocentric, concrete operational, and formal operational periods. See *Six Psychological Studies*, trans. Anita Tenzer and David Elkind (New York: Random House, 1968).

11. Little, *To Set One's Heart*. Little is dependent on Bruce Joyce and Marsha Weil, *Models of Teaching* (Englewood Cliffs, N.J.: Prentice-Hall, 1967). Joyce and Weil divide teaching models into information-processing, personal, social, and behavioral types. Little drops the behavioral type as not especially relevant to religious education, but she adds the indirect communication as particularly relevant.

12. See Lehmann, "Teaching and Learning Strategies," in Harder, *Guidebook for Writers*, pp. 18-21.

13. Harold Bessell et al., *Methods in Human Development, Theory Manual* (La Mesa, Calif.: Human Development Training Institute, 1973).

14. William Gordon, *The Metaphorical Way of Learning and Knowing* (Cambridge, Mass.: Synetics Education Systems, 1970).

15. Janet Litherland, *The Clown Ministry Handbook* (Colorado Springs: Meriwether, 1982).

16. Little, *To Set One's Heart*, pp. 80 ff.

17. Ibid., p. 78.

11. CURRICULUM

1. George H. Betts, *The Curriculum of Religious Education* (New York: Abingdon Press, 1924).

2. D. Campbell Wyckoff, *Theory and Design of Christian Education Curriculum* (Philadelphia: Westminster Press, 1961), p. 79.

3. Dale W. Brown, *Understanding Pietism* (Grand Rapids, Mich.: Eerdmans, 1978).

4. Winona Walworth, "Educational Curriculum," in Werner C. Graendorf, *Introduction to Biblical Christian Education* (Chicago: Moody Press, 1981), p. 294.

5. Ibid., pp. 283-90.

6. Mary Jo Osterman, "The Two Hundred Year Struggle for Protestant Education Curriculum Theory," *Religious Education* 75, no. 5 (1980):530. "The term 'Babel II' was first used [to my knowledge] by Dr. Dorothy Jean Furnish in her classes on 'Curriculum Designs for Christian Education' at Garrett-Evangelical Theological Seminary in the early 1970s. Babel II is characterized by a profound tendency of local churches to select materials irrespective of denominational source and to create or adapt materials to meet perceived local needs."

7. Mary Elizabeth Moore speaks of "disconnectedness in the curriculum system" in *Continuity and Change*, pp. 172 ff.

8. Maxine Greene calls for curricula that let people be actors. Maxine Greene, "Curriculum and Consciousness" in William Pinar, *Heightened Consciousness, Cultural Revolution and Curriculum Theory* (Berkeley, Calif.: McCutchan, 1974). Pinar also suggests that

curriculum focus on the person's experience. Dwayne E. Huebner makes a similar point in "From Theory to Practice: Curriculum," *Religious Education* 77, no. 4 (1982):363-74.

9. See William Pinar, ed., *Curriculum Theorizing: The Reconceptualists* (Berkeley, Calif.: McCutchan, 1975).

10. Allen Moore, "Liberation and the Future of Christian Education," in Seymour and Miller, *Contemporary Approaches to Christian Education*, pp. 117 ff.

11. See Harold S. Bender, *The Anabaptist Vision* (Scottsdale, Pa.: Herald Press, 1944), and Donald F. Durnbaugh, *The Believers' Church: The History and Character of Radical Protestantism* (New York: Macmillan, 1968).

12. Harder, *Guidebook for Writers*, p. 5.

13. Ibid.

14. Ibid., p. 6.

15. Ibid.

16. Evangelical Covenant Church of America, *Curriculum Evaluation: Measuring the Material* (Chicago, Ill.: Evangelical Covenant Church, 5101 N. Francisco Avenue, 60625, 1983).

17. Iris V. Cully, "Changing Patterns of Protestant Curriculum," in Marvin J. Taylor, ed., *Changing Patterns of Religious Education* (Nashville: Abingdon Press, 1984), p. 232.

18. Shirley J. Heckman and Iris L. Ferren, *Creating the Congregation's Educational Ministry* (Elgin, Ill.: Brethren Press, 1968).

19. William A. Dalglish, ed., *Media for Christian Formation* (Dayton, Ohio: Pflaum, 1969).

20. Freire, *Pedagogy of the Oppressed*.

21. Ibid.

22. See Allen Moore, "Liberation and the Future of Christian Education," in Seymour and Miller, *Contemporary Approaches to Christian Education*, p. 106.

12. ORGANIZING FOR LEARNING

1. For example, see Emil Brunner's discussion of "Ekklesia and the Church" in *The Christian Doctrine of the Church, Faith, and the Consummation: Dogmatics*, vol. 3 (London: Lutterworth Press, 1962), part 3, section I.

2. See Karl Barth, "The Holy Spirit and the Upbuilding of the Christian Community" in *Church Dogmatics*, vol. 2, trans. G. T. Thompson (Edinburgh: T. & T. Clark, 1948), section 67.

3. See Max Weber, *The Theory of Social and Economic Organization*, trans. A. M. Henderson and Talcott Parsons (New York: Oxford University Press, 1947).

4. See any of Westerhoff's books, e.g., *Liturgy and Learning*.

5. This sociological concept developed from the work of Max Weber. John Dewey gave an educational formation of the same idea.

6. See the discussion in the previous section.

7. Amitai Etzioni, *Modern Organizations* (Englewood Cliffs, N.J.: Prentice-Hall, 1964).

8. Carl S. Dudley, *Where Have All Our People Gone? New Choices for Old Churches* (New York: Pilgrim Press, 1979).

9. This typology follows Etzioni, *Modern Organizations*, pp. 32 ff.

10. See John Michael Miller, *The Contentious Community: Constructive Conflict in the Church* (Philadel-

phia: Westminster Press, 1978); Speed Leas and Paul Kittlaus, *Church Fights: Managing Conflict in the Local Chuch* (Philadelphia: Westminster Press, 1973).

11. Jean Piaget and Erik Erikson both have a conflict theory of learning. Loder, *The Transforming Moment*, also lifts up the importance of conflict in learning.

12. Regarding friendship, see Richards, *Theology of Christian Education*.

13. See Heckman and Ferren, *Creating the Congregation's Educational Ministry*.

14. Ibid.

15. Carl S. Dudley, "The Practice of Ministry," pp. 211-19, and James F. Hopewell, "The Jovial Church: Narrative in Local Church Life," pp. 68-83, in Carl S. Dudley, ed., *Building Effective Ministry: Theory and Practice in the Local Church* (San Francisco: Harper, 1983); Robert C. Worley, *A Gathering of Strangers: Understanding the Life of Your Church* (Philadelphia: Westminster Press, 1976).

16. Worley, *Gathering of Strangers*, offers suggestions for studying a congregation.

17. Hopewell, "The Jovial Church," in Dudley, *Building Effective Ministry*, pp. 68-83.

18. See Worley, *Gathering of Strangers*, chap. 3, pp. 31-44.

19. See Etzioni, *Modern Organizations*, chap. 2.

20. Community Congregational Church of Villa Park, Ill., mimeo.

21. James Michael Lee, *The Content of Religious Instruction: A Social-Science Approach* (Birmingham, Ala.: Religious Education Press, 1984).

22. Seymour, *From Sunday School to Church School.*

23. Worley, *Gathering of Strangers*, pp. 72 ff.

24. William B. Kennedy, "Education for a Just and Peaceful World," *Religious Education* 79, no. 4 (1984): 550-57.

25. Recent spokespersons for the paideia conception are Seymour, O'Gorman, and Foster, *Education of the Public.* Also Robert Bellah, Martin Marty, and Gabriel Moran.

26. Cully, *Education for Spiritual Growth.*

27. James D. Anderson and Ezra Earl Jones, *The Management of Ministry* (San Francisco: Harper, 1978), p. 78.

28. Weber, *Social and Economic Organization,* pp. 324-86.

29. Anderson and Jones, *Management of Ministry,* pp. 163-65.

30. Niebuhr, *Purpose of the Church,* pp. 79 ff.

31. Hamilton, *Maturing in the Christian Life,* pp. 22 ff.

32. Anderson and Jones, *Management of Ministry,* pp. 78-84.

33. Amitai Etzioni, *The Active Society: A Theory of Societal and Political Processes* (New York: Free Press, 1968), chap. 12.

34. Worley, *Gathering of Strangers,* laments that so few pastors are able to think organizationally.

35. Richards, *Theology for Christian Education.*

36. The comments here are based upon the discussion in Maria Harris, ed., *The DRE Reader: A Sourcebook in Education and Ministry* (Winona, Minn.: Saint Mary's Press, 1980).

37. Ibid., p. 30.

38. See Worley, *Gathering of Strangers,* p. 68.

39. Christine Long, "Understanding Church Organization," in Harris, *The DRE Reader,* pp. 146-49; Worley, *Gathering of Strangers,* pp. 72-79.

BIBLIOGRAPHY

Bibliography

Adorno, T. W., and Frenkel-Brunswick, Else. *The Authoritarian Personality*. New York: Harper, 1950.

Allport, Gordon W. *The Individual and His Religion, A Psychological Interpretation*. New York: Macmillan, 1950.

Alter, Robert. *The Art of Biblical Narrative*. New York: Basic Books, 1981.

Amadi, Elechi. *Ethics in Nigerian Culture*. Ibadan, Nigeria: Heinemann Educational Books, 1982.

Anderson, James D., and Jones, Ezra Earl. *The Management of Ministry*. San Francisco: Harper, 1978.

Arbuthnot, May Hill. *The Arbuthnot Anthology of Children's Literature*. Glenview, Ill.: Scott, Foresman, 1961.

Aristotle. *Ethics: The Nichomachean Ethics*. Trans. by J. A. K. Thomson. London: Allen & Unwin, 1953.

Augsburger, David W. *Caring Enough to Confront*. Glendale, Calif.: Regal, 1980.

381

Barth, Karl. *Church Dogmatics*. Trans. by G. T. Thompson. 4 vols. Edinburgh: T. & T. Clark, 1936–69.

Bellah, Robert N. *The Broken Covenant: American Civil Religion in Time of Trial*. New York: Seabury Press, 1975.

Bellah, Robert N., and Hammond, Phillip E. *Varieties of Civil Religion*. San Francisco: Harper, 1980.

Bender, Harold S. *The Anabaptist Vision*. Scottdale, Pa.: Herald Press, 1944.

Berger, Peter L. *The Noise of Solemn Assemblies: Christian Commitment and the Religious Establishment in America*. Garden City, N.Y.: Doubleday, 1961.

Berger, Peter L., and Luckmann, Thomas. *The Social Construction of Reality: A Treatise in the Sociology of Knowledge*. Garden City, N.Y.: Doubleday, 1967.

Bessell, Harold, and Palomares, Uvaldo H. *Methods in Human Development, Theory Manual*. La Mesa, Calif.: Human Development Training Institute, 1973.

Betts, George H. *The Curriculum of Religious Education*. New York: Abingdon Press, 1924.

Bonhoeffer, Dietrich. *The Communion of Saints: A Dogmatic Inquiry into the Sociology of the Church*. New York: Harper, 1963.

Bonino, Jose Miguez. *Doing Theology in a Revolutionary Situation*. Philadelphia: Fortress Press, 1975.

Boys, Mary. *Biblical Interpretation in Religious Education*. Birmingham, Ala.: Religious Education Press, 1980.

Brown, Dale W. *Understanding Pietism*. Grand Rapids, Mich.: Eerdmans, 1978.

Browning, Don S. *Generative Man: Psychoanalytic Perspectives*. Philadelphia: Westminster Press, 1973.

———. *The Morality Context of Pastoral Care*. Philadelphia: Westminster Press, 1976.

————. *Religious Ethics and Pastoral Care.* Philadelphia: Fortress Press, 1983.

————. *Practical Theology.* San Francisco: Harper, 1983.

Browning, Robert L., and Reed, Roy A. *The Sacraments in Religious Education and Liturgy.* Birmingham, Ala.: Religious Education Press, 1985.

Brueggemann, Walter. *The Creative Word: Canon as a Model for Biblical Education.* Philadelphia: Fortress Press, 1982.

Brunner, Emil. *Dogmatics.* 3 vols. London: Lutterworth Press, 1950-62.

Bultmann, Rudolf. *Theology of the New Testament.* New York: Macmillan, 1951.

Bushnell, Horace. *Christian Nurture.* New Haven, Conn.: Yale University Press, 1953.

Buttrick, George A.; Kepler, Thomas S.; Knox, John; May, Herbert G.; Terrien, Samuel; and Bucke, Emory S. *Interpreter's Dictionary of the Bible.* 5 vols. Nashville: Abingdon Press, 1962.

Caplow, Theodore; Bahr, Howard M.; Chadwick, Bruce A.; and Hoover, Dwight W. *All Faithful People: Change and Continuity in Middletown's Religion.* Minneapolis, Minn.: University of Minnesota Press, 1983.

Childs, Brevard. *Introduction to the Old Testament as Scripture.* Philadelphia: Fortress Press, 1979.

Chittister, Joan, and Marty, Martin E. *Faith and Ferment: An Interdisciplinary Study of Christian Beliefs and Practices.* Minneapolis, Minn.: Augsburg Publishing House, 1983.

Clements, William M., ed. *Ministry with the Aging.* San Francisco: Harper, 1981.

Cobb, John B., Jr., and Griffin, David Ray. *Process Theology: An Introductory Exposition.* Philadelphia: Westminster Press, 1976.

Coe, George Albert. *A Social Theory of Religious Education*. New York: Scribner's, 1917.

Cooley, Charles H. *Social Organization*. Glencoe, Ill.: Free Press, 1956.

Cox, Harvey G. *The Secular City: Secularization and Urbanization in Theological Perspective*. New York: Macmillan, 1965.

————. *Religion in the Secular City: Toward a Post-Modern Theology*. New York: Simon & Schuster, 1984.

Cully, Iris V. *Imparting the Word: The Bible in Christian Education*. Philadelphia: Westminster Press, 1962.

————. *Planning and Selecting Curriculum for Christian Education*. Valley Forge, Pa.: Judson Press, 1983.

————. *Education for Spiritual Growth*. San Francisco: Harper, 1984.

Dalglish, William A., ed. *Media for Christian Formation*. Dayton, Ohio: Pflaum, 1969.

Daniel, Eleanor A.; Wade, John W.; and Gresham, Charles. *Introduction to Christian Education*. Cincinnati, Ohio: Standard Publishing, 1980.

Dewey, John. *Experience and Education*. New York: Macmillan, 1952.

Dodd, Charles H. *The Apostolic Preaching and Its Development: Three Lectures by C. H. Dodd*. New York: Harper, 1944.

Duck, Ruth C. *Bread for the Journey*. Philadelphia: Pilgrim Press, 1981.

Dudley, Carl. *Where Have All the People Gone?: New Choices for Old Churches*. New York: Pilgrim Press, 1979.

————. *Building Effective Ministry: Theory and Practice in the Local Church*. San Francisco: Harper, 1983.

Durkheim, Emile. *The Elementary Forms of the Religious Life*. Trans. by Joseph Ward Swain. New York: Collier, 1954.

Durnbaugh, Donald F. *The Believers' Church: The History and Character of Radical Protestantism.* New York: Macmillan, 1968.

Dykstra, Craig R. *Vision and Character: A Christian Educator's Alternative to Kohlberg.* New York: Paulist Press, 1981.

Elliott, Harrison. *Can Religious Education Be Christian?* New York: Macmillan, 1940.

Erikson, Erik H. *Childhood and Society.* New York: W. W. Norton, 1950.

————. *Identity and the Life Cycle: Selected Papers.* New York: International Universities Press, 1959.

————. *Insight and Responsibility: Lectures on the Ethical Implications of Psychoanalytic Insight.* New York: W. W. Norton, 1964.

Etzioni, Amitai. *Modern Organizations.* Englewood Cliffs, N.J.: Prentice-Hall, 1964.

————. *The Active Society: A Theory of Societal and Political Processes.* New York: Free Press, 1968.

Evangelical Covenant Church of America. *Curriculum Evaluation: Measuring the Material.* Chicago: Evangelical Covenant Church, Department of Education, 1983.

Farley, Edward. *Theologia: The Fragmentation and Unity of Theological Education.* Philadelphia: Fortress Press, 1983.

Foster, Charles R. *Teaching in the Community of Faith.* Nashville: Abingdon Press, 1982.

Fowler, James W. *Stages of Faith: The Psychology of Human Development and the Quest for Meaning.* San Francisco: Harper, 1981.

————. *Becoming Adult, Becoming Christian: Adult Development and Christian Faith.* San Francisco: Harper, 1984.

Frankena, William K. *Ethics.* Englewood Cliffs, N.J.: Prentice-Hall, 1973.

385

Freire, Paulo. *Pedagogy of the Oppressed.* Trans. by Myra Bergman Ramos. New York: Herder and Herder, 1970.

Fuchs-Kreimer, Nancy. "The Authority of the Bible in Modern Jewish Thought." *Religious Education* 77, no. 5 (1982):477-85.

Furnish, Dorothy Jean. *Exploring the Bible with Children.* Nashville: Abingdon Press, 1975.

———. *Living the Bible with Children.* Nashville: Abingdon Press, 1979.

Gennep, Arnold van. *The Rites of Passage.* Trans. by Monika B. Vizedon and Gabrielle L. Caffee. London: Routledge & Paul, 1960.

Gilligan, Carol. *In a Different Voice: Psychological Theory and Woman's Development.* Cambridge, Mass.: Harvard University Press, 1982.

Goldman, Ronald. *Readiness for Religion: A Basis for Developmental Religious Education.* London: Routledge & Kegan Paul, 1965.

———. *Religious Thinking from Childhood to Adolescence.* New York: Seabury Press, 1968.

Gordon, William J. J. *The Metaphorical Way of Learning and Knowing.* Cambridge, Mass.: Synetics Education Systems, 1970.

Gottwald, Norman K. *The Tribes of Yahweh: A Sociology of the Religion of Liberated Israel, 1250–1050* B.C.E. Maryknoll, N.Y.: Orbis Books, 1979.

Graendorf, Werner C. *Introduction to Biblical Christian Education.* Chicago: Moody Press, 1981.

Grant, Robert M., and Tracy, David. *A Short History of the Interpretation of the Bible.* Philadelphia: Fortress Press, 1984.

Green, Robert W., ed. *Protestantism, Capitalism and Social Science: The Weber Thesis Controversy.* Lexington, Mass.: D. C. Heath, 1973.

Griggs, Donald L. *Teaching Teachers to Teach: A Basic Manual for Church Teachers.* Livermore, Calif.: Griggs Educational Service, 1974.

Griggs, Patricia. *Using Storytelling in Christian Education.* Nashville: Abingdon Press, 1981.

Groff, Warren F. *Christ the Hope of the Future: Signals of a Promised Humanity.* Grand Rapids, Mich.: Eerdmans, 1971.

————. *Storytime: God's Story and Ours.* Elgin, Ill.: Brethren Press, 1974.

Groome, Thomas H. *Christian Religious Education: Sharing Our Story and Vision.* San Francisco: Harper, 1980.

Gustafson, James M. *The Church as Moral Decision-Maker.* Philadelphia: Pilgrim Press, 1970.

————. *Ethics from a Theocentric Perspective.* 2 vols. Chicago: University of Chicago Press, 1981-84.

Gutierrez, Gustavo. *A Theology of Liberation.* Maryknoll, N.Y.: Orbis Books, 1973.

Hamilton, Neill Q. *Maturing in the Christian Life: A Pastor's Guide.* Philadelphia: Geneva Press, 1984.

Harder, Helmut. *Guidebook for Writers: Youth Curriculum, The Foundation Series.* Elgin, Ill.: Brethren Press, 1979.

Hare, Richard M. *The Language of Morals.* New York: Oxford University Press, 1968.

Harris, Maria, ed. *The DRE Reader: A Sourcebook in Education and Ministry.* Winona, Minn.: Saint Mary's Press, 1980.

————. *Portrait of Youth Ministry.* New York: Paulist Press, 1981.

Hauerwas, Stanley. *A Community of Character: Toward a Constructive Christian Social Ethic.* Notre Dame, Ind.: University of Notre Dame Press, 1981.

———. "The Family as a School for Character." *Religious Education* 80, no. 2 (1985):275-85.

Hayes, John H., and Holladay, Carl R. *Biblical Exegesis: A Beginner's Handbook.* Atlanta: John Knox Press, 1982.

Heckman, Shirley J. *On the Wings of a Butterfly: A Guide to Total Christian Education.* Elgin, Ill.: Brethren Press, 1981.

———. *Peace is Possible: A Study-Action Process Guide on Peacemaking.* New York: United Church Press, 1982.

Heckman, Shirley J., and Ferren, Iris L. *Creating the Congregation's Educational Ministry.* Elgin, Ill.: Brethren Press, 1976.

Highet, Gilbert. *The Art of Teaching.* New York: Alfred A. Knopf, 1952.

———. *The Immortal Profession.* New York: Weybright and Talley, 1976.

Huebner, Dwayne D. "From Theory to Practice: Curriculum." *Religious Education* 77, no. 4 (1982):363-74.

Joyce, Bruce, and Weil, Marsha. *Models of Teaching.* Englewood Cliffs, N.J.: Prentice-Hall, 1972.

Kalu, Ogbu, ed. *Christianity in West Africa: The Nigerian Story.* Ibadan, Nigeria: Daystar Press, 1978.

Kant, Immanuel. *Critique of Practical Reason and Other Writings in Moral Philosophy.* Trans. and ed. by Lewis White Beck. Chicago: University of Chicago Press, 1949.

Kennedy, William B. "Education for a Just and Peaceful World." *Religious Education* 79, no. 4 (1984):550-57.

Kierkegaard, Søren. *Training in Christianity.* Trans. by Walter Lowrie. Princeton, N.J.: Princeton University Press, 1944.

———. *Purity of Heart Is to Will One Thing: Spiritual Preparation for the Office of Confession.* Trans. by Douglas V. Steere. New York: Harper, 1948.

Knowles, Malcolm. *The Modern Practice of Adult Education: Andragogy Versus Pedagogy.* New York: Association Press, 1970.

Kohlberg, Lawrence. *Collected Papers on Moral Development and Moral Education.* Cambridge, Mass.: Moral Education Research Fund, 1973.

Leas, Speed, and Kittlaus, Paul. *Church Fights; Managing Conflict in the Local Church.* Philadelphia: Westminster Press, 1973.

Lee, James Michael. *The Shape of Religious Instruction: A Social-Science Approach.* Dayton, Ohio: Pflaum, 1971.

————. *The Flow of Religious Instruction: A Social-Science Approach.* Mishawaka, Ind.: Religious Education Press, 1973.

————. *The Content of Religious Instruction: A Social-Science Approach.* Birmingham, Ala.: Religious Education Press, 1985.

Lehmann, Paul. *Ethics in a Christian Context.* New York: Harper, 1963.

Litherland, Janet. *The Clown Ministry Handbook.* Colorado Springs: Meriwether, 1982.

Little, Lawrence, et al. *The Objectives of Christian Education.* New York: National Council of Churches, 1958.

Little, Sara. *To Set One's Heart: Belief and Teaching in the Church.* Atlanta: John Knox Press, 1983.

Loder, James. *The Transforming Moment: Understanding Convictional Experiences.* San Francisco: Harper, 1981.

Long, Edward Le Roy. *A Survey of Recent Christian Ethics.* New York: Oxford University Press, 1982.

Lynn, Robert W., and Wright, Elliott. *The Big Little School.* New York: Harper, 1971.

Mahler, Margaret S.; Pine, Fred; and Bergman, Anni. *The Psychological Birth of the Human Infant: Symbiosis and Individuation.* New York: Basic Books, 1975.

McFague, Sallie. *Metaphorical Theology: Models of God in Religious Language.* Philadelphia: Fortress Press, 1982.

Mead, Margaret. *Growing Up in New Guinea.* New York: New American Library, 1953.

———. *Coming of Age in Samoa.* New York: Morrow, 1971.

Meland, Bernard Eugene. *The Realities of Faith: The Revolution in Cultural Forms.* New York: Oxford University Press, 1962.

Melchert, Charles. "Theories as Practiced." *Religious Education* 78, no. 3 (1984):307-22.

Mill, John Stewart. *Utilitarianism.* New York: Macmillan, 1971.

Miller, Donald E. "Conscience and History." Ph.D. diss., Harvard University Press, 1962.

———. *The Wing-Footed Wanderer: Conscience and Transcendence.* Nashville: Abingdon Press, 1977.

Miller, John Michael. *The Contentious Community: Constructive Conflict in the Church.* Philadelphia: Westminster Press, 1978.

Miller, Randolph Crump. *The Theory of Christian Education Practice.* Birmingham, Ala.: Religious Education Press, 1980.

Moltmann, Jürgen. *The Theology of Hope.* New York: Harper, 1976.

Moore, Mary Elizabeth. *Education for Continuity and Change: A New Model for Christian Religious Education.* Nashville: Abingdon Press, 1983.

Moran, Gabriel. *Interplay: A Theory of Religion and Education.* Winona, Minn.: St. Mary's Press, 1981.

———. *Religious Education Development.* Minneapolis, Minn.: Winston Press, 1983.

Naisbitt, John. *Megatrends: Ten New Directions Transforming Our Lives.* New York: Warner Books, 1983.

Nelson, C. Ellis. *Where Faith Begins.* Richmond, Va.: John Knox Press, 1967.

The New England Primer. Ed. by Paul Leicester Ford. New York: Dodd, Mead, 1962.

Niebuhr, H. Richard. *The Social Sources of Denominationalism.* New York: Henry Holt, 1954.

————. *The Purpose of the Church and Its Ministry: Reflections on the Aims of Theological Education.* New York: Harper and Brothers, 1956.

————. *Radical Monotheism and Western Culture.* New York: Harper, 1960.

Osterman, Mary Jo. "The Two Hundred Year Struggle for Protestant Education Curriculum Theory." *Religious Education* 75, no. 5 (1980):528-38.

Pagliuso, Susan. *Understanding Stages of Moral Development: A Programmed Learning Workbook.* Ramsey, N.J.: Paulist Press, 1976.

Palmer, Parker J. *To Know as We Are Known: A Spirituality of Education.* San Francisco: Harper, 1983.

Parsons, Talcott, and Shils, Edward A., eds. *Toward A General Theory of Action.* New York: Harper, 1962.

Parsons, Talcott; Shils, Edward; Naegele, Kaspar D.; and Pitts, Jesse R., eds. *Theories of Society: Foundations of Modern Sociological Theory.* New York: Free Press of Glencoe, 1961.

Peatling, John H. *Religious Education in a Psychological Key.* Birmingham, Ala.: Religious Education Press, 1981.

Peters, R. S., ed. *The Concept of Education.* New York: Humanities Press, 1967.

Philibert, Paul J., and O'Connor, James P. "Adolescent Religious Socialization: A Study of Goal Priorities According to Parents and Religious Educators." *Review of Religious Research* 23, no. 3 (March 1982): 225-316.

Piaget, Jean. *The Moral Judgment of the Child.* Trans. by Majorie Gabain. Glencoe, Ill.: Free Press, 1948.

————. *Six Psychological Studies.* Trans. by Anita Tenzer and David Elkind. New York: Random House, 1968.

Pinar, William, ed. *Curriculum Theorizing: The Reconceptualists.* Berkeley, Calif.: McCutchan, 1975.

————. *Heightened Consciousness, Cultural Revolution and Curriculum Theory.* Berkeley, Calif.: McCutchan, 1974.

Plato. *The Republic of Plato.* Trans. by Francis Macdonald Cornford. London: Oxford University Press, 1961.

Poling, James N., and Miller, Donald E., *Foundations for a Practical Theology of Ministry.* Nashville: Abingdon Press, 1985.

Potter, Ralph B. "Justice and Beyond in Moral Education." *Andover Newton Quarterly* 19, no. 3 (January 1979): 145-55.

Ramsey, Paul, ed. *Faith and Ethics: The Theology of H. Richard Niebuhr.* New York: Harper, 1957.

Rawls, John. *A Theory of Justice.* Cambridge, Mass.: Harvard University Press, 1971.

Reuther, Rosemary Radford. *Sexism and God-Talk: Toward a Feminist Theology.* Boston: Beacon Press, 1983.

Richards, Larry O. *A Theology of Christian Education.* Grand Rapids, Mich.: Zondervan, 1975.

Ricoeur, Paul. *Interpretation Theory: Discourse and the Surplus of Meaning.* Fort Worth, Tex.: Christian University Press, 1976.

————. *The Philosophy of Paul Ricoeur.* Ed. by Charles E. Reagan and David Stewart. Boston: Beacon Press, 1978.

Rizzuto, Ana-Maria. *The Birth of the Living God.* Chicago: University of Chicago Press, 1979.

Sanneh, Lamin. *West African Christianity: The Religious Impact.* New York: Orbis Books, 1983.

Schleiermacher, Friedrich. *The Christian Faith.* Ed. by H. R. Mackintosh and J. S. Stewart. Edinburgh: T. & T. Clark, 1928.

Seymour, Jack L. *From Sunday School to Church School: Continuities in Protestant Church Education in the United States, 1860–1929.* Washington, D.C.: University Press of America, 1982.

Seymour, Jack L., and Miller, Donald E. *Contemporary Approaches to Christian Education.* Nashville: Abingdon Press, 1982.

Seymour, Jack L.; O'Gorman, Robert T.; and Foster, Charles. *The Church in the Education of the Public: Refocusing the Task of Religious Education.* Nashville: Abingdon Press, 1984.

Sheehy, Gail. *Passages: Predictable Crises of Adult Life.* New York: E. P. Dutton, 1976.

Sherrill, Lewis. *The Rise of Christian Education.* New York: Macmillan, 1944.

Smart, James D. *The Strange Silence of the Bible in the Church: A Study in Hermeneutics.* Philadelphia: Westminster Press, 1970.

———. *The Past, Present and Future of Biblical Theology.* Philadelphia: Westminster Press, 1979.

Smith, H. Shelton. *Faith and Nurture.* New York: Scribner's, 1941.

Snyder, Ross. *Young People and Their Culture.* Nashville: Abingdon Press, 1969.

———. *Contemporary Celebration.* Nashville: Abingdon Press, 1971.

Stackhouse, Max L. *Creeds, Society, and Human Rights: A Study in Three Cultures.* Grand Rapids, Mich.: Eerdmans, 1984.

Stokes, Kenneth, ed. *Faith Development in the Adult Life Cycle.* New York: W. H. Sadlier, 1983.

Tawney, Richard H. *Religion and the Rise of Capitalism.* New York: Harcourt Brace, 1926.

Taylor, Marvin J., ed. *An Introduction to Christian Education.* Nashville: Abingdon Press, 1976.

———. *Foundations for Christian Education in an Era of Change.* Nashville: Abingdon Press, 1976.

———. *Changing Patterns of Religious Education.* Nashville: Abingdon Press, 1984.

Thompson, Norma. *Religious Education and Theology.* Birmingham, Ala.: Religious Education Press, 1982.

Tillich, Paul. *A History of Christian Thought.* Ed. by Carl E. Braaten. New York: Harper, 1968.

———. *Systematic Theology.* 3 vols. Chicago: University of Chicago Press, 1950-63.

Toulmin, Steven. *Human Understanding.* Princeton, N.J.: Princeton University Press, 1972.

Towns, Elmer. *The Successful Sunday School and Teacher's Guidebook.* Carol Stream, Ill.: Creation House, 1976.

Tracy, David. *The Analogical Imagination: Christian Theology and the Culture of Pluralism.* New York: Crossroad, 1981.

Troeltsch, Ernst. *The Social Teaching of the Christian Churches.* Trans. by Olive Wyon. 2 vols. New York: Macmillan, 1956.

Turner, Victor. *The Ritual Process: Structure and Anti-Structure.* Ithaca, N.Y.: Cornell University Press, 1977.

Varenne, Herve. *Americans Together: Structured Diversity in a Midwestern Town.* New York: Teachers College Press, 1977.

Vieth, Paul H. *Objectives in Religious Education.* New York: Red Label Reprints, 1930.

Wagner, C. Peter. *Church Growth and the Whole Gospel: A Biblical Mandate.* San Francisco: Harper, 1981.

Weber, Max. *The Theory of Social and Economic Organization.* Trans. by A. M. Henderson and Talcott Parsons. New York: Oxford University Press, 1947.

——. *The Protestant Ethic and the Spirit of Capitalism.* Trans. by Talcott Parsons. New York: Scribner's, 1958.

Wehrheim, Carol A., ed. *Guide to Curriculum Choice.* Elgin, Ill.: Brethren Press, 1981.

Wellhausen, Julius. *Prolegomena to the History of Ancient Israel.* Trans. by J. S. Smith and C. A. Menzies. 1885. Reproduction. Magnolia, Ma.: Peter Smith, 1973.

Westerhoff, John H. III. *McGuffey and His Readers: Piety, Morality, and Education in Nineteenth-century America.* Nashville: Abingdon Press, 1976.

Westerhoff, John H. III, and Edwards, O. C., Jr. *A Faithful Church: Issues in the History of Catechesis.* Wilton, Conn.: Morehouse-Barlow, 1981.

Westerhoff, John H. III, and Neville, Gwen Kennedy. *Generation to Generation: Conversations on Religious Education and Culture.* Philadelphia: United Church Press, 1974.

Westerhoff, John H. III, and Willimon, William H. *Liturgy and Learning Through the Life Cycle.* New York: Seabury Press, 1980.

White, Burton L. *The First Three Years of Life: A Guide to Physical, Emotional, and Intellectual Growth of Your Baby.* New York: Avon, 1978.

Whitehead, Alfred North. *Adventures of Ideas.* New York: Macmillan, 1933.

Wilcox, Mary. *Developmental Journey: A Guide to Development of Logical and Moral Reasoning and Social Perspective.* Nashville: Abingdon Press, 1979.

Winter, Gibson. *The Suburban Captivity of the Churches.* Garden City, N.Y.: Doubleday, 1961.

World Council of Churches. *Baptism, Eucharist and Ministry.* Commission on Faith and Order, Faith and

Order Paper No. 111. Geneva: World Council of Churches, 1982.

Worley, Robert C. *A Gathering of Strangers: Understanding the Life of Your Church.* Philadelphia: Westminster Press, 1976.

Wren, Brian. *Education for Justice: Pedagogical Principles.* Maryknoll, N.Y.: Orbis Books, 1977.

Wyckoff, D. Campbell. *Theory and Design of Christian Education Curriculum.* Philadelphia: Westminster Press, 1961.

Yoder, John H. *The Politics of Jesus: Vicit Agnus Noster.* Grand Rapids, Mich.: Eerdmans, 1972.

INDEX